ᔥ Cultural Borders of Europe ᔥ

MAKING SENSE OF HISTORY

Studies in Historical Cultures

General Editor: Stefan Berger

Founding Editor: Jörn Rüsen

Bridging the gap between historical theory and the study of historical memory, this series crosses the boundaries between both academic disciplines and cultural, social, political and historical contexts. In an age of rapid globalization, which tends to manifest itself on an economic and political level, locating the cultural practices involved in generating its underlying historical sense is an increasingly urgent task.

For a full volume listing, please see back matter

CULTURAL BORDERS OF EUROPE

Narratives, Concepts and Practices in the
Present and the Past

Edited by Mats Andrén, Thomas Lindkvist, Ingmar Söhrman
and Katharina Vajta

berghahn
NEW YORK · OXFORD
www.berghahnbooks.com

Published in 2017 by
Berghahn Books
www.berghahnbooks.com

Library of Congress Cataloging-in-Publication Data
Names: Andrén, Mats, editor of compilation. | Lindkvist, Thomas, 1949-
editor of compilation. | Söhrman, Ingmar, editor of compilation. | Vajta,
Katharina, editor of compilation.
Title: Cultural borders of Europe : narratives, concepts and practices in the
present and the past / edited by Mats Andrén, Thomas Lindkvist, Ingmar
Söhrman and Katharina Vajta.
Description: New York : Berghahn Books, 2017. | Series: Making sense of
history : studies in historical cultures ; volume 30 | Includes
bibliographical references and index.
Identifiers: LCCN 2017018279 (print) | LCCN 2017024868 (ebook) | ISBN
9781785335914 (e-book) | ISBN 9781785335907 (hardback : alkaline paper)
Subjects: LCSH: Cultural pluralism--Europe. | Multiculturalism--Europe. |
Ethnicity--Political aspects--Europe. | Borderlands--Political
aspects--Europe. | Borderlands--Social aspects--Europe. |
Liberalism--Europe. | Democracy--Europe. | Europe--Ethnic
relations--Political aspects. | Europe--Politics and government--1989-
Classification: LCC D2009 (ebook) | LCC D2009 .C85 2017 (print) | DDC
306.094--dc23
LC record available at https://lccn.loc.gov/2017018279

British Library Cataloguing in Publication Data
A catalogue record for this book is available from the British Library

ISBN 978-1-78533-590-7 hardback
ISBN 978-1-78920-068-3 paperback
ISBN 978-1-78533-591-4 ebook

Contents

Part III   Mental Spaces and Barriers

Part IV   Scholars Making Borders

Figures and Tables

Figures

Tables

Introduction

Mats Andrén and Ingmar Söhrman

A new, more complex cultural landscape is evolving in Europe. However, these changes are often based on the past and we can now see how these borders have developed, changed and partly turned into new frontiers. A number of mental borders are becoming increasingly important, mostly based on imagined cultural differences that in some cases create new, and in other cases strengthen old, identities. There is also the desire to construct or re-establish cultural borders in order to reinforce these identities and cultural communities. Given that the ongoing integration process of the European Union poses endless occasions for disputes, avoidance, and encroachment of cultural borders, there is a growing need to understand the cultural dimension of their construction and reconstruction.

At first sight, these tendencies seem to contradict the idea of shrinking economic and legal borders in Europe. Although these borders between the nation-states of contemporary Europe have weakened, the cultural ones are more visible than ever, although it is not always possible to classify them in such a strict manner, given that they exist mostly in the realm of perception. The idea of culturally homogeneous states has never been true and it is now being fundamentally challenged by migration, new political concepts, and resurgent claims of the cultural components of national identities from long-neglected historical minorities.

The new landscape of presumed or real cultural borders is not easily identified on a map. It never was, but a globalized world has brought the issue to the fore. Due to the ongoing process, there is a need to understand the various dimensions of cultural borders, their construction and reconstruction. Questions may arise concerning culture, language and religion as markers of cultural borders. We need to know how and why cultural borders attain legitimacy; that is, how they are used. This is also the central question to which this book is offering tentative answers and providing examples from different parts of Europe and from different periods. The idea is to show a variety of relevant manifestations of cultural borders in modern and previous times in Europe that will help us to understand what is taking place now in different countries and regions.

The formation of cultural borders in contemporary Europe has entered a new phase. Historian Peter Burke (1998: 35–40; 2009) describes the period as one of cultural exchange and transformation, predicting that new cultural 'ecotypes' will emerge. More of these new patterns are now visible and they sometimes merge partly or totally with previous patterns and ideas. Cultural borders are formed as regional or local manifestations of a general European, or even global, pattern of increased emphasis on cultural diversity and regional cultural identity. This trend brings a sense of uncertainty to the liberal democratic traditions of European nation-states and the institutions of the EU. It also challenges the concepts of legitimacy and political representation, as well as the cultural and legal bases for citizenship. Thus, thorough research on cultural borders and their consequences in Europe is of the utmost importance, not only as an academic exercise, but also as a way to achieve a broader understanding and promote the evolution of democracy. Greater awareness of the ways that cultural borders are dealt with in Europe requires a more profound insight into their relationship with issues of belonging and loyalty, as well as the strategies that have emerged to deal with this task.

'Europeanization' needs to be redefined, given that it involves the merging of specific sets of national cultures. This becomes problematic when it excludes its Muslim and Jewish heritage and suppresses the continent's religious diversity and identities that are not perceived as connected to a nation. Another complex, widely discussed issue is whether economic and legal integration also requires cultural coalescence. In recent decades the EU has striven to create and define a framework for a common culture and identity by means of symbols such as a flag, an anthem and the concept of European citizenship (Shore 2000; Fornäs 2012). Meanwhile, the proliferation of European cultural identities must be understood in order to grasp the meaning and consequences of changing cultural borders. Of central importance to this book on the cultural borders of Europe is to discuss and present important aspects of these identities, as well as cultural borders, as a means of establishing a common set of values.

The book is intended for academics and advanced students of European studies who need a broader background on which to base their research and papers. It will also serve as a source for journalists and eager readers with a wider interest in these cultural borderlands. It differs from other books dealing with this topic in that it gives a very broad perspective in regard to specific cases.

Proceeding from the Concepts of Border and Culture

The history of the concepts of *border* and *culture* offers a number of insights that might seem surprising. It also provides us with an initial framework from which we can embark upon this endeavour. The etymology of the word 'border' can be traced back to the far-flung no man's land between the English and the Scots in the fourteenth and fifteenth centuries, as the term 'border' referred not only to the dividing line between the two countries but also to the surrounding areas. 'Limit' (from the Latin *limes*) originally meant 'legal limitation on power or authority', and is slightly older than 'border' (about 1400, from the Old French *bordëur*, which was derived from the Frankish *bord/bort* = side), as it goes back to the Roman fortifications in Africa and Europe, which were called *limites* (Barnhart 1988: 434).

There is a crucial difference between the two meanings of border. The first refers to a link with that which lies beyond; the second refers to a frontier, a line that must not be crossed – the legal system of a state and the power of its ruler end there. In other words, a border represents both that which it circumscribes and that which it excludes, but the exclusionary aspect has grown stronger and gained the upper hand during the last two centuries. Dimensions of this trend can be identified in the conscious creation of national languages and cultures (Andersson 1991; Liedman 1997: 153ff; Berger and Lorenz 2010; Hirschi 2012: 105). Literature and folkloristic perceptions are of the utmost importance in cultivating and promoting the culture, creating a basis of political and cultural differences. The role of literature is often downplayed in these discussions, but it has an impact as a means of both describing a complex cultural crossroads and promoting a regional or recently unified language, as has been the case in Rhaeto-Romance Switzerland (Grisons), where literature is written both in various Romance varieties and in the unified language of Rumantsch Grischun. This is also the case in the Basque Country in Spain. Basque author Bernardo Atxaga stresses that literature has an important role to play in countering the predominant political discourses of contemporary society (Atxaga 2013: 54–56). Images and ideas are easily manipulated for various purposes, and they need to be recognized for what they are.

Johann Gottfried Herder stands out as the main philosopher of the reconstructed concept of border in symbiosis with culture. Herder's idea was that national borders stemmed from autochthonous cultures. German culture was the product of history, strengthened by the creation of a national language (Herder 1965: 259f, 272f, 385–92, 484f). He emphasized cultural borders, whereas his philosophy included the idea of *Humanität* shared by all human beings (ibid.: 157ff, 375ff). From Herder's perspective, cultures set specific borders while humanity violated them, but he did not advocate a world without borders; national cultures were to be preserved. His ideas were taken up by Romantic nationalists, who interpreted them as vital to promoting national identity, especially among those peoples – Poles, Hungarians, Czechs, Italians – who did not have their own state (Andrén 2001: 85ff). Presently other peoples, such as the Samis, Galicians, Basques, Bretons, Catalans, Flemings, Scots and Roma, are stateless. Most are not demanding their own state, but one can still wonder how far this fragmentation into small homogeneous states should continue.

The modern concept of border emerged from this tension between cultural dividing lines and an all-embracing universalism. Two observations are relevant at this point. First, if cultural borders are regarded as a given, the problem is how to deal with them. The hypothesis advanced by Samuel P. Huntington that future conflicts will arise from cultural and religious tenets is based on such an assumption (Huntington 1993) – as are the ideas of tolerance and multiculturalism. However this last concept may refer to both legal recognition and a norm. In analysis it is more accurate to use multiculturalism as a more neutral term related to the current situation without any ideological implications. The ongoing controversy about these two terms infuses the management of cultural borders with a great deal of conflict. Second, if universalism is seen as the fundamental concept, cultural borders should not exist – perhaps they are actually evil and a source of conflict. Ideas such as cosmopolitanism, universalism and globalism are essential to such a perspective, but it is also important to know their purpose. While globalism and universalism might seem ideal for many people, they can also be tools for undermining regional cultures and minority languages. Many nineteenth-century liberals and socialists saw these regional languages and cultures as atavisms that should have been allowed to die out as soon as possible. Signs in the bars of early twentieth-century Brittany warned, 'Défense de cracher par terre et de parler breton' (Spitting on the floor and speaking Breton is prohibited) (Piriou 1977: 9–46).

Objections need to be raised to the above juxtaposition of cultural borders and an all-embracing universalism. These concepts do not have equal empirical status. Cultural borders belong to the real world, having consequences for contemporary society, but they are nevertheless human artefacts that change over time. Their importance varies depending on the person you are talking to and the particular context. Although someone may be highly influenced by their cultural identity, s/he still has a choice of remaining within this framework, taking on another identity or living with both. If it is a question of religious identity, moving to another part of the world can be a way of maintaining it (such as non-conformist European Protestants who left for America in the seventeenth century) or removing oneself from the predominant society. This can entail anything from an accent to a dress code, either voluntary or the result of peer pressure, gender-related or not. Nothing is as simple as it appears. The answers are often very complex. Anthropologists have paid a great deal of attention to the ways that cultural borders are politicized, whereas political and economic borders can be culturalized (Wright 1998; Ivanescu 2010). Furthermore, cultural borders may be fixed to a greater or lesser degree and for longer or shorter periods of time. Meanings are always in flux – administrative and legal borders sometimes clash with cultural identities (e.g. Eder 2006; Delanty 2006).

The national cultures of contemporary Europe need to be redefined as the nation-states become more multicultural due to an awareness of immigrant groups and national minorities, as well as their demands and rights. So attentiveness is demanded when talking about 'national borders', as the accurate expression is mostly 'state borders'. Particularistic identities are rapidly emerging, relaxing some borders while enforcing others. 'Multiculturalism' may refer to parallel cultures, which may or may not accept each other, but always on terms set by the majority (Söhrman 2004: 65–80). Literature is often a reliable reflection of how these situations are perceived by various groups. References to 'second generation immigrants' or a 'regional minority' may leave them with a feeling of not belonging anywhere. The very concept gives the impression that the origin of one's parents is all that matters, even though one may have spent one's whole life in the country. It would be more appropriate to be specific – for example, 'first generation Germans'. At least that label is inclusive. So much prejudice and exclusion is abetted by the use of 'ethnic' terms. This is surely one of the factors that led (and leads) to riots in European cities such as London, Paris and Stockholm. Such social, economic and political borders are difficult to separate from cultural borders. But this book will focus on identities, especially national identities, that have an ideological and historical basis, and cultural borders that have appeared and disappeared as a result of historical currents, ideological awareness, and relationships with neighbouring peoples who do not belong to the same cultural community even though there may not be political borders between them. The situation in the former Yugoslavia shows how complex the issue is. The old Serbian majority that dominated the army is spread out across most of the new countries and has become a minority in these new states. The same is true for many Russians in the Baltic countries.

The transition from a powerful majority to a subservient minority is not easy, affecting self-esteem and the sense of national identity. Have these new minorities maintained their old national identities? Are new cultural borders emerging? In the case of old minorities and a linguistic majority in a neighbouring country, the issue of identity arises. Does the Hungarian minority in Transylvania have a Hungarian identity or one of their own? Is the Russian-speaking minority in eastern Ukraine Russian or just Russian-speaking? Whose interests do these various definitions serve? Many ideological and personal interests are at stake. The examples – Belgium, Luxemburg, Northern Ireland, Switzerland, and so on – are legion.

Meanwhile 'universalism', also referred to as 'Europeanization' and 'cosmopolitization' by Ulrich Beck and Edgar Grande (Beck and Grande 2004), is a growing phenomenon in politics and in the society as a whole. When political projects and civic responsibility go beyond the cultural borders of nation-states, cultural identities and borders become blurred. Such changes are immanent with possibilities both of new openness and threats of intolerance. Anthropologist Arjun Appadurai (2006) and other scholars have warned of the dangers associated with current modes of cultural and national identification, all the more relevant in light of the financial crisis of 2008 and its long aftermath.

The crossroads between cultural borders and national identities represents an important field for further empirical and theoretical research. One objective in this anthology is to embark on such research. We are well aware of its pitfalls; a Scandinavian, German or French researcher who relates national identity to a nation-state without considering old minorities with varying ideas and with cultural borders (the Samis in northern Scandinavia, Sorbs in Germany, Alsatians in France, etc.) will probably carry different ideological baggage from a Spanish researcher who is aware of turbulent national activism in Catalonia, the Basque Country and Galicia. Researchers may like or dislike these discourses, but there is no way around them as they threaten the very existence of the Spanish state. Extremists in many European countries accept neither immigrants nor national minorities. Thus, awareness of these identities and cultural borders, their interrelationships and complexity, is essential to the understanding of modern society. The promotion of one particular standpoint can easily be used for political purposes that were never the intention of the researchers who came up with the standpoint.

Previous Literature as a Springboard

The chapters in this volume explore the cultural borders of Europe in their relation to the construction of European ideas, identities and institutions, both past and present. But why is there a need for yet another book on borders in Europe? Before we answer that question, let us first recall the evolution of the field over the last twenty years.

Research on the borders of Europe expanded considerably during the 1990s, including scientific articles and special issues of journals, new departments at universities, and research funding by European institutions. The apparent catalysts were the emergence of new borders during the decade; the acceleration of the rate at which goods, information and people crossed borders; the changing status of geographic regions; and the creation of new ones (Anderson, O'Dowd and Wilson 2002). A series of conferences, forums and anthologies were devoted to the borders associated with the integration of Western Europe, while many examined the emerging ethnic borders of post-Communist Eastern Europe (Kurti and Langman 1997; Anderson and Bort 1998; Wilson and Donnan 1998).

Since that time, a great deal of research has been devoted to legal and territorial borders. One approach has been to stress the ongoing significance of such borders in a 'borderless' Europe – see the works of geographer Henk van Houtum (van Houtum 2002; van Houtum and Pijpers 2007); an anthology entitled *Europe without Borders: Remapping Territory, Citizenship and Identity in a Transnational Age* (Berezin and Schain 2003); and *Territorial Choice: The Politics of Boundaries and Borders* (Baldersheim and Rose 2010) in which political scientists inquire into the shifting scales of local government in Europe. Some research goes beyond territorial borders and examines social change on a continent in the process of transformation; political sociologist Chris Rumford (2006a, 2012) emphasizes the continual differentiation of borders. Cultural aspects of territorial borders have attracted the attention of various social scientists, including those who conduct social anthropological studies that look at the identities of people and places along borders (Berdahl 1997; Wilson and Donnan 1998). Such enormous interest in borders has raised awareness in the social sciences of their multifaceted character, which has led to the conclusion that such studies need to expand beyond the issue of territoriality (Rumford 2012).

Ever since the 1990s, research in the humanities has increasingly addressed the question of the cultural borders of Europe (see e.g. Andrén et al. 2009). The explicit focus has often been on identity rather than borders. An anthology entitled *Beyond Boundaries: Language and Identity in Contemporary Europe* examines language as an integral part of contemporary identity. Other works focus on the central phenomenon of multilingualism; see John Edward's classic *Multilingualism* (1994), an anthology entitled *Multilingualism in European Bilingual Contexts* (Gibbons and Holt 2002) and many others (e.g. Lundén 2006; Lagasabaster and Huguet 2007). Historian Karl Schlögel (2007) views borders and the cultures with which they are associated as a learning process. In the case of European cultural borders, he points not only to the evolution of specific cultures but to a long history of Europeanization and the crossing of borders through mutual learning. Philosopher Étienne Balibar (2002, 2009) describes the 'dead ends' of a territorial concept of European borders now that political spaces are overlapping and 'the territorial concepts of "interior" and "exterior" are no longer completely separable'.

The chapters in this anthology address processes of defining European cultural borders, as well as their dependence on, and relation to, various kinds of European belonging and national identity. By proceeding from cultural borders as the object of investigation, we open the door to a range of cases that is both broader and more complex than the ambit of territorial borders. The fact that this anthology combines studies on a great variety of cultural borders – literary, linguistic, religious, historiographical and ideological among others – is also new. A closely related development is the growing complexity of identities and the multiplicity of border making, including phenomena such as linguistic complexity, religious diversity and regional affinity.

This anthology brings together scholars from Britain, Luxembourg and Sweden whose research focuses on Europe's cultural borders. It takes advantage of these scholars' frontier work in their fields of expertise, and presents a considerable amount of new empirical data. By virtue of the fact that the authors represent eight different disciplines – archaeology, history of ideas, political science, sociology and history of religion, as well as English, French and Spanish linguistics – the anthology offers a multidisciplinary account of cultural borders. In an attempt to capture the complex realities and cultural images involved as fully as possible, the approach is more wide-ranging than other books on the subject.

One trend in current social and political research is the proliferation of meanings of the word 'border'. Distinctions are made between *borders, borderlines, boundaries* and *frontiers*, between *bordering, re-bordering* and *de-bordering*, and between *soft* and *hard* borders (Eder 2006; Agnew 2009; Janczak 2011).[1] This has to do with an apparent need to go beyond a demarcating approach that defines borders in an oversimplified manner in accordance with a line on a map, the tradition of a particular discipline or an attempt to understand a specific tendency. While the concepts explored by research about borders are often pigeonholed into specific disciplines, we want to promote conceptual studies that stimulate genuine interdisciplinary collaboration. David Newman (2006) suggests that 'boundary demarcation, the nature of frontiers, borderlands and transition zones' are useful concepts. However, they all imply objects that are both completed and relatively constant, which is not the case when it comes to cultural borders; they are always under construction and will never be etched in stone.

We define cultural borders broadly and consider them to be more than simply legal or political constructs. A historical, linguistic and cultural analysis suggests that people will always need borders to define themselves in relation to others but that borders operate in different ways and at different levels; moreover, the degree to which they influence society changes over time. We subscribe to the premise that there is a need for a 'radical break with substantialist notions of Europe's borders and identity' (Eder 2006) in favour of a focus on their cultural constructions. The intention of this anthology to contribute to border research and its further development is based on three hypotheses that consider: (1) the construction of cultural borders, (2) the foundation of nations, and (3) the Janus-faced nature of borders.

The first hypothesis is that borders have a strong tendency to be constructed as narratives, concepts and practices. Narratives, both literary and otherwise, arguably invest borders with credibility in several ways. Ideas of national culture, like those of European identity, are rooted in narratives of origin and an imagined community of the future (Hobsbawn and Ranger 1983). Arguments for or against cultural diversity are advanced as narratives, and the cultural borders of Europe are upheld by constructing narratives of difference (e.g. Berger and Lorenz 2015). Shared stories are of the utmost importance for constructing and maintaining the borders of Europe – even more so than the strength of political institutions (Eder 2006).

However, narratives are insufficient to construct sustainable cultural borders. The *concepts* needed to contain narratives are subject to dispute. The concept of Europe is controversial in itself – the various definitions are supported by arguments and theories that have differing degrees of cogency. The concept of multiculturalism is central to contemporary ideological discussions of the ways in which cultural borders in Europe should be handled, as well as how and why they can help to define Europe as both a continent and an idea.[2]

Narratives and concepts are both embedded in various practices that are indispensable to the maintenance of cultural borders (Parker, Vaughan-Williams et al. 2009). Religious practices may promote contempt or fear. Linguistic practices may uphold borders even after formal legal and territorial dividing lines have been dismantled. Such practices reveal how this process of dismantling is perceived by people of varying national identities. Is it simply formal and superficial or does it reflect a deeper level of unification? It is also important to study the ways that religious and linguistic practices, as well as narratives and concepts, support or oppose each other. In contemporary Europe, migration and greater awareness of minority rights have reshaped the linguistic landscape in ways that render existing borders more complex (Extra and Gorter 2001; Söhrman 2009). New practices may be blurring and redefining cultural borders (Delanty 2006). Old cultural borders do not always disappear as new ones emerge. Often they are reinterpreted to suit a specific ideological agenda.

If it is correct to assume that narratives, concepts and practices are important, our understanding of borders takes on a new character. The narratives, concepts and practices associated with borders are constructions of history that are embedded in European languages. Even fixed territorial borders are culturally constructed and need to be understood as such. In other words, learning about the cultural, historical and linguistic dimensions of borders is an urgent imperative.

The second hypothesis is that the search for the starting point of nations – the time and place of 'absolute origin', an ethnic legend – is crucial to the making of European borders. Such a starting point is inherently controversial, given that conscious historical constructions incorporate powerful projections of contemporary interests and notions of borders from the past. Is the starting point for Italy the Roman Empire of the first century CE, Dante's essay on Latin and the vernacular (*De vulgari eloquentia*)[3] in 1306, or the unification of the Italian state in 1861? Several chapters of this anthology argue that such starting points, albeit disputable per se, are essential to defining borders.

The third hypothesis is that European borders are Janus-faced – they invite both conflict and integration. The process of defining borders in contemporary Europe is closely tied to issues of identity and thereby to the description of difference. The mobility of today's Europeans does not suggest that borders have disappeared, but rather that they have taken on other forms. Even a unified Europe is likely to have borders. The three hypotheses recur throughout the various chapters and are re-examined in the conclusion.

Outline of the Book

This anthology aims to establish a further understanding of the multifaceted character of cultural borders, rather than setting a tight research agenda on one of its specific aspects or mapping the cultural borders of the whole continent. Therefore a basic idea of this anthology has been to invite researchers from different fields in order to attack the notion of cultural borders from many different perspectives, thus offering a complex and intriguing picture. The chapters present representative cases from the area that composes today's European Union, and although most are from Western and Central Europe, they also offer glimpses of Estonia and Romania. The book deals with both historical and contemporary perspectives of European society, and how history is used and influences the modern concept of cultural borders. The cases illuminate ways to attain legitimacy and establish a common set of values. The contributions are accordingly organized into sections: by religion; by linguistic practices; by mental spaces and barriers; and, finally, by scholars' constructions of cultural borders.

The intersections, frictions and conflicts between territorial and religious borders are the focus of Part I. There is a complex balance of power and influence between Orthodoxy, Catholicism and the heterogenic Protestantism, as well as a complex relationship to Islam. The complexities do not facilitate our understanding of the situation or our understanding of what has really taken place and what this means to modern society. Historically, the different brands of Christianity were territorially organized and of great importance to creating a feeling of community. However, what is the relationship between religious identification and territorial belonging in modern Europe marked by the integration process? In Chapter 1, Linda Berg presents the relationship between territorial and religious identification. Protestants tend to identify with the state, whereas Catholics and Orthodox Christians identify with the local community, state and European institutions. It is particularly noteworthy that Muslims are much more likely to identify with Europe as a whole than with the state in particular. This gets complicated, as a central issue for the contemporary construction of European identity is whether it should include Muslims and Islam. A 2010 discussion in London, as described in Chapter 2 by Göran Larsson and Riem Spielhaus, was rife with stereotypes of what constitutes 'a European', as well as a narrative of Europe that included Muslims and one that did not. The dilemma posed by these kinds of debate is the apparent demand for clear-cut cultural borders, although they are actually flexible and negotiable, and are likely to remain that way. The modern dichotomy of European versus Islamic becomes less cogent within the European narrative of Islamic philosophy and the neo-Platonic heritage of Islam. In Chapter 3, Klas Grinell focuses on the borders between European and Islamic thought, which are more like meeting grounds than strict epistemological lines. A sincere dialogue aimed at transcending cultural borders should emphasize the local nature of identities and the fact that European thought is a grey area with a history that includes Islam. The idea of multiculturalism requires reflection, as it is crucial to the discussion of Muslims in Europe and must brave the winds of Eurocentricity.

The links between national identities and cultural borders are often strengthened by stereotypes, which make an appearance in many different contexts of linguistic practices, and are the focus of Part II of the volume. Of special interest are foreign language textbooks, as they purportedly convey a basic sense of another culture. They may be regarded as loci at which national characteristics and cultural demarcations are defined. It may not be so surprising that language textbooks often perpetuate cultural stereotypes, given that national identity has included the principle of monolingual states and national programmes for schools. The intercultural quest – as explicitly mandated by the national curriculum, UNESCO and the Council of Europe – has not yet attained its objectives. The textbooks present cultural borders as they are seen as national in character rather as an opportunity to promote communication and understanding. Katharina Vajta, in Chapter 4, addresses these issues, using the example of French textbooks used in Swedish schools. However, the merging of national identities with cultural borders throughout the twentieth century has been challenged by other cultural borders that do not fit into the nation-state paradigm. The main examples are Bavarians who are considered German in the same way as Catalans are often regarded as Spaniards, and Scotsmen as British, but all of whom also have a strong regional identity of their own. The Bavarians in the heart of Europe are often overlooked, and this group also entails a special feature as they are closer – linguistically, historically and politically – to their Austrian neighbours to the south than to their fellow countrymen to the north, a fact that is frequently neglected. Barbara Loester, in Chapter 5, discusses the Bavarian claim to a distinct historical identity, and examines the interaction of cultural and national identities in Bavaria.

Furthermore, linguistic competence and performances have the ability to create illusions associated with the notion that cultural borders are stable and based on an eternal ethnic myth. It is well worth considering how these illusions, and particularly the lack of language skills, interfere with adequate media coverage of foreign countries. Journalists and analysts are often complacent about receiving second-hand information that propagates stale stereotypes. Ingmar Söhrman argues in Chapter 6, the concluding chapter of Part II, that borders are very much a product of ignorance and shallow thinking. His discussion draws attention to the Balkans, often portrayed as impossible for Westerners to understand.

Part III of the anthology turns to mental spaces and barriers that are due to cultural borders in their relation to national identities. An illuminating example of the cultural complexity that emerges in a borderland is the construction of national identity in Luxembourg, a small country situated on a border over which modern Europe has frequently fought. The cultural identity and mental space of Luxembourg was invented as a kind of hybrid at the beginning of the twentieth century, paving the way for subsequent ideals of openness and Europeanization, and later 'Luxembourgish' was promoted as a national language and as a means of strengthening the cultural border to neighbouring countries – a complex process that Fernand Fehlen analyses in Chapter 7.

An aspect of living with cultural borders is the making and transgressing of mental spaces and barriers. Literary narratives often reflect the images and transgressions of these borders, and are deemed less pretentious as they do not claim to report reality but rather to reflect the intellectual ambiance at a certain time and place. An excellent historical example is the Finnish writer Aino Kallas, who had been assimilated into Estonian culture by the turn of the twentieth century, and who was ostracized at times by native Finnish and Estonian writers alike. Kallas exemplifies a number of different identities and thereby transgresses 'silent cultural rules or borders'. In Chapter 8, Katarina Leppänen interprets Kallas's persona as 'a site of cultural confrontation'. Nowadays, images also constitute an important part of contemporary narratives of bordering, and society is replete with powerful images of which its members are rarely aware on a conscious level. Johan Järlehed, in Chapter 9, presents an illustrative contemporary example of the production of images represented by logos of a Basque-language community. The study of logos, as well as the specific example of annual festivities at Basque middle schools – which have been adopted by other European linguistic minorities – underscores the contemporary nature of border practices.

Part IV of the book is dedicated to the topical issue of how scholars have been constructing European borders and identities. The historical construction of national borders is instrumental to this process. It is often emphasized that historians did play an important role in the conceptualization of national borders and the exploration of their origins. It is less studied, but nevertheless of utmost importance, how archaeologists contributed to and took part in the construction of cultural borders. Per Cornell, in Chapter 12, stresses border practices and narratives by examining German and Austrian archaeologists who elaborated upon concepts that defined the nation all the way back to prehistoric times. It is worrying to notice that the arguments resemble some of those in the contemporary debate in Europe on cultural borders. For example, Gustaf Kossina stressed Nordic culture as the focus area of Germany, and his Austrian counterpart Oswald Menghin emphasized a larger German cultural sphere that included Austria, however it excluded historical minorities, specifically the Jews.

Today, scholars are deeply involved in the bordering of Europe, for which the concept of European identity is fundamental; this is not circumscribed by its geographic characteristics, but evolves from cultural constructs. The concept has been promoted by the institutions of the EU since the 1980s and is still enthusiastically supported by leading intellectuals, as well as politicians. The idea is that European identity will bring greater acceptance and willingness to engage in further integration based on consciousness of a common destiny, mission and sense of solidarity. The intellectuals who define European identity trace its origin to various times and places. Each of them concentrates on cultural borders as a means of defining European identity. Mats Andrén analyses this mechanism in Chapter 10. The overall project of European integration has not only encompassed the construction of a European identity but also of an outer border. Proceeding from political philosophy, and especially from some aspects of Carl Schmitt's thinking about the border of a large political space, Jon Wittrock in Chapter 11 highlights various cultural aspects of Europe's political borders and the question of their legitimacy. A vital issue is how the EU can legitimize its outer borders and whether it should supplement its liberal ideal with rituals surrounding core symbols, as the individual states have done, in order to strengthen the sense of European identity.

A proper understanding requires knowledge of the details. The chapters of this book show the ways that cultural borders and national identities interact, and how they are sometimes difficult to distinguish. They influence society and ideas about it, not only on a local or national level, but on a continental level, as seems to be the intention of many European intellectuals and policy makers these days. The examples offered in the various chapters make it clear that the themes are complex, interacting in ways that are not always possible to foresee.

Acknowledgements

The Swedish Foundation for Humanities and Social Sciences kindly supported this project with a starting grant that made is possible to arrange three workshops and coordinate the group.

Mats Andrén is professor of history of ideas and science at the University of Gothenburg, and former director of the Centre of European Research at this same university (CERGU http://www.cergu.gu.se//); he was the deputy dean 2011–2016. His latest book is *Nuclear Waste Management and Legitimacy: Nihilism and Responsibility* (Routledge, 2012), and he has published seven monographs and twelve anthologies. He is also guest editor for special issues – e.g. on European Nihilism in *European Review* 2 (2014), with Jon Wittrock.

Ingmar Söhrman is Professor Emeritus of Romance Languages at the University of Gothenburg. Among his publications is *Diachronic and Typical Perspectives on Verbs* (2013, with Folke Josephson), and he has written on syntax, semantics, cultural contacts and nation-building in the Romance world.

Notes

1. The distinction between soft and hard borders also applies to legal and political borders – see Zielonka 2002; Debardeleben 2005; Delanty 2006.
2. The method of conceptual history has recently been advocated in European studies. See http://www.europaeum.org/europaeum/?q=taxonomy/term/357 on the European Conceptual History Research Project, initiated in 2008.
3. http://www.danteonline.it/english/opere.asp?idope=3&idlang=UK.

References

Agnew, J. (2002) 2009. *Making Political Geography*. Lanham, MD: Rowman & Littlefield.
Anderson, J., L. O'Dowd and T. Wilson. 2002. 'Why Study Borders Now?', *Regional and Federal Studies* 12(4): 1–12.
Anderson, M., and E. Bort (eds). 1998. *The Frontiers of Europe*. London: Wellington House.
Andersson, B. 1991. *Imagined Communities: Reflections on the Origin and Spread of Nationalism*. London: Verso.
Andrén, M. 2001. *Att frambringa det uthärdliga: studier kring gränser, nationalism och individualism i Centraleuropa*. Hedemora: Gidlunds förlag.
Andrén, M., et al. (eds). 2009. *Cultural Identities and National Borders*. Gothenburg: Gothenburg University.
Appadurai, A. 2006. *Fear of Small Numbers: An Essay on the Geography of Anger*. Durham, NC: Duke University Press.
Atxaga, B. 2013. 'El país vasco es, o fue, un territorio imaginario' *Tiempo*, (1.610), 5–11 July 2013, pp. 54–56.
Baldersheim, H., and L.E. Rose (eds). 2010. *Territorial Choice: The Politics of Boundaries and Borders*. New York: Palgrave MacMillan.
Balibar, E. 2002. 'World Borders, Political Borders', PMLA 1, pp. 68–78.
———. 2009. 'Europe as Borderland', *Environment and Planning D: Society and Space* 27(2): 190–215.
Barnhart, R.K. 1988. *The Barnhart Dictionary of Etymology*. New York: H.W. Wilson Co.
Beck, U., and E. Grande. 2004. *Das kosmopolitische Europa*. Frankfurt am Main: Suhrkampf.
Berdahl, D. 1999. *Where the World Ended: Re-Unification and Identity in the German Borderland*, Berkeley, CA: University of California Press.
Berezin, M., and M. Schain (eds). 2003. *Europe without Borders: Remapping Territory, Citizenship and Identity in a Transnational Age*. Baltimore, MD: The Johns Hopkins University Press.
Berger, S., and C. Lorenz. 2010. *Nationalizing the Past: Historians as Nations Builders in Europe*. Basingstoke: Palgrave Macmillan.
Burke, P. 1998. *Kultureller Austausch*. Frankfurt am Main: Suhrkamp.
———. 2009. *Cultural Hybridity*. Cambridge: Polity Press.
Council of Europe. 2006. Recommendation 1735, 'The Concept of Nation', http:/www.coe.int/.
Dante, A. ~1306. *De vulgari eloquentia*, http://www.danteonline.it/english/opere.asp?idope=3&idlang=UK
Debardeleben, J. 2005. *Soft or Hard Borders? Managing the Divide in an Enlarged Europe*. Aldershot: Ashgate.
Delanty, G. 2006. 'Borders in a Changing Europe: Dynamics of Openness and Closure', *Comparative European Politics* 4: 183–202.

Eder, K. 2006. 'Europe's Borders: The Narrative Construction of the Boundaries of Europe', *European Journal of Social Theory* 9(2): 255–271.

Edwards, J. 1994. *Multilingualism*. London and New York: Routledge.

Extra, G., and D. Gorter. 2001. *The Other Languages of Europe: Demographic, Sociolinguistic and Educational Perspective*. Clevedon: Multilingual Matters Ltd.

Fornäs, J. 2012. *Signifying Europe*. Bristol: Intellect.

Gibbons, P., and M. Holt (eds). 2002. *Beyond Boundaries: Language and Identity in Contemporary Europe*. Clevedon: Multilingual Matters Ltd.

Herder, J.G. 1965. *Ideen zur Philosophie der Geschichte der Menschheit I–II, 1784–91*. Berlin: Aufbau-Verlag

Hirschi, C. 2012. *The Origins of Nationalism: An Alternative History from Ancient Rome to Early Modern Germany*. Cambridge: Cambridge University Press.

Hobsbawn, E., and T. Ranger (eds). 1983. *The Invention of Tradition*. Cambridge: Cambridge University Press.

———. 2002. 'Borders of Comfort: Spatial Economic Bordering Processes in the European Union', *Regional and Federal Studies* 12(4): 37–58.

Houtum, H. van, and R. Pijpers. 2007. 'The European Union as a Gated Community: The Two-Faced Border and Immigration Regime of the EU', *Antipode* 39(2): 291–309.

Huntington, S.P. 1993. 'The Clash of Civilizations?', *Foreign Affairs* 72(3): 22–49.

Ivanescu, C. 2010. 'Politicised Religion and the Religionisation of Politics', *Culture and Religion* 11(4): 309–325.

Janczak, J. (ed.). 2011. *De-Bordering, Re-Bordering and Symbols on the European Boundaries*. Berlin: Logos.

Kurti, L., and J. Langman (eds). 1997. *Beyond Borders: Remaking Cultural Identities in the New East and Central Europe*. Boulder, CO: Westview Press.

Lagasabaster, D., and Á. Huguet (eds). 2007. *Multilingualism in European Bilingual Contexts*. Clevedon: Multilingual Matters Ltd.

Liedman, S.-E. 1997. *I skuggan av framtiden: modernitetens idéhistoria*, Stockholm: Bonnier.

Lundén, Thomas (ed.). 2006. *Crossing the Border: Boundary Relations in a Changing Europe*. Eslöv: Gondolin.

Newman, D. 2006. 'Borders and Bordering: Towards an Interdisciplinary Dialogue', *European Journal of Social Theory* 9(2): 171–186.

Parker, N., N. Vaughan-Williams et al. 2009. 'Lines in the Sand? Towards an Agenda for Critical Border Studies', *Geopolitics* 14(3): 582–587.

Piriou, Y.B. 1977. *Défense de cracher par terre et de parler Breton*. Paris: P.J. Oswald.

Rumford, C. 2006a. 'Rethinking European Spaces: Territory, Borders, Governance', *Comparative European Politics* 4 (2–3): 127–140

———. 2006b. 'Theorizing Borders', *European Journal of Social Theory* 9(2): 155–169.

———. 2012. 'Towards a Multiperspectival Study of Borders', *Geopolitics* 17(4): 887–902.

Schlögel, K. 2007 . 'Europe and the Culture of Borders: Rethinking Borders after 1989', in M. Hildermeier (ed.), *Historical Concepts Between Western and Eastern Europe*, New York: Berghahn 2005, pp. 73–84.

Shore, C. 2000. *Building Europe: The Cultural Politics of European Integration*. London: Routledge.

Söhrman, I. 2004. 'Intercultural Communication or Parallel Cultures? The Swiss Example with Special Regard to the Rhaeto-Romance Situation', in J. Allwood and B. Dorriots (eds), Intercultural Communication at Work. Papers in *Anthropological Linguistics* 29, Gothenburg.

———. 2009. 'Where, When and What is a Language', in Andrén et al. (eds), *Cultural Identities and National Borders*. Gothenburg: University of Gothenburg, pp. 15–34.

Wilson, T.A., and H. Donnan (eds). 1998. *Border Identities: Nation and State at International Frontiers*. Cambridge: Cambridge University Press.

Wright, S. 1998. 'The Politicization of "Culture"', *Anthropology Today* 14(1): 7–15.

Zielonka J. (ed.). 2002. *Europe Unbound: Enlarging and Reshaping the Boundaries of the European Union*. London: Routledge.

Part I

THE CHALLENGES OF RELIGIOUS BORDERS

CHAPTER 1

Territorial and Religious Identifications in Europe

LINDA BERG

Questions about who we are and where we belong are essential to most people. When asked in survey studies, people tend to respond that family, gender and occupation are among the most important categories. These categories, however, are closely followed by collective identities marked by territorial and cultural borders (such as attachment to country and religious affiliation). Given the long historical importance of territory and religion for societal development and peoples' identifications, not least in Europe, this is not very surprising (Bruter 2005; Checkel and Katzenstein 2009; Raudvere, Stala and Willert 2012; Rasmussen 2013).

European history is marked by power struggles over territory, between religious denominations, and between church and state. Issues regarding religious and territorial identity have furthermore raised concern about the European integration process, as seen, for example, in the British 'Brexit' referendum campaign. Territorial state borders have been challenged from above by European integration and from below by increased sub-state autonomy, leading to questions about the role of territorial identity (Hooghe and Marks 2001; Bruter 2005; Checkel and Katzenstein 2009). Similarly, the historical Christian Democratic foundations of the (original member states of the) European Union are being challenged by the Protestant and secular north, new orthodox member states in the east, and a complex relationship with Islam in light of both immigration and candidate countries such as Turkey (Foret and Riva 2010; Modood 2010; see also Chapter 2 in this

Notes for this section begin on page 37.

volume). Meanwhile, the religious–secular debate has been stirred by an increased focus on moral values (Berger, Davie and Fokas 2008).

This chapter will explore the relationship between individuals' feelings of religious and territorial identification in order to examine whether belonging to particular religious denominations tends to coincide systematically with specific forms of territorial identification.

Some scholars have asked to what extent different religious beliefs – as well as atheism – can be harboured within the European Union (EU) as integration deepens (Foret and Riva 2010; Foret and Itçaina 2012). The basic idea behind such questions is similar to the catalyst for research on European identity over the past decade; namely that a deepening integration that affects the everyday lives of Europeans is argued to demand greater cohesion and public support than in the early days of market integration (Ferrera 2005). The so-called 'permissive consensus' is no longer enough as issues of solidarity, redistribution of wealth and values become part of the EU policy-making process (Checkel and Katzenstein 2009). The euro crisis and its aftermath, as well as the results of the 2014 European Parliament elections and the 'Brexit' referendum, have highlighted issues of identity, and the lack of solidarity, across Europe. As emphasized in theories of system building and democracy, the more a political system evolves, the greater the need for legitimacy in the eyes of the public (Dahl 1989; Bartolini 2005). David Easton (1965: 176) described the relationship this way: 'Underlying the functioning of all systems, there must be some cohesive cement – a sense of feeling of community amongst the members. Unless such a sentiment emerges, the political system itself may never take shape – or if it does, it may not survive'.

This 'sense of feeling of community' may also be referred to as group identification. Both religious and territorial belonging are possible sources of such identification, sharing the ambiguity of serving either a positive or negative function. Group identification can serve the positive function of linking people emotionally, potentially serving the purpose as the 'emotional', or in Easton's words 'affective', part of political system support, balancing the more short-sighted utilitarian support (Easton 1975). Thus, such identification may help society to function better by creating a lasting support for the political institutions, acceptance of majority decisions, and support for redistributive measures (Dahl 1989; Offe 2000; Bartolini 2005; Ferrera 2005). The consequences of a lack of group identification among Europeans have been noticeable in debates about the euro crisis and the unwillingness to help other EU member states. Turning instead to religion, it has in a similar manner traditionally been seen as vital to social integration and solidarity by toning down self-interest (Durkheim [1912] 1975). All world religions preach the virtue of caring for the less fortunate.

However, the relationship between religion and democratic societies has been much debated. Some scholars have raised questions about the societal impact of particular religions, especially Islam (Huntington 1996; Inglehart and Norris 2003). But history makes it clear that negative consequences, even horrors such as genocide and wars, can be justified in the name of any religion – or any type of territorial identity. Neither religion nor territorial identity is intrinsically good or bad, but they share the ability to serve as mental spaces or barriers. Thus, they can arouse emotions in groups of people for either better or worse. Moreover, because religious and territorial borders may or may not coincide, religious and territorial identifications may either reinforce or counteract one another.

Although rarely studied empirically, there is an assumption about a connection between territorial identification and religion which is almost taken for granted. In some parts of Europe, territorial and religious borders coincide, most notably in the case of state religions. Religion may also be seen as intrinsic to identity, as Catholicism is in Ireland. In other cases religion forms a strong cleavage within a country, exemplified by the traditional Dutch system of pillarization. Thus, religious borders may intersect national borders. Finally, religion may be regarded as wholly independent of the state, neither reinforcing nor intersecting territorial borders but seen as a strictly personal matter (Coakley 2007; Foret and Itçaina 2012).

Territorial and Religious Identifications

The European Union is often described as a multi-level political system (Hooghe and Marks 2001) in which cultural borders, old and new, may become more sharply delineated. Such borders may or may not overlap territorial borders, promoting either tension or shoring up of feelings of identification. The concepts of identification and identity beg to be defined. The word 'identity' has become extremely popular in a wide range of academic disciplines, with a tendency to be used indiscriminately (Brubaker and Cooper 2000). Thus, it is important to distinguish between its various forms and definitions.

First, an important aspect is the division between collective identity and individual identity. Collective identities are usually seen as encompassing all, or almost all, of the individuals in a particular community, and can be found in and analysed via symbols and specific cultural features. This is most commonly found in studies of nationalism (Cederman 2001). Religion may also be studied from a mainly collective, symbolic point of view. It has, for example, been described as 'a part of collective culture that functions as a reservoir of meaning, to be freely used for whatever purpose' (Foret and Riva 2010).

Turning to the individual aspects, the word 'identification' is more commonly used to signify individuals' feelings of emotional attachment to a community, whether defined mostly in relation to territorial or cultural borders. Other common concepts are belonging and sentiments. Taking the individuals' feelings as a starting point, the identifications thus tend to vary across persons and situations, even within the same community (Brodsky and Marx 2001; Bruter 2005; Berg 2007). This individually based identification is the focus of this chapter.

Second, the object of identification needs to be defined. This chapter focuses on identifications connected to territorial and religious borders. The term 'territorial identification' is used to encompass individuals' emotional feelings of belonging to different political (administrative) units, demarcated by territorial borders such as local (municipality, town, city), regional (district, county), national (state) and European (EU).[1] Similarly, the term 'religious identification' captures feelings of affinity or belonging to various faiths – for example, Roman Catholic, Protestant, Jewish and Muslim (Modood 2010).

A distinct feature of territorial identification is that the units may also be regarded as levels within a European multilevel system, highlighting the question of how strongly people simultaneously identify with *more than one* territorial level (Hooghe and Marks 2001; Berg 2007). Previous studies of multilevel identifications have mainly compared national and European identifications (McManus-Czubinska et al. 2003; Bruter 2005). Research on identification with lower (i.e. sub-state) levels focuses mainly on countries with strong historical regions, such as Catalonia and Scotland (Díez Medrano and Gutiérrez 2001; McEwen 2005; Henderson 2007). Theoretically there are different models explaining how individuals may identify with multiple territorial levels – for example, a model of concentric circles ('The Russian doll model'), a 'marble cake' model of overlapping identities, and so on. There are also people who do not identify with any of these territorial levels (Herrmann, Risse and Brewer 2004; Bruter 2005).

In contrast to territorial identification, individuals are not expected to identify with more than one religion at a time. Converting from one faith to another is often highly restricted and relatively uncommon, and most religions demand loyalty, and thus not simultaneously belonging to another faith. Research on religion in Europe focuses on the major faiths – Protestantism, Catholicism, Greek Orthodoxy, Islam and Judaism – as an empirical approach to understanding the role of religion in society (Nelsen, Guth and Highsmith 2011; Foret and Itçaina 2012). Of course, many people are not religious. In fact, some scholars argue that non-religious individuals may be the most distinct in terms of values and political support compared to people of faith, regardless of their religious denomination (Modood 2010).

Third is the issue of how strongly a person identifies with each territorial level, or their degree of religiosity. Lawler suggests two different rules. First, the proximal rule indicates that identification will be strongest towards the lowest, or closest, level – for example, one's home town, gradually weakening with distance (Lawler 1992). Second, the distal rule expects stronger identification with the level(s) that possess the resources and power to provide for a citizen's well-being. Thus, individuals are expected to feel most strongly attached to a higher level, such as a state, if it is responsible for their well-being. Regarding the strength of religious identification, scholarly interest typically concerns commitment, usually focusing on the extent of attendance at religious services as an indicator (Foret and Riva, 2010; Nelsen, Guth and Highsmith 2011).

The theoretical expectations regarding the relationship between territorial and religious identifications may be elaborated on by considering the distinction between 'thick', 'ethnic' or 'cultural' forms of identification on the one hand, and 'thin' or 'civic' forms of identification on the other. Bruter (2005) defines cultural identities as associated with phenomena such as language, history, religion and myths, whereas civic identities are more related to legal/political aspects, and the rights and obligations of individuals. Using such a definition clarifies how and why religious identification may support and strengthen territorial identification for some individuals, whereas the relationship may be the opposite or unrelated for others. When territorial identifications are associated with cultural aspects – like religion – the two may reinforce one another, whereas a more civic form of identification may cut across, or be unrelated to, religious identifications.

Moreover, we can find similarities in the expected consequences for society of religious and territorial identifications; for example, people of faith tend to be more supportive of existing political regimes (Inglehart and Norris 2003; Meyer, Tope and Price 2008). Religious beliefs have also been shown to influence attitudes towards European integration, but with somewhat mixed results for the various religious denominations (Nelsen, Guth and Highsmith 2011).[2] Similarly, territorial identifications have been shown to impact trust in political systems (Berg 2007). The strongest resistance to European integration has been found among people who identify primarily with their state, whereas the most positive attitudes are among those who feel European (Hooghe and Marks 2004; McLaren 2004).

However, few studies have combined religious and territorial identifications. When combined, the studies are usually of countries or regions where religion is important to a conflict (for example, Northern Ireland), or, as in the case of Spain, closely connected with the state's identity (Coakley 2007; Muñoz 2009). If the religion and identity are combined in a study, religious beliefs tend to be treated as an explanatory factor for phenomena such as the persisting Protestant influence on identity in Northern Ireland. Foret and Riva (2010: 794) argue that 'the re-activation of the religious references can serve many purposes. It is rarely used to celebrate the nation in an exclusivist way, as this leads to political marginalisation. It is often mobilised in the negotiation of the nation's attachment to Europe'.

The least theorized group consists of non-religious people. Given the secular tradition of many European states, one might expect non-religious people to have strong 'civic' identifications with their country and Europe. But some scholars point to secularism, particularly in its radical form, as the least tolerant of any religious belief (Modood 2010). Moreover, if the initial ideas from system-building theory are correct, this group can be expected to display less territorial identification than others. Some preliminary expectations about the relationship between religious belonging and territorial identification can be summarized as follows:

Belonging to a religion that is dominant in one's country and/or Europe
  • More likely to be proud to be a citizen of one's country and/or Europe
  • More likely to identify with the state and/or Europe
  • More likely to feel multilevel identification
Belonging to a religion that is not dominant in one's country/Europe
  • Less likely to be proud to be a citizen of one's country and/or Europe
  • More likely to identify with higher territorial levels (Europe, the world)
Being non-religious
  • Less likely to be proud to be a citizen of one's country and/or Europe
  • More likely to be unattached / not identify with any territorial levels

Study Design

As this chapter focuses on the overall relationship between religious and territorial identifications across countries and individuals, the material consists of comparative opinion study data. The benefit of studying overall patterns in this manner comes at a price. As with all opinion study data, we lose qualitative, in-depth insights while gaining the opportunity to generalize. Identification is a complex phenomenon, and we will not be able to capture the inner sentiments of an individual when answering questions about being proud of one's country or the meaning of religious feelings. Moreover, precise concepts such as nation and state are predefined in the surveys. Thus, some of the comments on results in this chapter will concern less optimal concepts than desired. Another critique of this approach is that the strength and importance of identification may differ according to changing situations. Although that is a relevant concern, the relationship between two questions that have been asked at the same time is of interest here, which makes situational variation less problematic. Two sets of opinion studies, which combine questions of territorial and religious identifications, will be used for the analyses in this chapter: the International Social Survey Programme (ISSP) 2003 and the European Values Study (EVS) 2008.[3] For purposes of simplification, the chapter will use graphs and tables to illustrate the overall patterns discussed.

The survey questions used in the analyses will be discussed next. The first question asks the respondent to rank the groups that s(he) identifies with (out of several different categories), providing a good indication of how important various identifications, like religion and territory, are in comparison with one another.[4]

Focusing specifically on the aspect of *territorial* identification, this chapter will then rely on one of the most common measures used in survey studies: 'proud to be a [country] citizen', and 'proud to be a European citizen', with four response alternatives from 'very proud' to 'not at all proud'. Another question measures the respondents' identification with different territorial levels, ranging from the local to Europe, using two different measures: 'Which of these geographical groups would you say you belong to first of all? And secondly?'[5] The third question asks: 'How close do you feel to: "your town/city", "your county", "your country" and "Europe"'.[6]

These questions are useful in their original form, as well as offering the opportunity to create a new measure of multilevel territorial identifications, where respondents are categorized according to which territorial level, or levels, they most strongly identify with. The categories of multilevel territorial identifications are: unattached, primarily sub-state identification, all domestic identification (i.e. a person who identifies equally strongly with the state and all sub-state levels); primarily state identification; primarily European identification; and 'all levels equal' (identifies equally strongly with all levels). These categories are mutually exclusive; that is to say, they are all coded as one (1) if a person belongs to the category, or zero (0) if s/he does not.[7]

Religious affiliation is more straightforward to measure. The questions in the two surveys are worded very similarly: 'Do you belong to a religious denomination?' (yes/no), and if 'yes', 'Which one?' The answers have been coded according to the major world religions, plus a category for 'other'.[8] In the ISSP, there is also a question about religious attendance: 'Apart from weddings, funerals and christenings, about how often do you attend religious services these days?' The seven response alternatives range from several times a week to never, and these are then recoded down to just three categories: often (several times a week, once a week), seldom (2–3 times a month, once a month, several times a year, once a year), and never (less frequently, never).

Results

Starting with a cross-country comparison of identifications connected to either territorial or cultural borders, some interesting patterns emerge. Out of a list of ten possible objects of identification, individuals in each country have chosen their top three alternatives.[9] Showing only the proportion of people who indicate territorial and cultural identifications (in this case, one of the response alternatives 'nationality' and 'part of country', or 'ethnicity' and 'religion') in Figure 1.1, there are some interesting variations across European countries. In most countries, territorial identifications (nationality and part of country) are indicated by a larger proportion of the population than the proportion that indicates more cultural identifications (ethnicity and religion). There are some notable exceptions, including Latvia, where the cultural alternatives dominate. In some countries, citizens have more mixed answers, creating a pattern where cultural and territorial alternatives are equally important. Religion is considered important for many people in Slovakia, Poland, the Netherlands and Ireland. The category 'nationality' is considered important by approximately one-third of the people in all countries except Hungary and Latvia.

In most countries, there are historical reasons for this variation. For example, Sweden, Finland and Denmark have a long history of state formation and relative cultural homogeneity. Cultural aspects are typically seen as more important by a larger proportion of the population in countries that have ongoing border conflicts with neighbours, in recently independent states, and where the Catholic Church has a large influence and religion has been historically important, such as Ireland.

Turning more specifically to the aspect of religion, Figure 1.2 offers an overview of the total proportion of people in each country who feel that they belong to a religious denomination. It also gives insight into the distribution of belonging across different religions, as well as the proportion of people who answer that they do not belong to any denomination at all. The highest number of people who feel that they do not belong to any religion is found in the Czech Republic (70 per cent), closely followed by Estonia (65 per cent). For countries like France and Belgium, with a 'laïcité' tradition, it might be less surprising to find that over 40 per cent of the respondents say that they do not feel they belong to any religion. Secularism, albeit in a different form, is also common in the UK and the Nordic countries. This corresponds to the relatively high proportion of non-believers in these countries, apart from Denmark, which has a surprisingly low proportion of non-believers – only 12 per cent. In contrast, it is as expected that very few people in Cyprus, Malta, Greece, Romania or Poland are non-believers.

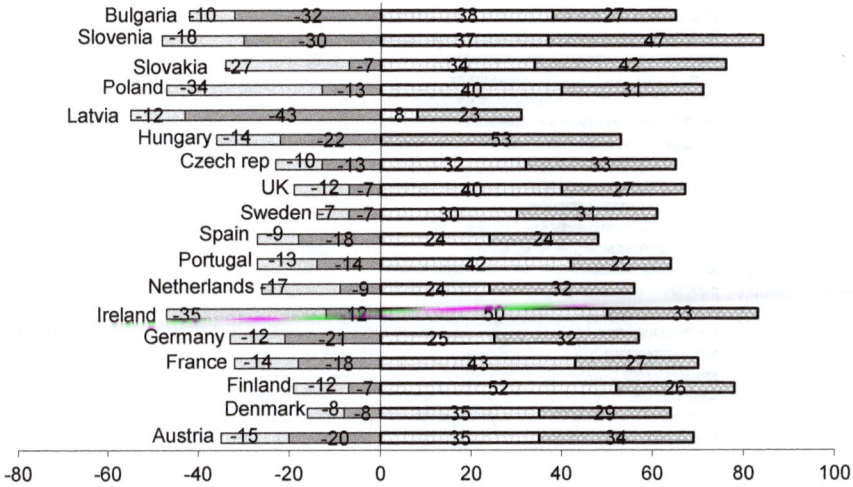

Figure 1.1 Ethnicity, religion, nationality or part of country as one of three most important aspects of identification, per country (per cent).

Comment: ISSP 2003. The question is: 'We are all part of different groups. Some are more important to us than others when we think of ourselves. In general, which in the following list is most important to you in describing who you are? And the second most important? And the third most important?' The alternatives are: your current or previous occupation, race/ethnic background, gender, age group, religion (or being atheist), preferred political party, nationality, family or marital status, social class and the part [of the country] you live in. In the figure only four categories are displayed (ethnic, religion, nationality and part of country), representing the proportion of people in each country indicating each of these four as one of their three most important groups of belonging. Due to the option for each individual to provide up to three answers, the aggregated percentages for each country do not total 100. Only EU countries have been included in the analysis, and only the eighteen countries that participated in the ISSP 2003.

Another noticeable pattern is that a large majority of people in most countries regard themselves as belonging to the same religion, such as Orthodoxy in Greece, Catholicism in Poland and Protestantism in Denmark. Some similarities in the overall pattern can be found when comparing the feelings of religious belonging (Figure 1.2) to the distribution of national pride across the EU countries (Figure 1.3). One example is that certain countries – including Malta, Cyprus and Greece – have both a high number of people who are religious and of people who feel very proud to be citizens of their respective countries. At the other end of the spectrum, the similarities are less striking, but there are nonetheless certain countries in the upper parts of figures 1.2 and 1.3 (the Netherlands, Belgium, Germany, the Czech Republic, etc.) with lower levels of both religiosity and national pride.

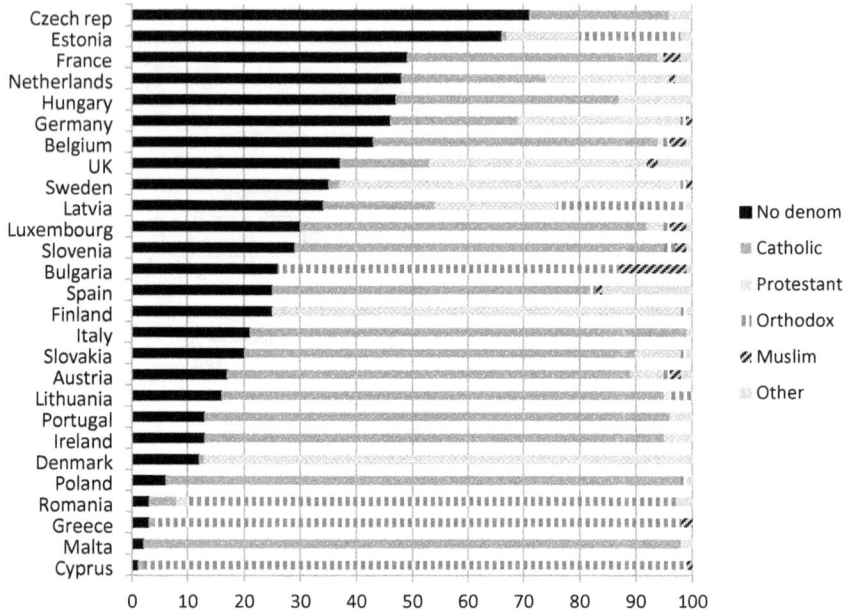

Figure 1.2 Religious denomination (none, Catholic, Protestant, Orthodox, Muslim or other), per country in the EU27 (per cent).

Comment: EVS 2008. The figure is based on two questions. The first one: 'Do you belong to a religious denomination?' Response alternatives are yes/no. Those who answer yes receive the follow up question: 'Which one?' The answers have later been categorized into the major world religions, plus a category 'other'. Respondents answering Jew, Hindu or Buddhist have also been included in the category 'other' as there were too few respondents in these categories. In addition, people answering 'no' to the first question were given their own category of 'no denomination'.

Looking at the overall distribution for all twenty-seven EU member states in Table 1.1, we see the pattern more clearly: people who claim to be non-religious also tend to be less proud to be citizens of their country than people who feel that they are religious. The non-religious group also has the highest proportion (17 per cent altogether) of people who are 'not very' or 'not at all' proud to be a citizen of their country.

The group with the highest proportion of people who feel proud to be a citizen of their country is the Roman Catholics, with a net balance of 84 when the number of those who are not proud has been subtracted from those who feel proud. Protestants also tend to be proud to be citizens of their country, with a net balance of 80. Among religious people, Muslims have a slightly lower net balance; in particular, the proportion of 'very proud' people is lower than for all other religions, although they are slightly

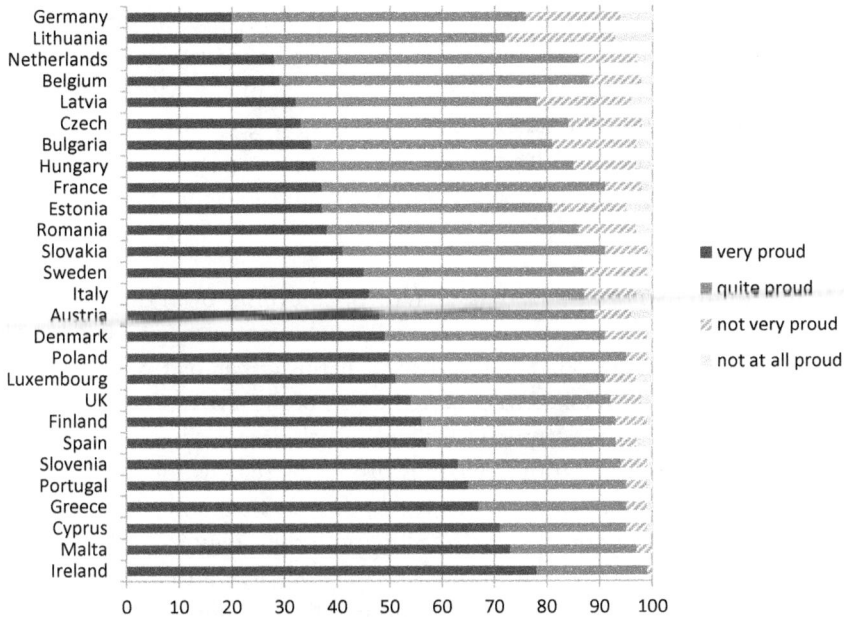

Figure 1.3 National pride, per country in the EU27 (per cent).

Comment: EVS 2008. The figure is based on the question: 'How proud are you to be a [country] citizen?' The response alternatives are displayed in the figure.

Table 1.1 Religious denomination (none, Catholic, Protestant, Orthodox, Muslim or other) and national pride, in the EU27 (per cent)

	Non-religious	*Catholic*	*Protestant*	*Muslim*	*Orthodox*	*Other*	*Total*
Very proud	34	52	48	35	51	46	46
Quite proud	49	40	42	51	37	42	43
Not very proud	13	6	8	10	10	9	9
Not at all proud	4	2	2	4	2	3	2
Sum	100	100	100	100	100	100	100
N	10,295	15,083	5,438	337	4,811	698	36,662
Balance	*66*	*84*	*80*	*72*	*76*	*76*	*78*

Comment: EVS 2008. For information about religious denomination, see Figure 1.2. The question about pride is: 'How proud are you to be a [country] citizen?' The response alternatives are displayed in the table. The balance measure subtracts the proportion of people who answer 'not very proud' or 'not at all proud' from those who answer 'very proud' or 'quite proud'.

more proud than the non-religious group. However, the total number of Muslim respondents is just 337, so the results must be interpreted cautiously. Moreover, it should be noted that large segments of the Muslim population in the EU member states are first or second generation immigrants. Identification with either their country or Europe may therefore be more challenging, as Göran Larsson and Riem Spielhaus discuss in Chapter 2.

Different Territorial Levels

Moving on to identifications with all territorial levels – from the town one lives in to the world as a whole – we explore the extent to which religiosity corresponds with such identifications. In the upper half of Table 1.2, respondents have been asked to choose the two of the five territorial alternatives to which they have strongest feelings of belonging. There is very little variation between the various religious groups as regards identifying with one's town. But for higher territorial levels, there is a tendency for Catholics and Protestants to identify somewhat more with their region, the Orthodox more with their country, and Muslims, people belonging to other religions and the non-religious to identify a bit more with the highest levels (Europe and the world).

However, it should be noted that this type of question forces respondents to choose two territorial levels to which they belong. Not only does such a question imply a ranking that the respondent may not regard as appropriate, but a respondent is not able to indicate identification with more than two levels. Hence, another survey question is used in the lower part of the table in which the respondents are asked to answer the question 'How close do you feel to: Your town/city, your county/region, your country, Europe?', with response alternatives ranging from very close to not close at all. Only the percentages for those answering 'very close' to each territorial level are displayed in the table.

As can be seen, the pattern in the lower half of Table 1.2 is somewhat different to the upper half. For example, we find the lowest proportion of people who feel 'very close' to any of the four levels among those who are non-religious (mean 25). The only exception to this pattern is slightly lower identification with the regional level among Protestants. The mean score is also relatively low for people with an 'other' religion (27) and Protestants (29), indicating on average low numbers of people feeling 'very close' to any level. However, almost half of Protestants feel very closely attached to their country. Stronger feelings are generally found among the Orthodox and Catholics. The highest proportion of people who feel close to Europe is found among the Muslims. This result might initially seem surprising, but it is in accordance with the distal theory to expect Muslims to feel attached to a higher (or larger) territorial area than national or regional entities.

Table 1.2 Religious denomination and geographical belonging/feeling very close to different territorial levels, in EU27 / 18 European countries (per cent)

	Non-religious	Catholic	Protestant	Orthodox	Muslim	Other	Total	N
Your town	64	69	64	66	62	60	66	13,303
Your region	41	44	46	31	36	42	41	16,225
Your country	64	66	69	79	64	62	67	26,389
Europe	19	14	14	14	21	16	15	6,029
The World	13	8	8	9	17	20	10	3,775
N	11,081	15,990	5,556	5,280	482	776	39,165	
Your town	30	46	33	49	44	29	39	8,294
Your region	23	39	21	41	36	26	31	6,548
Your country	32	51	48	57	43	35	46	9,828
Europe	14	23	15	27	28	16	19	3,936
Mean	25	40	29	44	38	27	34	
N	4,709	9,828	4,861	1,143	255	390	21,186	

Comment: For information on religious denomination, see Figure 1.2.

Upper half of the table: EVS 2008. The wording of the question concerning geographical belonging is: 'Which of these geographical groups would you say you belong to first of all? And secondly?' The figures indicate the percentages of people mentioning each of the five alternatives as first or second groups of belonging.

Lower half of the table: ISSP 2003. The wording of the question concerning closeness is 'How close do you feel to: Your town/city, your county/ region, your country, Europe?' The response alternatives are very close, close, not very close, and not close at all.

Table 1.3 Correlations between religious denominations and territorial identifications in 18 European countries

	How close do you feel to:			
	Your town	Your region	Your country	Europe
Non-religious	−0.1189★	−0.1394★	−0.1749★	−0.0984★
Roman Catholic	0.1390★	0.2134★	0.1161★	0.1485★
Protestant	−0.0659★	−0.1353★	0.0303★	−0.0883★
Orthodox	0.0466★	0.0457★	0.0404★	0.0234★
Muslim	0.0130	0.0075	−0.0150	0.0205★
Other	−0.0319★	−0.0229★	−0.0408★	−0.0253★

Comment: ISSP 2003. For information on religious denomination, see Figure 1.2. The wording of the question concerning closeness is: 'How close do you feel to: Your town/city, your county/region, your country, Europe?' The response alternatives are very close, close, not very close, or not close at all. The correlations are weighted according to population size; significant results are marked ★.

The pattern is further supported by correlations between the same variables, which can be seen in Table 1.3. Here it is clear that non-religiosity correlates negatively with closely identifying with all four territorial levels. Catholicism correlates positively with all levels, as does the Orthodox group, albeit weaker. Protestantism correlates negatively with all levels – apart from country. Having a Muslim denomination is insignificantly correlated to all territorial levels apart from Europe, which is weakly positive. Finally, 'other' religions correlate negatively with all territorial levels.

Answers to the question presented in the lower half of Table 1.2 can also be used to categorize people according to the level or levels to which they feel most attached. Respondents can be assigned to one of six categories: unattached, primarily sub-state identification, all domestic identification (equally strong identifications with all sub-state and state levels), primarily state identification, primarily European identification, and 'all levels equal' (identifies equally strongly with all levels). Table 1.4 presents this categorization in relation to religious belonging (percentages and correlations). The results show that the non-religious, Muslims and 'other' religions are over-represented in the 'unattached' category (i.e. those who do not identify with any of the four territorial levels). They are also somewhat over-represented in the group who primarily identify with Europe, and thus tend to identify less with the domestic levels.

Another pattern which is even more apparent in this table is that Protestants identify more strongly with their country and more weakly with levels above or beneath the state. In contrast, the Catholics and the Orthodox tend to have most multilevel identifications, with a high percentage among them identifying equally strongly with all territorial levels.

Table 1.4 Religious denomination and different categories of multilevel attachments, in 18 European countries (per cent, correlations)

Identification	Non-religious	Roman Catholic	Protestant	Orthodox	Muslim	Other	Total	N
Unattached	7	2	4	4	7	8	4	884
	0.0814★	−0.0883★	0.0104	−0.0027	0.0226★	0.0287★		
Primarily sub-state	17	14	12	9	11	15	14	2,890
	0.0436★	−0.0002	−0.0244★	−0.0348★	−0.0059	0.0056		
All domestic	15	20	14	21	10	15	17	3,729
	−0.0292★	0.0579★	−0.0431★	0.0222★	−0.0214★	−0.0083		
Primarily state	22	20	34	19	12	22	23	5,047
	−0.0176★	−0.0832★	0.1398★	−0.0256★	−0.0327★	−0.0048		
Primarily European	18	13	15	13	17	21	15	3,044
	0.0417★	−0.0388★	0.0041	−0.0134	0.0020	0.0223★		
All levels equal	16	27	14	28	26	16	21	4,619
	−0.0652★	0.1280★	−0.1026★	0.0361★	0.0127	−0.0226★		
Total	100	100	100	100	100	100	100	100
N	4,827	9,991	5,030	1,154	264	403	4,827	21,669

Comment: ISSP 2003. For information on religious denomination, see Figure 1.2. The categorization of multilevel identifications is based on the survey questions used in Table 1.3. The category unattached is constituted by those answering 'not very close' or 'not at all close' to all levels in the original question. The other categories are based on which (one or more) level(s) a person indicated as their strongest identification ('very close'): primarily sub−state identification, all domestic identification (equally strong identifications with all sub−state and state levels), primarily state identification, primarily European identification and 'all levels equal' (identifies equally strongly with all levels). More information can be found in the section *Study Design*. The correlations are weighted according to population size; significant results are marked ★.

Conclusion

This chapter has explored the relationship between individuals' territorial and religious identifications in Europe. As both territorial and cultural borders have caused tensions and conflict throughout history, it is important to learn more about their influence on individuals' identifications. In the wake of the economic crisis, the European integration process has been called into question. Issues relating to territorial and religious borders influence the political agenda. Hence, it is important to understand how and when religious identifications reinforce, counteract or are unrelated to territorial identifications.

The results in this chapter show some interesting similarities between territorial and religious identifications, as well as differences or oppositions. Large-scale cross-country survey data offer the opportunity to explore this relationship across European countries, as well as across various religious denominations and territorial levels of identification. Among the notable results are that Roman Catholics tend to have stronger feelings of identification with all territorial levels, from the local to the European level. Orthodox identifications display a somewhat similar, but weaker, pattern. Protestantism, on the other hand, tends to be associated mainly with state identification – especially in the predominantly Protestant countries – and a general lack of identification with Europe. This pattern corresponds to the historical development whereby Protestant countries tended to have a very strong relationship between church and state. In comparison, the Catholic Church more often offered a non-state, universalistic and multilevel alternative of power. The data contain many fewer people with a Muslim identification such that the results need to be interpreted cautiously. However, the tendency is for this group to have weak or non-existent identification with the state and to identify instead with higher territorial levels such as Europe and the world – or not to identify with any of them. This should be understood in relation to the predominant immigrant background among Muslims in the EU member states. However, in response to previous academic concerns, there is little support in these data for an inherent lack of identification with Europe among Muslims.

These initial results point to potentially fruitful future research about this relationship. Theoretical concerns by some researchers about a challenge to European cohesion by Islam are not supported by these results. Instead the group with no religious or territorial identifications merit further attention for anyone interested in emotional support for European integration. One preliminary conclusion is that religious borders matter for national or lower territorial identifications, especially among people who belong to the predominant religion in a country. But in terms of European integration, the cause for concern is less a matter of reinforcing or counteracting cultural and territorial identifications, or the possible coexistence of various religions, as a lack of feeling of community among certain groups of Europeans.

Linda Berg is a senior lecturer in the Department of Political Science and director of the Centre for European Research (CERGU) at the University of Gothenburg, Sweden (www.cergu.gu.se). She is the author of 'National Identity and Political Trust' (with Mikael Hjerm), in *Perspectives on European Politics and Society* (2010, 4). Her work is also featured in the journals *European Politics and Society*, *Policy Studies* and *Electoral Studies*. She has edited four books and authored more than twenty chapters, including in the book *Regional and National Elections in Western Europe: Territoriality of the Vote in Thirteen Countries* (eds. Regis Dandoy and Arjan H. Schakel), Palgrave Macmillan, 2013.

Notes

1. The theoretical concept used in this chapter is 'region'. However, due to variations across Europe, country-specific questionnaires use different words to better reflect the appropriate societal level in each country. When writing a chapter in English, the English version of the questionnaires is referred to. For the EVS2008 study, there is an English basic questionnaire, in which the word 'region' is used, whereas the English version of the questionnaire for ISSP 2003 is the UK version, in which the word 'county' is used. For simplicity, and since the main purpose of this chapter is to give an overview across many countries with different regional structures, the concept 'region' will be used throughout the text, even when 'county' appears in a table or in a reference to a full formulation of a survey question.

2. One study found that Catholics, especially religious ones, supported the EU; Protestants were strongly opposed unless they were religious; and Muslims were opposed if religious.

3. Both are large-scale, cross-country programmes for international and/or European comparative attitude studies, with approximately one thousand respondents in each country – fewer in small countries like Luxembourg, and more in Germany. The ISSP 2003, 'Aspects of National Identity II', is useful as it covers a variety of aspects of territorial identification and some questions about religion. The study covers thirty-three countries, but only the eighteen current EU member states are included in the analyses of this chapter. The EVS 2008 covers forty-seven states, but only the current twenty-seven EU member states are included in the analyses. The EVS 2008 included several questions concerning religion, and some concerning territorial identification.

4. The categories are: occupation, race/ethnicity, gender, age group, religion, political party, nationality, family/marital status, social class, and the part of country the respondent lives in.

5. The five alternatives are 'locality or town where you live', 'region or county where you live', 'your country', 'Europe' and 'the world as a whole'. This item is recoded in order to capture whether any of the alternatives have been mentioned at all, regardless whether it was the first or second group of belonging (EVS 2008).

6. Four response alternatives are presented for each territorial level: 'very close', 'close', 'not very close' and 'not close at all' (ISSP 2003).

7. See Berg 2007 for more details on coding and theoretical justification of the groups.

8. Due to the small number of respondents, people answering Jew, Hindu or Buddhist have been recoded to the 'other' category, whereas people answering 'no' to the first question have their own category, referred to as 'no denomination'.

9. The alternatives in the ISSP 2003 were: current or previous occupation, race/ethnic background, gender, age group, religion (or being an atheist), political party, nationality, family or marital status, social class and the part of the country you live in.

References

Bartolini, S. 2005. *Restructuring Europe: Centre Formation, System Building and Political Structuring between the Nation-State and the European Union*. Oxford: Oxford University Press.

Berg, L. 2007. *Multi-level Europeans: The Influence of Territorial Attachments on Political Trust and Welfare Attitudes*. Gothenburg: University of Gothenburg.

Berger, P., G. Davie and E. Fokas. 2008. *Religious America, Secular Europe? A Theme and Variations*. London: Ashgate.

Brodsky, A.E., and C.M. Marx. 2001. 'Layers of Identity: Multiple Psychological Senses of Community within a Community Setting', *Journal of Community Psychology* 29(2): 161–78.

Brubaker, R., and F. Cooper. 2000. 'Beyond "Identity"', *Theory and Society* 29: 1–47.

Bruter, M. 2005. *Citizens of Europe? The Emergence of a Mass European Identity*. New York: Palgrave Macmillan.

Cederman, L.-E. 2001. 'Nationalism and Bounded Integration: What It Would Take to Construct a European Demos', *European Journal of International Relations* 7(2): 139–74.

Checkel, J.T., and P.J. Katzenstein. 2009. *European Identity*. Cambridge: Cambridge University Press.

Coakley, J. 2007. 'National Identity in Northern Ireland: Stability or Change?', *Nations and Nationalism* 13(4): 573–97.

Dahl, R.A. 1989. *Democracy and its Critics*. New Haven, CT: Yale University Press.

Díez Medrano, J., and P. Gutiérrez. 2001. 'Nested Identities: National and European Identity in Spain', *Ethnic and Racial Studies* 24(5): 753–78.

Durkheim, E. (1912) 1975. *The Elementary Forms of the Religious Life*. London: George Allen & Unwin Ltd.

Easton, D. 1965. *A Systems Analysis of Political Life*. Chicago: The University of Chicago Press.

———. 1975. 'A Re-Assessment of the Concept of Political Support', *British Journal of Political Science* 5: 435–57.

Ferrera, M. 2005. *The Boundaries of Welfare: European Integration and the New Spatial Politics of Social Protection*. Oxford: Oxford University Press.

Foret, F., and X. Itçaina. 2012. *Politics of Religion in Western Europe: Modernities in Conflict?* London: Routledge / ECPR Studies in European Political Science.

Foret, F., and V. Riva. 2010. 'Religion between Nation and Europe: The French and Belgian "No" to the Christian Heritage of Europe', *West European Politics* 33(4): 791–809.

Henderson, A. 2007. *Hierarchies of Belonging: National Identity and Political Culture in Scotland and Quebec*. Montreal and Kingston: McGill-Queen's University Press.

Herrmann, R.K., T. Risse and M.B. Brewer (eds). 2004. *Transnational Identities: Becoming European in the EU*. Oxford: Rowman & Littlefield.

Hooghe, L., and G. Marks. 2001. *Multi-level Governance and European Integration*. Lanham, MD: Rowman & Littlefield.

———. 2004. 'Does Identity or Economic Rationality Drive Public Opinion on European Integration?', *PS: Political Science & Politics* 37(3): 415–20.

Huntington, S.P. 1996. *The Clash of Civilizations and the Remaking of World Order*. New York: Simon & Schuster.

Inglehart, R., and P. Norris. 2003. 'The True Clash of Civilizations', *Foreign Policy* 135: 62–70.

Lawler, E. 1992. 'Affective Attachments to Nested Groups: A Choice-Process Theory', *American Sociological Review* 57(3): 327–39.

McEwen, N. 2005. *Nationalism and the State: Welfare and Identity in Scotland and Quebec*, Vol. 5. Brussels, Bern, Berlin, Frankfurt am Main, New York, Oxford and Vienna: P.I.E. Peter Lang

McLaren, L. 2004. 'Opposition to European Integration and Fear of Loss of National Identity: Debunking a Basic Assumption Regarding Hostility to the Integration Project', *European Journal of Political Research* 43: 895–911.

McManus-Czubinska, C., et al. 2003. 'Understanding Dual Identities in Poland', *Political Studies* 51: 121–43.

Meyer, K., D. Tope and A.M. Price. 2008. 'Religion and Support for Democracy: A Cross-National Examination', *Sociological Spectrum* 28: 625–53.

Modood, T. 2010. 'Moderate Secularism, Religion as Identity and Respect for Religion', *The Political Quarterly* 81(1): 4–14.

Muñoz, J. 2009. 'From National-Catholicism to Democratic Patriotism? Democratization and Reconstruction of National Pride: The Case of Spain (1981–2000)', *Ethnic and Racial Studies* 32(4): 616–39.

Nelsen, B.F., J.L. Guth and B. Highsmith. 2011. 'Does Religion Still Matter? Religion and Public Attitudes toward Integration in Europe', *Politics and Religion* 4, 1–26.

Offe, C. 2000. *The Democratic Welfare State: A European Regime under the Strain of European Integration*. Vienna: Institut für Höhere Studien, Abt. Politikwissenschaft. Retrieved from http://nbn-resolving.de/urn:nbn:de:0168-ssoar-246586.

Rasmussen, S.W. 2013. *Religion and Identity in Europe: The Makings of Religious Enemies in Antiquity and Today*, Vol. 24. Odense: University Press of Southern Denmark.

Raudvere, C., K. Stala and T.S. Willert. 2012. *Rethinking the Space for Religion: New Actors in Central and Southeast Europe on Religion, Authenticity and Belonging*. Lund: Nordic Academic Press.

CHAPTER 2

Europe with or without Muslims

Creating and Maintaining Cultural Boundaries

GÖRAN LARSSON AND RIEM SPIELHAUS

With a detailed analysis of a specific public debate, this chapter will demonstrate that Islam and Muslims play an important role in the current public imagining of what Europe means and how European idéntities are constructed and played out in public debates. We will argue that the construction of 'us' and 'them', and with it the drawing of cultural boundaries, has grown in importance over the last few decades, and that this dichotomy has been reinforced by the construction of the European Union. Today Europe is not only a geographical entity, it is a political and economic construction that strives to cultivate a specific shared European identity. The lack of a common language and competing national histories mean that the construction of a common identity is a difficult task to undertake. This might be why the topos of values shared by all Europeans has become such an important narrative. As we will show in the following analysis, this is often done by portraying ethnic or religious minorities – in this case, people of Muslim faith and immigrants from Muslim majority countries – as different, while ascribing values to them that are perceived and constructed as contrary to those of Europe. Another way of moulding European identities would be to stress Europe's diversity and heterogeneous composition in what we would call an inclusive narrative.

Debates about how to define Europe, its boundaries and the content of its identities and values, are currently gathering steam. A growing number of populist parties and politicians in Europe benefit from xenophobic, anti-Roma and anti-Muslim prejudice. The 2014 European Parliament elections are just one example. Established and mainstream parties and politicians are revisiting the question of how much multiculturalism and pluralism Europe can handle. In recent years, initially small groups of activists in the Netherlands, France, Denmark, Germany, Austria and Switzerland have developed a pan-European narrative that combines warnings about the Islamization of Europe with anti-EU and anti-elitist sentiments while drawing on a transnational network based on social media, personal contacts and meetings that allow the exchange of arguments, images, slogans and campaigns. In some cases they manage to convey their messages to the mainstream media and set the tone for popular images of a Europe based on common values created through stereotypes of a Muslim enemy (Shooman and Spielhaus 2010). Meanwhile, initiatives against discrimination at the local, national and EU levels have taken up the topic by articulating a counternarrative of a Europe that includes Muslims.

Locating Muslims in Academic Research

These two narratives are entrenched in academic literature as well. On the one hand, academic literature by and large highlights the migration of Muslims to Western Europe and presents them – sometimes in very subtle forms – as immigrants. On the other hand, a growing number of researchers are arguing that this interprets the past and reduces Europe to Western Europe, overlooking the Muslim presence on the Iberian Peninsula from the eighth century and the Baltic Rim from the fifteenth century (cf. Larsson and Račius 2010; Tsitselikis 2013). During the last two decades, research on the 'new Islamic presence in Europe' (Gerholm and Lithman 1988) has produced a wealth of publications with great diversity of approaches and focal points. However, the presence of Muslims in Europe is mostly presented as a part of postwar migration starting with workers arriving in France, the Netherlands, Belgium, Austria, the UK and Germany, and later the Nordic countries as well. Hence, the Muslim presence in Europe is portrayed as a rather recent phenomenon that primarily involves workers, their families, and refugees. According to many introductions to Islam in Europe, this process began after the Second World War but has only recently been affecting southern European countries such as Italy, Spain and Greece. A few studies and introductory textbooks counter this perception and present the evolution of Muslim communities in other parts of Europe, especially central, eastern, and northern Europe (cf. Larsson and Račius 2010; Tsitselikis 2012; Nordbruch and Ryad 2014).

How to write up the history of Europe and its inhabitants is therefore a sensitive topic that can lend it self to different political projects. So without developing the argument, it is fair to say that the study of Islam and Muslims in Europe has become highly politicized and the academic field is increasingly drawn into political debates and policy decisions.

Debating the Motion that 'Europe is Failing its Muslims'

The following case study centres on the public discussion entitled 'Europe is failing its Muslims', arranged by Intelligence Squared, a global forum for live debate, 'dedicated to creating knowledge through contest' in cooperation with the British Council and BBC. The debate took place on 23 February 2010 at Cadogan Hall in London in front of a large audience and was streamed online, as well as broadcasted by BBC World News.[1] This debate involved Muslim scholar Professor Tariq Ramadan of Oxford University and former Dutch diplomat Petra Stienen, who both spoke in favour of the motion that 'Europe is failing its Muslims', while British writer and policy maker Douglas Murray and the cultural editor of the Danish newspaper _Jyllands-Posten_ Fleming Rose both argued against.

We chose this debate because it contains positions and a certain set of themes and arguments that frequently recur when Islam is publicly discussed. Among many typical features, this debate reveals the notion of 'us' versus 'them', alluding to the questions of who is a European, who to include and who to exclude. Thus, it presents an argument about the cultural borders of Europe.

We will first outline Ramadan and Stienen's arguments, followed by those of Murray and Rose. Finally, we will analyse various interactions between the panellists and the audience during the question and answer session. The chapter ends with a comparison of the conflicting narratives about Europe and its Muslims. If no other references are given, the quotes are taken from the debate between Ramadan/Stienen and Murray/Rose that was broadcast by BBC and is available in its entirety on the Intelligence Squared website.

'Europe is failing its Muslims' – For the Motion

Ramadan explains that Europe is failing its Muslims by denying them the feeling of belonging, along with social deprivation – thus both symbolic or discursive, and material exclusion. He identifies the major problems in the current debate as the negative image of Islam and Muslims in Europe coupled with social deprivation, exclusion of, and racism against, Muslims, and the fact that Islam is blamed for these problems. In order to demonstrate his point, he bases his statement on four major arguments by which he claims to counter the fictions of public debate with reality. He points out that Europeans associate Islam and Muslims with problems and conflicts, beginning with the negative perception of Muslims:

Let me start by saying that we are living in a difficult situation. If you listen to what is said in the European countries, the perception is very bad. 75 per cent for example of French people are associating Islam with violence. The perception is that Islam is a problem and that Muslims are creating problems. They are not really perceived at home in Europe. Every single European society has its own debate, its own controversies around the Muslim presence. The first one is the way Europe is defining itself. The general discourse is that Muslims are not European citizens.

Secondly, Ramadan argues that the prevailing public discourse holds that the European continent does not have any Muslims. For instance, in the debate about the accession of Turkey to the EU, Muslims are seen as 'people who are coming from outside, not acknowledging the fact that we already have Europeans who are Muslims in our countries'. The fact that Europe is the home to millions of Muslims, Ramadan argues, is ignored and the Muslim presence in the Balkans and Eastern Europe is downplayed or denied in the collective memory of Europe. Hence, Western Europe is the model, and large parts of the continent and its history are either forgotten or excluded. 'It is as if, because they [the Bosnians] are Muslims they are less Europeans'. In his introduction Ramadan analyses his imagined opponent's argument – 'as if these new citizens are problematic because of their religion'. According to Ramadan, being both a Muslim and a European is deemed to be impossible in today's Europe.

A third major obstacle that Ramadan mentions is that Europe appears to be positive and open to fresh money and food cultures, but afraid of colour and differences: 'Money and food are fine, but colour and dress, no'. This selective pattern is contributing to growing discrimination against immigrants, creating an environment for anti-Muslim opinions and parties to benefit from public fear. Consequently, all socio-economic problems appear to be Islamized, and few discussions address the fact that immigrants suffer from discrimination, segregation and failed attempts to resolve unemployment and social problems.

Furthermore, Ramadan claims, the new visibility of Muslims and Islamic institutions, especially mosques, is cited as evidence

> showing that they just don't want to integrate. In fact it is exactly the opposite. As they are visible, millions are visible, it means that they are at home. So when you have mosques, when you have organizations, it's not because you don't want to integrate. It's exactly the opposite. You feel at home, you build your mosque.

According to Tariq Ramadan, it is because of this misconception that the media and public discourse become obsessed with problems, and they forget that many positive things are also happening at grassroots level.

When it comes to the media it's as if here we are only dealing with problems, and we are dealing with these controversies every day. We are talking about violence, the minarets, the headscarf – all the problems, but not talking about what is being done at the grassroots level, the positive actions of the Muslims. Millions are silent and are constructive and contributing to the reality of our country ... The Muslims are understanding the West and Europe much better than before, they are understanding their religion much better than before.

According to Ramadan, it is just a matter of time before the 'positive reality' triumphs over the political discourse and media coverage, which focus on stories of strife and conflict. Here his line of reasoning appears to be at least partly inconsistent with his support for the motion 'Europe is failing its Muslims'. Ramadan apparently does not fully commit to the underlying premise of a major problem or conflict facing Europe and 'its Muslims' that is implicit in the idea behind his argument.

In her opening statement Petra Stienen, a former Dutch diplomat in Egypt and Syria, asks whether Europe will be capable of 'looking beyond the colour of religion'. Based on her experience as a diplomat, she acknowledges major deficits in freedom, knowledge and participation of women in the Middle East. 'The question though is: Are these wrongs really connected to Islam?' She then turns to her experiences after 2001 in the Netherlands with polemical political parties and fears that were raised by her friends:

They warn me not to be naive. They say that the danger now is among us. Like an Islamic Trojan horse? I wonder though, and this would be a question from me to Douglas, what do we do with the people who don't want to adhere to your ideas of enlightenment? Do we send them away? Do we re-educate them? So I'm wondering: Are we actually addicted to our own stereotypes? Over and over again we hear the same warning: 'We are sleeping! Europe will turn into a certain EurArabia. Islam is about to take over'. I believe that this one-sided, one-dimensional story is really failing Muslims in Europe miserably.

Building on Ramadan's statement, Stienen argues that, with its over-whelmingly negative and stereotypical portrayal of Islam and Muslims as the problem, Europe neglects the other side of the story, the good examples and success stories – for example, the lawyer Famile Arslan, who wears a headscarf, was on the cover of *Time* magazine. Other examples are Ahmed Aboutaleb, the mayor of Rotterdam, and football player Ibrahim Afellay. Failing to note these success stories means that we risk alienating current and future generations. Furthermore, Stienen asks about the extent to which the problems of social cohesion, segregation, discrimination and unemployment are related to a specific religion, and the extent to which they might be explained by the fact that a certain percentage of the European population is Muslim.

One of the common features of the opening statements of Ramadan and Stienen is that they refer extensively to dominant media representations of

Muslims while also presenting many of the arguments they want to counter. At the same time, it remains unclear just exactly what or who the Europe is that is failing its Muslims. Both Ramadan and Stienen repeatedly refer to an unspecified 'us' in their statements. For instance, when Stienen says: 'What do *we* do with the people, who don't want to adhere to your ideas of enlightenment? Do *we* send them away? Do *we* re-educate them?', a closer look at this use of 'we' shows that she is referring to Europeans, and the alleged group behind this personal pronoun is ambivalent about the inclusion of Muslims. Similarly, Ramadan – even though he speaks as a Muslim – uses the first person plural only to refer critically to the actions of (non-Muslim) Europeans rather than to active populations of any religion: '*We* Islamize socio-economic problems', and '*We* are talking about violence, the minarets, the headscarf – all the problems, but not talking about what is being done at the grassroots level'. Hence, in a surprising twist, Stienen and Ramadan perpetuate the very techniques of the discourse that they criticize. It seems impossible for them to present a European 'we' that is inclusive of Muslims.

'Europe is failing its Muslims' – Against the Motion

Douglas Murray, director of the Centre for Social Cohesion – which according to its website strives to promote integration and also has a special focus on radicalization[2] – begins his opening remarks by addressing Ramadan's presentation. According to Murray, it is not at all strange that many Europeans associate Islam with violence: 'That is, Islam *is* associated with violence. It was not Buddhists who flew planes into the Twin Towers, it was not Hindus or Jews that blew up the London underground and buses a few years ago'. To acknowledge this, according to Murray, is essential 'before you are even going to start a dialogue'. It is also necessary to understand that Europe has welcomed a very large number of migrants over the last decades, so to say that it has failed its Muslims is unfair.

On the contrary, the Muslims have failed Europe. Instead of building parallel societies and asking for Islamic laws and groups rights, 'they' have to realize that they have

> no right to be intolerant towards other minorities, religious or sexual, or to disrespect freedom of speech, or to discriminate half of the population, that is, the women, of Europe … And the call once more for parallel legal systems within Britain and European societies – this is nonsense. No other group behaves like this, asking for parallel laws.

However, according to Murray the situation is not entirely without hope. 'This is not solely something that we have to say we cannot reconcile. Of course we can reconcile this. We need to be honest about it. We have to be frank about it and we cannot avoid things just because they are unpleasant.' Here Murray employs a rhetorical element which claims that important aspects of Muslim life are deliberately hidden or ignored in order to avoid causing offence. Murray continues:

> If there were one thing that I would wish Muslims in Europe would learn today, as fast as possible, it would be this: You have no right in this society not to be offended. You have no right to say that because you don't like something you turn to violence, or you would like something to be stopped, or censored. You have no right to have more hate laws, or hate crime laws, or hate speech laws, just to defend Islam. You have to realize, Muslims in Europe have to realize, that the society in which even your deepest feelings can be trodden upon, is the only society worth living in. And the sooner we can learn that, the sooner that Islam can learn that within Europe, the better.

For Murray, the fundamental problem that putting European values at risk is a 'clash of values'. Therefore the non-Muslim population of Europe needs to be aware of this danger. Murray argues: 'It is a problem between a society, Western Europe that believes that laws are based on reason, and Islam that believes that they are based on revelation'. Consequently, 'it is not Europe that has failed its Muslims. It is Islam that has failed Europe. I'd argue that Islam has failed its Muslims.'

As the last speaker, Fleming Rose, the journalist and editor who published the Muhammad cartoons that caused a major uproar in Denmark, mounts the rostrum. He begins his statement against the motion 'Europe is failing its Muslims' with an acknowledgement that every Muslim is 'first and foremost an individual endowed with certain rights and obligations'. This 'serves … as a foundation of liberal democracies in Europe'. This also means that Muslims enjoy rights such as freedom of expression, freedom of religion, equal treatment before the law and secular government. While explaining the tension between Muslims and Europe, Rose like Murray quickly speaks about values and explains that some Muslims cannot enjoy the rights they are granted by European societies and that this is the fault of their own communities:

> It also means that Muslims, as other Europeans, have the freedom to choose. But unfortunately within too many Muslim communities in Europe, European Muslims are not able to exercise the rights they are being granted by the European governments and societies. And I see this as a big problem. So on the one hand in a liberal democracy you enjoy the freedom of expression, you enjoy the freedom of religion which includes the right to leave your religion, you treat women and men equally. But at the same time Muslims within their own communities are not able to exercise that right. And it is controversial among Muslim communities to leave Islam. And you have ex-Muslims and descending Muslims in their own communities who are living in fear because they are being accused of apostasy – apostasy, according to Islamic law, being a capital crime. So if a Muslim decides to leave his religion, he risks social exclusion, stigmatization, or maybe even worse.

Rose portrays Europe as enlightened (even though the word is not mentioned once during the whole debate) and highlights that secular and liberal societies allow Muslims freedom of religion. Furthermore – and he states this as a fact – men and women are treated equally in Europe. Equality and freedom, however, are not available within Muslim communities throughout Europe, Rose argues, mentioning the treatment of apostasy as an example.

> May I remind you, that it is human beings who enjoy human rights, not religions, cultures and certain versions of history? And I do believe in the notion of universal human rights. And I think that this notion has served Europeans, Muslims and non-Muslims well – one consequence being that Muslim citizens in Europe are, in fact, enjoying more freedom and more rights than any Muslim in any Muslim-majority country.

Even though Rose is presenting in the same camp as Murray, it is notable that he – much more than Murray – acknowledges individual rights and freedom of choice as well as personal responsibility, explicitly including Muslims. The Muslims of Europe should be seen foremost as individuals and 'not as some kind of homo-Islamicus'. Like all other citizens of Europe, Muslims have certain rights, but 'they need to understand', as Murray argues, that these rights can also be used for criticizing or debating religious beliefs and that all individuals in Europe have the opportunity to choose alternative lifestyles that might go against a religious belief and still be respected. At this point Rose asks a rhetorical question: 'Who is failing the Muslims in Europe?' His answer is that it is rather the Muslims who are failing Europe – and here his argument comes close to that of Murray.

Two Different Narratives of Europe

By comparing how the participants in the Intelligent Square debate argue during their presentations and question and answer session, we can more fully grasp the two different narratives of Europe and its Muslims. On the one hand, we see that Ramadan and Stienen claim that the Muslims of Western Europe are suffering from discrimination and exclusion. Both of them contend that there are major social problems that need to be addressed, but these problems could not be explained by pointing the finger only at Islam or Muslims. This notion is challenged by Murray and Rose, who stress that multicultural society has failed, that Muslims and Islam are the major reason for Europe falling apart, and that it is high time for the public to understand this problem instead of sacrificing European values on the altar of multiculturalism. A breakdown of these arguments reveals the diametrically opposed positions of the two narratives of Europe.

In Murray's talk 'we' refers to 'proper' Europeans who adhere to secular, liberal and rational values, while 'they' refers to Muslims, who are not followers of these traditions but are religious, bound by revelation and thus unable to change. The presentation by Murray takes the form of a lecture, designed to let Muslims know what 'they' have to learn and respect. 'They' have to adapt to European values and norms with apparently little room for dialogue or mutual responsibility. As members of the audience point out during the question and answer session, individuals of non-European ethnic and cultural backgrounds, and Muslims who already adhere to the norms and values that Murray mentions, are ignored in this presentation. Similarly Europeans without an immigrant − or any other religious or cultural − background, who reject 'European' values, are also neglected. This is, however, pointed out by Stienen, Murray's opponent, who gives an example of unequal treatment of women by non-Muslims which has − despite being widely known − not led to public outrage: 'In the Netherlands we have a political party in parliament that doesn't allow women to run for office. And I don't hear the same voices about this party as I hear about Muslim women'.

In response to a question by the moderator about the freedom of Muslim women, Ramadan admits that there are problems within Muslim communities, but not without pointing to the positive developments: more autonomy, access to Islamic knowledge appropriation and leadership for Muslim women. Ramadan also stresses the link between human rights and Islamic values, claiming that the headscarf should be a free choice according to both Islamic conviction and human rights:

> When it comes to forced marriage, we had campaigns in Europe against forced marriages. And then when it comes to anything to do with reading the text, being able to comment, and to get a sense of autonomy for women, this is happening. It is said, in some countries, when you wear the headscarf, by definition you can't be a free Muslim woman because of the way you dress. I think that is wrong! Let the people decide and let them speak for themselves. And listen − because sometimes they speak but are not listened to.

Ramadan's strategy is to admit that there are problems like forced marriage and the headscarf in order to point to how they are tackled within Muslim communities and what solutions could look like. In the following exchange with a Muslim woman from the audience, Murray also admits to problems, such as discrimination, racism and social deprivation; however he quickly shifts the focus and insists instead on freedom of expression, implicitly presented as a European value.

> Muslim woman from the audience: I'm a British female. I love this country and I gave to this country. Now you call me a problem. I don't think I am, I think you are! As a Muslim female, my parents might not let me go out late at night, because people are racist to me. They tell me to go back home. I got hit by two white guys and they laughed at me and called me a 'scarfy'.

Murray: Nobody, nobody thinks that any physical attacks or any such things could be a good thing to happen. Of course not! Let's be absolutely clear about this. Prejudice undoubtedly exists in society. It exists across racial groups including from minorities to other minorities after all, which is one of the things that we see increasingly in Great Britain these days. And it is also the case that people, particularly from lower socio-economic groups, are likely to feel hatred [by] other groups. That is one of the things that has to be tackled, and everyone I think in this hall, I am sure, we are in agreement that it has to be tackled. But, do not mix up somebody – a thug, a racist and so on – attacking somebody in the street with the right of Fleming and me to see what we see in the Quran, what we think of Muhammad, and maybe even asserting our right to say so.

Apart from Murray's suggestion that by pointing to her experience of being physically assaulted, the member of the audience intended to deny his right to criticize Islam or Muhammad, this reply is interesting as an example of a semantic shift which often occurs in debates about migration, Islam and Muslims. Questions and problems that used to be related to migration, integration and social cohesion of ethnic groups and society in general, are now related to issues of Muslims and Islam in what can be called the 'Islamization of the integration debate' (Allievi 2005; Johansen and Spielhaus 2012; Spielhaus 2011). This shift means that social problems are not associated with racism, segregation or the position of disadvantaged groups in society, but rather with religious belonging – i.e. Islam. This means that problems of social cohesion are not perceived in the context of prevailing structures or power relations but are seen as being instigated by actual or assumed religious affiliation. According to this strand of the discourse, Islam is ascribed an explanatory value, and being Muslim is considered far beyond an identity or religious belonging as a static habitus and set of problematic practices.

If we compare Murray and Rose's presentations with those of Ramadan and Stienen, there are other relevant differences. For Ramadan and Stienen, individuals with a Muslim cultural background are part of the European fabric. Tensions do not arise from different religious identities, but from the failure of society to put its core values into practice. For Europe to live up to the Human Rights Declaration, the ideal of freedom of religion and actual equality among its citizens, it is necessary to recognize fundamental structures, particularly the social and economic problems from which Muslim citizens are suffering in Europe today.

The basic assumption of Murray's and Rose's statements, as well as some comments from the audience, is that Muslims – at least many of them – do not share European values, and therefore, as Murray maintains, cannot be Muslim and European at the same time.[3] In this part of the discussion, Murray repeats a frequent accusation that Ramadan is speaking with a forked tongue – meaning that he says one thing when addressing a non-Muslim, mixed or public audience, and another thing when speaking to Muslims. When Ramadan rejects this allegation, Murray replies, 'You can't pretend that you have two identities'. However, the exchange begins with Ramadan accusing Murray of fostering a 'sense of alienation' among Muslims and not allowing them to feel that they are at home in Europe, and with Ramadan objecting to phrases like 'in their home countries':

> Ramadan: I'm sorry. I am at home. I am at home. What are you talking about? Talk to me! I'm sorry. Talk to us or talk to me as a fellow European. And not as someone who is an outsider infiltrating the freedom of expression and using it!
> Murray: No, I'm not saying you are not a European. But I would appreciate the following, which is this: Don't come to this hall and say you are a European and then go and talk to an Islamic audience as Islamic brothers. Because that is what you have spent your career doing [*noises from the audience*].
> Ramadan: What is wrong with that?
> Murray: Let me finish this. Tariq comes here one day and says 'We fellow Europeans' – he will speak to you as a fellow European. And another day he speaks to Muslims audiences and says 'We as Muslims'. Which is it Tariq? Which is it? You can't pretend you have two identities!

Murray presents the question of identity as a choice between being Muslim and being European. Ramadan does not agree that there is any contradiction between simultaneously being Muslim and European – a fact that he repeatedly emphasizes throughout the debate.

In his reply to this discussion, Rose tries to balance Murray's attack on Ramadan by admitting that one can very well be Muslim and European at the same time; however, Islam should not be seen as a race, because if it were, people would not be able to change it. Consequently it is rather like an ideology comparable to Communism. 'Islam', Rose argues, 'is a set of ideas' that constitute an ideology. At this point the moderator asks Stienen to reply by stressing both the challenge and value of accepting people and thoughts that are significantly different:

> Stienen: It almost seems as if the only good Muslim would be an ex-Muslim. And so for me: How enlightened are we if we only welcome people who are like us? Like you and me. Can we actually accept people who think differently? I think this is when our values are really tested. And of course when people are thinking differently and don't want to change religion. That is also a universal human right.

While stressing the responsibility of Muslims to adhere to European laws and regulations, Stienen criticizes Murray and Rose for not addressing the legitimacy of being religious in Europe, which also includes Muslims. To neglect this would be a violation of the European value of freedom of religion.

Members of the audience point out that the plurality of opinions among Muslims has been downplayed, especially in Murray's statements. Whilst extremist ideas were suggested as being the only authentic interpretation of Islam, Muslim communities showed a 'humongous diversity' and could not be 'judged by a few fringe people'. Rejecting the opponents of the motion, several audience members contested the idea that it would be impossible to be secular, moderate or feminist and Muslim at the same time, and that the Qur'an proclaimed women's rights 'long before women in the West were burning their bras'.

Conclusions

This chapter has analysed the debate on the motion 'Europe is failing its Muslims', which was arranged by the Intelligence Squad, British Council and BBC in London on 23 February 2010. According to our analysis, the debate reveals that inclusive and exclusive narratives of Europe are largely interdependent, and that Muslims are often used as tools for constructing European identity and values. By arguing about who belongs and who does not, the speakers contribute to an imagined ideal and thereby a homogenous Europe, reinforcing notions of what are considered to be core European values: freedom of expression, freedom of religion and equal treatment of everybody regardless of gender, sexual orientation or religion. One of the narratives presents a notion of Europe that leaves out or intentionally neglects the diverse ways that values and their implementation are discussed by contemporary European society when it comes to minorities. The other narrative not only offers an inclusive perspective, but argues for the recognition of a diversity of positions, both among Muslims and Europeans, and highlights the fact that the European project is based on many cultures and traditions. The main differences between these two positions and narratives about Europe are where the borders are drawn, and who and what should be considered to be insiders and outsiders. In the first notion, it is simply the difference between Muslims and non-Muslims that excludes adherents of particular beliefs from the European project. The second notion allows for different and more inclusive lines that pay attention to legal rights, such as freedom of religion, and determine the inclusion of Muslims according to their individual stances on basic values. By analysing this debate, we have shown how narratives of cultural difference are used to maintain borders vis-à-vis those who are perceived and constructed as immigrants and newcomers or those who reject the notions of diversity among Muslims and religious plurality in Europe. We argue that the ways in which participants in public debates refer to the Muslim presence in Europe, and whether or not they view Muslims as part of Europe, is a useful case that can help us to understand how borders and mental maps are drawn.

Göran Larsson is professor of religious studies at the University of Gothenburg, Sweden. His research focuses on Islam and Muslims in Europe in both past and present times, with publications in main journals, such as *Journal of Muslims in Europe*, *Islam and Christian–Muslim Relations* and *Method and Theory for the Study of Religions*; he has also written on religion and media, youth culture and Islamic theology.

Riem Spielhaus is head of the department Textbooks and Society at the Georg Eckert Institute for International Textbook Research and professor of Islamic studies at the Georg-August-Universität Göttingen. Her research includes topics such as the production of knowledge about Muslims in Europe, female authorities in Islam and the institutionalization of Islam.

Notes

1. The entire debate can be listened to and seen at http://www.tariqramadan.com/ Intelligent-Square-Debate-Europe,11043.html?lang=fr (accessed 28 January 2012). See also http://www.intelligencesquared.com/events/europe-muslims (accessed 27 January 2012).

2. Concerning the Centre for Social Cohesion, see http://www.socialcohesion.co.uk/ (accessed 28 January 2012).

3. Amir-Moazami (2011) observes a similar notion in her analysis of the German Islam Conference organized by the German government, based on the argument that Muslims need to be taught German as well as European or universal values.

References

Allievi, S. 2005. 'How the Immigrant has Become Muslim: Public Debates on Islam in Europe', *La Revue européenne des migrations internationales* 21: 135–63.

Amir-Moazami, S. 2011. 'Pitfalls of Consensus-orientated Dialogue: The German Islam Conference (Deutsche Islam Konferenz)', *Approaching Religion* 1: 2–15.

Gerholm, T., and Y.G. Lithman (eds). 1988. *The New Islamic Presence in Western Europe*. London: Mansell.

Johansen, B.S., and R. Spielhaus. 2012. 'Counting Deviance: Revisiting a Decade's Production of Surveys among Muslims in Western Europe', *Journal of Muslims in Europe* 1: 81–112.

Larsson, G., and E. Račius. 2010. 'A Different Approach to the History of Islam and Muslims in Europe: A North-Eastern Angle, or the Need to Reconsider the Research Field', *Journal of Religion in Europe* 3: 350–73.

Nordbruch, G., and U. Ryad (eds). 2014. *Transnational Islam in Interwar Europe: Muslim Activists and Thinkers*. New York: Palgrave Macmillan.

Shooman, Y., and R. Spielhaus. 2010. 'The Concept of the Muslim Enemy in the Public Discourse', in J. Cesari (ed.), *Muslims in Europe and the United States after 9/11*. London & New York: Routledge, pp. 198–228.

Spielhaus, R. 2011. *Wer ist hier Muslim? Die Entwicklung eines islamischen Bewusstseins in Deutschland zwischen Selbstidentifikation und Fremdzuschreibung*. Würzburg: Ergon Verlag.

Tsitselikis, K. 2012. *Old and New Islam in Greece: From Historical Minorities to Immigrant Newcomers*. Leiden: Brill.

———. 2013. 'European Islams and Muslim Europes: Some Thoughts about Studying Europe's Contemporary Islam', in *Yearbook of Muslims in Europe*, Vol. 5. Leiden: Brill, pp. 1–18.

CHAPTER 3

Ilm al-Hududiyya

Un-Inheriting Eurocentricity

KLAS GRINELL

L'Europe est moralement, spirituellement indéfendable
—Aimé Césaire, *Discours sur le Colonialisme*

Prologue: Borders

Borders are a key to understanding European modernity. Borders might even be claimed to be a political and epistemological invention of European modernity, politically established by the Westphalian order and spread around the world by imperial colonialism, and epistemologically established by Cartesianism during the same period (Mignolo 1999; *ISR* 2000). In different areas, dichotomies and trenches were created between 'us' and 'them' – this nation and that nation, this culture and that culture, Europe and Africa, Christianity and Islam, civilized and barbarian, man and woman, mind and body, either–or (Grinell 2010).

Within a modern/colonial framework, borders tend to look natural, and the people who trespass those borders are easily seen as less natural, as deviations and problems (Malkki 1992). The renegotiation of borders produced by contemporary globalization is seen as creating something new. As we learn from the introduction to this book, the etymology of the word 'border' comes from the frontiers of Scotland and England, more blurry meeting grounds than sharp epistemic lines. In a longer historical perspective and from a less Eurocentric point of view, boundaries are returning to a weaker form. Instead of definite dividing lines, there are borderlands. In the words of Judith Butler: '[W]hat was thought of as a border, that which delimits and bounds, is a highly populated site ... confounding identity in what may well become a very auspicious direction (Butler 2004: 49).

Etymology can also take us in other directions: the Arabic word for border (and restriction) is *hadd* (plural *hudud*). Its meaning is closest to that of the English/Latin 'limit'. *Hudud* is the line separating *haram* (sanctuary, private, forbidden) from *halal* (lawful, permissible); it is also the name of a category of crimes in traditional Islamic law, including murder, theft, fornication and apostasy. *Hudud* crimes have become infamous, mainly because of the harsh physical punishments for them. One explanation of why they are called *hudud* crimes is that they are acts that violate God's limits. Some Islamic scholars argue that they should rather be interpreted as prescribing restrictions on the severe retaliation of pre-Islamic society (Esack 1999). In this interpretation, *hudud* is less about separation than about setting a limit for excesses. *Hadd* or *hudud* is also the contemporary Arabic word for geopolitical border(s). Borderland can be translated as *hududiyya*, *tugur* or *takhum*, the latter two being older words, connected with marshes, and thus closer to the concept of border (Brauer 1995).

The epistemological problematization of the concept of borders via its etymology might not be as convincing as we would like it to be. What is the argumentative value of etymology/history? It tends to be used when it serves our purposes. Ananda Abeysekara tries to refute the assumption that knowledge of history can help us to create a more just society. With the concept of 'un-inheriting', he questions the belief that genealogical problematization can distil the true essence of heritage and disconnect it from historical abuses. There are always other genealogies. Un-inheriting is similar to Gayatri Spivak's definition of deconstruction as 'a constant critique of what you cannot not want' (Spivak 1994: 285). But Abeysekara suggests that we are now at a post-deconstruction stage where we can only mourn the inheritance that we cannot reconstruct, dismiss, or disassociate ourselves from. Un-inheriting is the alternative we face after deconstruction. This means that we cannot escape Eurocentricity, that we must find ways of living with our inheritance of a hegemonic, partial, perspective: Eurocentricity as an aporia, an inheritance that we cannot escape, solve, dismiss or salvage (Abeysekara 2008).

Introduction

The title of this chapter, 'Ilm al-Hududiyya', is a construction alluding to the inherited knowledge of the borderlands, a metaphorical translation of what Walter Mignolo has developed under the name of 'border gnoseology' or border thinking, of which more will be said later (Mignolo 1999).[1] The locus of enunciation for this argument is in the Euro-Islamic borderlands; it is labelled *ilm al-hududiyya* to convince us that our thinking is not locked into the modern dichotomy of European and Islamic. The solution does not lie in presenting a more accurate etymology/genealogy of a specific Europe, but in un-inheriting the aporetic locations we inhabit. We cannot do anything about it. It is not a problem about which we are privileged to make a decision. Rather we are haunted by a heritage that we cannot control, by relationships to forefathers that cannot be repaired or denied (Abeysekara 2008). But we are free to find new friends in the borderlands and create new futures.

This chapter investigates the borderlands of European knowledge: historically via a narrative about the Eurocentric reception of neo-Platonist and Islamic philosophy, and a contrasting *hududiyya* narrative of these philosophies; theoretically via short inventories of delinking arguments and critiques of Eurocentricity.

Polycentric Knowledge

The broad critique of European modernity during the last thirty to forty years has often set out to show the biases of scientific, positivist, objectivist and universalist discourses. This work has been very important. But is there not a certain Eurocentrism to these critical investigations? The focus is still on European history and its legacy, albeit confrontational rather than chauvinistic. But do we not still treat 'Europe as the categorical universal for the world' (Asante 2007: 107)?

At the heart of most critical theories vaguely describable as postmodern is a realization that all understanding is local, that knowledge is situated. There is a contradiction here that has caught the attention of many critics. How can you state that all knowledge is situated without simultaneously invalidating your own claim (Kitching 2008)? Much of this critique comes off as overconfident and somewhat misinformed about its opponents. The concept of 'situated knowledges' was developed by Donna Haraway, who clearly saw the contradiction:

> '[O]ur' problem is how to have *simultaneously* an account of radical historical contingency for all knowledge claims and knowing subjects, a critical practice for recognizing our own 'semiotic technologies' for making meanings, *and* a no-nonsense commitment to faithful accounts of a 'real' world – one that can be partially shared and friendly to earth-wide projects of finite freedom, adequate material abundance, modest meaning in suffering, and limited happiness. (Haraway 1991: 187, emphasis added)

What the construct *ilm al-hududiyya* tries to capture is a ground for such a partially shared commitment to a common (un-inherited) heritage, and common projects for new futures.

Post-theories have seldom been about total relativization or denial of reality as it is lived. The broad and well-articulated claim that knowledge and understanding are tied to the specific circumstances of their (often male) expression has been made by many different propagators (Calhoun 1995). Even if we are convinced by their arguments and believe in a polycentric and pluriversal world, every position creates a need to universalize our values and statements. As Immanuel Wallerstein says, we must accept 'the need to defend their particularist roots against the incursion of the particularist perceptions, analyses, and statements of values coming from others who claim they are putting forward universals' (Wallerstein 2006: 49).

It is possible to describe the emergence of critiques of Eurocentrism from a more materialistic point of view – including anti-colonial struggles, the voices of new countries at the UN, environmental devastation, the so-called 'oil crises', movements for racial equity, the second wave of feminist activism, gay rights activism – all exposing the darker sides of European modernity. One response to this massive critique of modernity/coloniality was the concept of delinking. Walter Mignolo argues that:

> de-linking presupposes to a move toward a geo- and body politics of knowledge that on the one hand denounces the pretended universality of a particular ethnicity (body politics), located in a specific part of the planet (geo-politics), that is, Europe, where capitalism accumulated as a consequence of colonialism. De-linking then shall be understood as a de-colonial epistemic shift leading to other-universality, that is, to pluri-versality as a universal project. (Mignolo 2007: 453)

The concept of delinking comes from Samir Amin's 1985 book *Delinking: Towards a Polycentric World.* Amin is a leading scholar on connections between underdevelopment in the Third World, colonial imperialism and the Eurocentric system of nation-states. Amin is a political economist, and his theory questions whether the Western model of developed capitalism can, or by historical necessity will, be generalized to the whole world. But Amin's concept of delinking is broad and vague, postulating an indistinct universalism, a polycentric system along with autocentric, self-reliant economies (Nederveen Pieterse 2010). The most radical interpretation of delinking is an emphatic disconnection from the European legacy and its modern expression, what Molefi Kete Asante calls 'a locative thesis, which does not adapt to the overarching ideas of European hegemony' (Asante 2007: 3).

I sympathize with this wish to break with European hegemony, but not at the expense of disavowing European ideas, history or problems. We have all inherited modernity, and Eurocentricity along with it. What we can do is mourn and try to 'un-inherit' it, escape its dichotomies, while remembering that the reliance on clear borders supporting arguments like those set forth by Asante is also modern.

This chapter is also an effort to follow Amin on the path of investigating the potential of non-hegemonic historical narratives and identities in a polycentric world, which includes the relationship between Islamic and European traditions. Can they reveal opportunities for a situated (decolonial, post-secular, non-chauvinistic), un-inherited Eurocentricity?

Un-inherited Eurocentricity: Post-secularism?

As stated by Spanish philosopher Eugenio Trías, the modern era can be described as the 'age of the modern prophecy'. Within European modernity, the term 'modern' was used in a prophetic way as a solution and alternative in almost every field. The term had an aura of the coming of a new age – a very prophetic quality.

Modern prophecy attached a kind of messianic hope to reason and science that remains unfulfilled. In the post-prophetic era, there is less certainty, creating a need to acknowledge the non-reducible aspects of life and experience (Trías 1997).

This modern messianic hope was expressed in classical modern/bordering theories of secularization that foresaw three different developments as interdependent. The first development consisted of a historical differentiation between social spheres, whereby religion was separated from politics, economy and science. The second development was a decline in religiosity. The third development was the privatization of religion. Thus, a society based on reason and science would arise. A strict boundary between religion and politics was created – in theory at least (Casanova 1994). Religion (Islam) was seen as archaic, to be discarded rather than inherited and brought into the rational public sphere of Europe (Grinell and Strandberg 2012).

This theory was based on an Enlightenment-centred analysis of European history. Like many sociological models, it was intended to be a universal social law. This was a Eurocentric mistake. But even in the European context, the theory seems to be mistaken. Organized religion is increasingly more visible in public spaces; it appears that the secularist claim that religion and politics should be separated was neither scientific nor analytical, but ideological. This very idea of religion as a discrete sphere of life is itself a Eurocentric conception (Asad 1993). Most people's lives are situated in indistinct borderlands where the analytical categories of politics and religion are indistinguishable from one another.

Eurocentric Narratives of the History of Philosophy

The history of philosophy genre, which was important in ancient Greece with Diogenes Laërtios as a prime representative, became part of the Christian-European tradition during the Renaissance. In 1470, a Latin translation of Diogenes' book was published. But the history of philosophy as a separate genre was not thoroughly established until the turn of the nineteenth century (Santinello et al. 1993). One of its leading proponents was Georg Wilhelm Friedrich Hegel and his *Vorlesungen über die Geschichte der Philosophie*. Like his other historical lectures, it traces the worldly realization of the Spirit (*Geist*). The presentation includes the thinkers who have been a part of the Spirit's self-realization process. The narrative is teleologically and unilinearly Eurocentric. The little that Hegel has to say about Arabic philosophy is under the heading of Medieval Philosophy. The only individual philosopher who receives any kind of attention in Hegel's presentation of Islamic-Arabic philosophy is Moses Maimonides, a Jewish Aristotelian (Abu Amran Musa, 1135–1204). About two-thirds of the 1–3 page sections are dedicated to a presentation of Maimonides's *Dalalat al-Ha'irin* (A Guide for the Perplexed). Hegel also emphasizes the importance of the Arabic transmission of Aristotle to the Christian world, mentioning thinkers such as Alkendi (al-Kindi, 801–873), Alfarabi (al-Farabi, ca 870–950), Avicenna (Ibn Sina, 980–1037), Algazel (al-Ghazzali, 1058–1111) and Averroes (Ibn Rushd, 1126–1198) as examples of commentators on Aristotle (Hegel 1986).[2]

This has become the standard operating procedure for European introductions to the history of philosophy. Arabic-Islamic philosophy is presented only as a step in the evolution of European thought. Ideas and thinkers that did not become part of the Christian-Latin tradition are rarely mentioned. Ernest Renan famously said that what has commonly been called Arabic science was actually Arabic in language only. Its content was Greek or Persian, since the Arab race and Islam did not have the power to think scientifically. A single Islamic philosopher (al-Kindi) was born Arab, and the Arabs and Turks who have ruled Muslim empires were all hostile to philosophy and science (Hourani 1962; Keddie 1983).

Hans Georg Gadamer, one of the leading thinkers on the subject of the Western tradition and its role in contemporary Europe, is not as chauvinistic as Renan. Who would dare to claim that European art is better than any other art, Gadamer asks rhetorically, claiming that the language of art is relative and culture-bound. Still, he draws the same straight teleological line from ancient Greece to modern Germany as Hegel did, adding: 'The kind of science and concepts inherent to the philosophically informed understanding of the world has uniqueness, advantages and a specific mission, which can be found in European civilization and the world only after they were adopted and made inherent by Christianity (Gadamer 1989: 14).

The conclusion is similar to Renan's: European civilization is better than others. In other parts of the text of his book, entitled *The European Heritage*, Gadamer emphasizes that European uniqueness was developed by the Ancient Greeks. The argument makes a direct connection from ancient Greece to modern European civilization. There is not a single word about the role of Greek heritage in Islamic civilization. Gadamer follows Hegel – as do most other historians of philosophy (Grinell 2009).

A *Hududiyya* Narrative of the History of Philosophy

Around 450 CE, Probha of Antioch translated Aritotle's *On Interpretation* (*Peri Hermeneias*, better known under its Latin name *De interpretatione*) and *Prior Analytics* (*Analutika Protera*, or *Analytica Priora*) into Syriac. He was followed by other translators, the most important of whom was Sergius of Reshayna in the early sixth century, who translated more Aristotelian texts into Syriac, as well as translating thinkers like Porphyrios, Ptolemy, Isocrates and Plutarch. The incentive for these translations was to develop tools for Christian textual exegesis. Thus, they had no interest in more narrowly philosophical texts (Peters 1968). Dimitri Gutas argues that there is a widespread misconception that the transmission of Greek knowledge into Arabic went through Syriac translations. Before the Abbasid dynasty founded Baghdad as its capital in 762, relatively few non-religious Greek texts had been translated into Syriac. The majority of Greek scientific and philosophical texts translated into Syriac were part of the ninth-century Abbasid translation movement in Baghdad (Gutas 1998).

The Umayyad Dynasty, which preceded the Abbasids, set up its capital in the ancient city of Damascus in 661. Out of necessity, they kept the Greek-speaking functionaries and administrative language until around 700, when an Arabic administrative vocabulary was developed by bureaucrats like Sargun ibn Mansur. At this time, Greek 'Mirrors for princes' were translated into Arabic, as well as the correspondence between Aristotle and Alexander of Macedonia. In Egypt and Greater Syria, Greek remained an important language for trade and commerce well into the eighth century, and many contracts were drawn up in both Greek and Arabic. It is uncertain whether any scientific or philosophical texts were translated from Greek to Arabic as early as the Umayyad Era (Gutas 1998).

With the Christianization of the Roman Empire, a gradual Christianization of the Hellenistic culture also took place. Up to the mid sixth century, Greco-Roman culture had been slowly transformed into a

Christian culture and worldview. Yegane Shayegan calls this an epistemic transformation by which the cyclical understanding of time in the Hellenic conception of the world was replaced by a linear and historic interpretation of time. Christian suppression of heathen customs also affected philosophy in other ways. Around 500, Ammonius, leader of the Alexandrian school of philosophy, was forced to sign an agreement with Alexandrian pope Athanasios II to stop commenting on Platonic dialogues. Because of the explication of Plato by Proclus, Ammonius's teacher, they had been regarded as connected to heathen polytheism. Ammonius started working on Aristotle's less controversial texts instead, producing what are now known as the neo-Platonic commentaries (Shayegan 2001).

Shayegan indicates that this period was very important to the history of philosophy. The neo-Platonist Aristotle of Ammonius was the one whom Nestorian Christians later introduced to the early Islamic tradition. Other important neo-Platonist commentators of Aristotle in pre-Islamic Hellenic Greater Syria and Persia were Alexander of Aphrodisias, Simplicius, Olympiodorus and Philoponus.

The neo-Platonic philosophy of late antiquity is more creative than its role in the Eurocentric narrative and canon reveals. Arabic-Islamic philosophy explains why the philosophical work in the Eastern regions during these years should be presented as something more than merely commentaries on Aristotle. New arguments that were also crucial to the later European-Christian challenge of Aristotelian physics in the sixteenth century were developed in these neo-Platonic works as absorbed by the Islamic tradition (Schmitt 1987). This change of perspective also challenges the elimination of the mystical and religious elements of the Greek heritage. This narrative also supports Kostas Vlassopoulos's critique of the 'Athenocentric, Hellenocentric and Eurocentric study of Greek history', which sets Athenian *demos* apart from its historical context, constantly elevating it as a starting point for all things European (Vlassopoulos 2007).

Hellenic traditions are not an exclusively European inheritance; they are part of a historic Afro-Euro-Asian world system and a past shared with Islam (Sherratt 2004). It is often said that European thinking is based on Athens (Greek), Rome (Roman) and Jerusalem (Abrahamitic, Jesus). Islam is similarly based on Athens (Greek), Jerusalem (Abrahamitic), Ctesiphon (Sassanid) and Mecca/Medina (Muhammad) (Lapidus 2002: 183). There is no clear boundary (*hudud*) between Europe and Islam, just differences of emphasis in a shared intellectual landscape.

The point of this brief *hududiyya* narrative is not to identify a truer history of our past but to provide alternatives; to show that we can choose what we want to learn from our inheritance, and that it does not have the power to impose identities on us.

'The West Alone Knows How to Think'

Histories of philosophy, science, politics, sociology, critical theory, beauty
and most other subjects tend to be narrated as phenomena emanating from
Europe, a perspective Aimé Césaire ironically described as: 'the West alone
knows how to think; at the borders of the Western world begins the
shadowy realm of primitive thinking' (Césaire 1972: 19). This is one aspect
of (or perspective on) our European inheritance. The problem addressed in
this chapter can be described as methodological. What happens if European
scholars take Césaire's critique, and subsequent post-colonial critique, seriously? To be able to really take this critique in, we need to un-inherit
Eurocentricity.

Dipesh Chakrabarty has said that only old, European, male thinkers
are alive in modernity. Thinkers from other traditions can be studied as
dead objects, but theoretical arguments are possible only in connection
with a European–Western canon stretching from the ancient Greeks to
the present. To be an academic anywhere in the world, you need to work
with this European canon, this European inheritance. Indian history, for
example, is thought to be analysable through categories obtained from
Europe, while a corresponding claim that we should associate European
histories with the concepts of Indian thinkers such as Gangesa, Batrihari
and Abhinavagupta is unthinkable (Chakrabarty 2000). European narratives do not need to see their connections to others. But such imagined
transcanonical thinking could be stimulating and fruitful, possibly a way of
un-inheriting Eurocentricity.

Eurocentrism is not merely a question of science, research, histories and
ideas. 'In no place where Europe has appeared with non-European people
has Europe sought to live in mutual peace with other people. Everywhere
Europe has sought domination, defeat, ethnic cleansing, and conquest',
writes Molefi Kete Asante (2007: 107). Even if we allow some exceptions
to Asante's narrative of conquest and domination, can we – with such a historical legacy – defend a continuous centring on Europe that is not deeply
critical? Do we have any alternatives?

Asante, in *An Afrocentric Manifesto*, also says that to escape from particular
European experiences, 'the researcher must take an auto-locative stance in
order to know where she or he stands in the process' (Asante 2007: 25). The
main thrust of his manifesto is the establishment of 'the African agency as
comparable to that of any other human in the world' (ibid.: 47), but what
could it mean for someone firmly situated as a European? Asante's claim for
the strategic need to have a strong Afrocentric initiative in order to desta-
bilize the Eurocentric framework, which continues to rule in the United

States, is convincing (ibid.: 81). But how does this translate into a European context? How can white, male Europeans adopt an auto-locative stance without becoming 'self-absorbed in some notion of Europe as the categorical universal for the world' (ibid.: 107)?

A somewhat gentler critique of the universalizing aspects of Eurocentrism has been formulated by Chakrabarty in his book *Provincializing Europe*. He states that historical and linguistic differences always matter; the 'universal' ideas of European modernity were misnomers, formulations of specific circumstances of European histories. He talks about 'the multiple pasts of Europe', and the adaptation of modern concepts in new localities as a source of new configurations when encountering pre-existing concepts, categories, institutions and practices. Chakrabarty also shows that critiques of Eurocentrism tend to mistake their own *place*, their own provincial belonging. 'They presumably produce their criticism from "nowhere" or – what is the same thing – from the "everywhere" of capitalism that always seems to be global in scope' (Chakrabarty 2007: xvi). Chakrabarty claims that we are always somewhere. Since an auto-locative stance inevitably places this text within European geo-history, it cannot be part of Asante's project. Still, even academics situated in this 'region of the world that we call Europe' can allow for other perspectives and agencies as equal to their own, and strive for a provincial, un-inherited Eurocentricity. Besides the universalization of its own peculiar history, the creation of borders is claimed to be a fundamental aspect of Eurocentrism or European modernity. But the universality of modern borders is being questioned: they are losing their economic and epistemological validity. Politically they are being renegotiated, both strengthened and weakened at different levels. As geographer John Agnew argues, 'political and social boundaries have not simply disappeared; they are being reconstituted around and across long-established ones' (Agnew n.d., 3–4; Anderson 2005). This means that identifications and belongings are also renegotiated and reconstituted. When identities are under threat, resistance comes rather naturally. In contemporary Europe, we see all kinds of Eurocentric, atavistic and nationalistic defences against perceived threats to the borders drawn by European modernity.

It is important to stress that European modernity is a constructed ideal, and as such has never encompassed all Europeans – it can never be portrayed as a subject with an agency of its own. In critical reflections as broad as this one, there is always a risk of reifying the phenomenon being critiqued. Europe has no agency, nor has Eurocentrism. We must be careful not to conflate different aspects of European history. No tradition is monolithic; there are always anti-hegemonic forces that resist universalization.

Life in the Borderland

Chicana feminist Gloria Anzaldúa claimed the borderland as a place to have a full identity. She did not accept the assertion that purity and one-sided belonging is essential for a qualitative identity (Anzaldúa 1999). To develop a practice of border thinking (*ilm al-hududiyya*), this text is situated in the borderlands (*hududiyya*) where European-Christian and Islamic traditions are fairly indistinguishable. *Ilm al-hududiyya* is intended to be a kind of deconstructivist or decolonial understanding, where meaning is situated in the marshlands between the poles of perceived dichotomies. The European aspect of border thinking is informed by an array of post-theories, feminist critiques and critical hypotheses. Post-secularism in particular creates an opening towards European anti-hegemonic diversities and borderlands that have been trapped within the nationalist borders of the secular-modernist model.

This is not to say that life in the borderlands is easy or always friendly; Anzaldúa's narrative is certainly not cheerful:

> Though I'll defend my race and culture when they are attacked by non-Mexicanos, *conozco el malestar de mi cultura* [I know the malaise of my culture], I abhor some of my culture's ways, how it cripples women, *como burras* [like donkeys] … I abhor how my culture makes *macho* caricatures of its men. … What I want is an accounting with all three cultures – white, Mexican, Indian. (Anzaldúa 1999: 43–44)

There are many blurred antagonisms between tradition and change, religion and sexual liberation, men and women, and so on. But antagonistic forces are not the same thing as binary oppositions; presenting them in terms of a simple conflict in which we need to take sides is to hide and deny the complexities that we live in and by (Butler 2009).

In order to situate ourselves as Europeans in partially shared, marshy borderlands, we also need to emphasize the marginality and opacity of our own local histories. It is important for all of us to trace, and to focus on, the contrapuntal histories of our traditions. As Euro-Islamic scholar Tariq Ramadan has argued, '[i]t is impossible to start earnest dialogue about present diversity if one persists in denying the plural reality and the diversity of one's own past' (Ramadan 2009: 307).

No tradition has ever been monolithic, and there are always dissidents against privilege and ideologies of supremacy with whom we can identify (Martín Alcoff 2000). As Asante says, 'the more fully we know our ancestors, the rounder, the more powerful our sense of identity' (Asante 2007: 158). But he goes on to argue against efforts such as border thinking: '[W]e cannot have a double consciousness'. Those of us who speak from positions of power might need to learn to live with weaker identities, with a consciousness that is fragmented rather than double. This makes it obvious how different the struggle to un-inherit Eurocentricity is from Asante's Afrocentric project. This does not mean that un-inheriting should be more advanced or informed. But it points to the importance of seeing the connection between self-knowledge and social critique. Asante's Afrocentricity is a powerful, personal social critique originating from a specific location. Identity politics is a way to gain power. When used by those who need to un-inherit their positions of power, it has other effects, as can be seen in the nationalistic, nation-centric movements of many European countries.

My need for an auto-locative approach is more aligned with Ramadan's insistence on self-critique and Haraway's understanding that 'the knowing self is partial in all its guises, never finished, whole, simply there and original; it is always constructed and stitched together imperfectly, and *therefore* able to join with another, to see together without claiming to be another' (Haraway 1991: 193). Understanding and recognition can only come about when we reveal our inability to achieve self-identity ('I do not know why I am who and how I am'). 'I need to be forgiven for what I cannot have fully known, and I will be under similar obligation to offer forgiveness to others, who are also constituted in partial opacity to themselves' (Butler 2005: 42). This is a starting point for the elaboration of a social critique that compels us to recognize our ethical obligations to one another.

Our ancestors are never only ours; our location does not have to be on one side of a dichotomous trench (*hadd*) – it is always in the marshy borderlands (*hududiyya*) where outcasts have hidden and found room to live. Un-inheriting Eurocentricity means acknowledging this, mourning it, remembering our situatedness and provincialism, and working on trans-canonical, pluriversal epistemologies, identities and futures.[3]

Klas Grinell is associate professor in history of ideas at the University of Gothenburg and curator of contemporary global issues at the Museum of World Culture in Gothenburg. Among his recent publications are *Reflections on Reason, Religion and Tolerance: Engaging with Fehullah Gulen's Ideas* (New York: Blue Dome Press, 2015).

Notes

1. *Ilm al-hududiyya* is my construction/invention; it is not found in any dictionaries and it seems odd to Arabic speakers – but so does 'border gnoseology' to most English speakers.

2. In that edition, the arabophone Aristotle commentators are not mentioned, as they are in Hegel 1979: 523. For a discussion of the various versions of the lectures on the history of philosophy, see Beiser 1995 and Grinell 2007.

66   *Klas Grinell*

3. The chapter is a revised and adapted version of my chapter 'Islamisk filosofi och västerländsk idéhistoria: Om Suhrawardis frånvaro och synen på den grekiska filosofins vidare öden', in Katarina Leppänen and Mikaela Lundahl (eds), *Kanon ifrågasatt: Kanoniseringsprocesser och makten över vetandet.* Hedemora: Gidlunds förlag (2009).

References

Abeysekara, Ananda. 2008. *The Politics of Postsecular Religion: Mourning Secular Futures.* New York: Columbia University Press.
Agnew, John. n.d. 'A World That Knows No Boundaries? The Geopolitics of Globalization and the Myth of a Borderless World'. CIBR Working Papers in Border Studies, no. 9.
Anderson, James. 2005. 'Borders, Fixes, and Empires: Territoriality in the New Imperialism'. CIBR Electronic Working Paper Series, no.15.
Anzaldúa, Gloria. 1999. *Borderlands/La Frontera: The New Mestiza.* San Francisco: Aunt Lute Books.
Asad, Talal. 1993. *Genealogies of Religion: Discipline and Reasons of Power in Christianity and Islam.* Baltimore, MD: The Johns Hopkins University Press.
Asante, Molefi Kete. 2007. *An Afrocentirc Manifesto.* New York: Blackwell.
Beiser, Frederick C. 1995. 'Introduction to the Bison Book Edition', in Hegel, *Lectures on the History of Philosophy 1: Greek Philosophy to Plato.* Lincoln: University of Nebraska Press, pp. xi–xl.
Brauer, Ralph W. 1995. 'Boundaries and Frontiers in Medieval Muslim Geography', in *Transactions of the American Philosophical Society,* 85 (6), 1–73.
Butler, Judith. 2004. *Precarious Life: The Powers of Mourning and Violence.* London: Verso.
———. 2005. *Giving an Account of Oneself.* New York: Fordham University Press.
———. 2009. *Frames of War: When is Life Grievable?* London: Verso.
Calhoun, Craig. 1995. *Critical Social Theory: Culture, History, and the Challenge of Difference.* London: Blackwell.
Casanova, José. 1994. *Public Religions in the Modern World.* Chicago: University of Chicago Press.
Césaire, Aimé (1955) 1972. *Discourse on Colonialism.* New York and London: Monthly Review Press.
Chakrabarty, Dipesh. 2000. *Provincializing Europe: Postcolonial Thought and Historical Difference.* Princeton, NJ: Princeton University Press.
———. 2007. 'Preface to the 2007 Edition: Provincializing Europe in Global Times', in *Provincializing Europe: Postcolonial Thought and Historical Difference.* Princeton, NJ: Princeton University Press, pp. ix–xxii.
Esack, Farid. 1999. *On Being a Muslim: Finding a Religious Path in the World Today.* London: Oneworld Publications.
Gadamer, Hans Georg. 1989. *Das Erbe Europas: Beiträge.* Frankfurt am Main: Suhrkamp Verlag.
Grinell, Klas. 2007. 'Hegel Reading Rumi: The Limitations of a System', in *Medeniyet ve Klasik,* ed. Sami Erdem. Istanbul: Klasik Yayinevi, pp. 103–118.
———. 2009. 'Islamisk filosofi i västerländsk idéhistoria: Om Suhrawardis frånvaro och synen på den grekiska filosofins vidare öden', in Kanon ifrågasatt: kanoniseringsprocesser och makten över vetandet, ed. Katarina Leppänen and Mikela Lundahl. Hedemora: Gidlunds förlag, pp. 52–75.
———. 2010. 'Border Thinking: Fethullah Gülen and the East–West Divide', in *Islam and Peacebuilding: Gulen Movement Initiatives,* ed. Ihsan Yilmaz and John Esposito. New York: Blue Dome Press, pp. 65–84.

Grinell, Klas, and Urban Strandberg. 2012. 'Expressions, Mediations, and Exclusions in Post-secular Societies: Introduction', *European Review* 20(1): 68–76.

Gutas, Dimitri. 1998. *Greek Thought, Arabic Culture: The Graeco-Arabic Translation Movement in Baghdad and early Abbasid Society*. London and New York: Routledge.

Haraway, Donna J. 1991. 'Situated Knowledges: The Science Question in Feminism and the Privilege of Partial Perspective', in *Simians, Cyborgs, and Women: The Reinvention of Nature*. London: Free Association Books, pp. 183–202.

Hegel, Georg Wilhelm Friedrich. (1825–26) 1979. *Vorlesungen über die Geschichte der Philosophie II, Werke 19*. Frankfurt am Main: Suhrkamp Verlag.

———. (1825–26) 1986. *Vorlesungen 9: Vorlesungen über die Geschichte der Philosophie 4: Philosophie des Mittelalters und der neueren Zeit*. Hamburg: Felix Meiner Verlag.

Hourani, Albert. 1962. *Arabic Thought in the Liberal Age: 1798–1939*. London: Oxford University Press.

ISR (International Studies Review). 2000. Special issue – 'Continuity and Change in the Westphalian Order', *International Studies Review* 2(2).

Keddie, Nikki R. 1983. *An Islamic Response to Imperialism: Political and Religious Writings of Sayyid Jamal al-Din al-Afghani*. Berkeley: University of California Press.

Kitching, Gavin. 2008. *The Trouble with Theory: The Educational Costs of Postmodernism*. University Park, PA: Penn State University Press.

Lapidus, Ira M. 2002. *A History of Islamic Societies*, 2nd edition. Cambridge: Cambridge University Press.

Malkki, Liisa. 1992. 'National Geographic: The Rooting of People and the Territorialzation of National Identity among Scholars and Refugees', *Cultural Anthropology* 7(1): 24–44.

Martín Alcoff, Linda. 2000. 'What Should White People Do?', in *Decentering the Center: Philosophy for a Multicultural, Postcolonial, and Feminist world*, ed. Sandra G. Harding and Uma Narayan. Bloomington: Indiana University Press, pp. 262–82.

Mignolo, Walter D. 1999. *Local Histories/Global Designs: Coloniality, Subaltern Knowledges, and Border Thinking*. Princeton, NJ: Princeton University Press.

———. 2007. 'Delinking: The Rhetoric of Modernity, the Logic of Coloniality and the Grammar of De-coloniality', *Cultural Studies* 21(2): 449–514.

Nederveen Pieterse, Jan. 2010. *Development Theory: Deconstructions/Reconstructions*, 2nd edition. London: Sage.

Peters, F.E. 1968. *Aristotle and the Arabs: The Aristotelian Tradition in Islam*. New York: New York University Press.

Ramadan, Tariq. 2009. *Radical Reform: Islamic Ethics and Liberation*. New York: Oxford University Press.

Santinello, Giovanni, et al. 1993. *Models of the History of Philosophy: From its Origins in the Renaissance to the 'Historia Philosophica'*. Dordrecht: Kluwer Academic Publishers.

Schmitt, Charles. 1987. 'Philoponus' Commentary of Aristotle's *Physics* in the Sixteenth Century', in *Philoponus and the Rejection of Aristotelian Science*, ed. Richard Sorabji. London: Duckworth, pp. 210–27.

Shayegan, Yegane. 2001. 'The Transmission of Greek Philosophy to the Islamic World', in *History of Islamic Philosophy*, ed. Seyyed Hossein Nasr and Oliver Leaman. London and New York: Routledge.

Sherratt, Andrew. 2004. 'Trade Routes: Growth of Global Trade. Urban Supply Routes, 3500 BC–AD 1500', *ArchAtlas*, Edition 4, http://www.archatlas.org/Trade/WStrade.php (accessed 23 January 2012).

Spivak, Gayatri Chakravorty. 1994. 'Bonding in Difference: An Interview with Alfred Ortega', in Alfred Ortega, ed., *An Other Tongue: Nation and Ethnicity in the Linguistic Borderlands*. Durham, NC: Duke University Press, pp. 273–86.

Trías, Eugenio. 1997. *Penser la Religión*. Barcelona: Ediciones Destino.

Vlassopoulos, Kostas. 2007. *Unthinking the Greek Polis: Ancient Greek History beyond Eurocentrism.* Cambridge: Cambridge University Press.

Wallerstein, Immanuel. 2006. *European Universalism: The Rhetoric of Power*. New York: The New Press.

Part II

LINGUISTIC BORDERS IN PRACTICE

CHAPTER 4

When the Intercultural Goes National

Textbooks as Sites of Struggle

———————

KATHARINA VAJTA

— Bonjour. Je m'appelle Luc, et toi? [*Hello, my name is Luc, and yours?*]
— Je m'appelle Sophie. Tu es français? [*I'm Sophie. Are you French?*]
— Oui, je viens de Marseille, et toi? [*Yes, from Marseille. And you?*]
— Je viens de Suède, d'Uppsala. [*I'm from Sweden, from Uppsala.*]
— C'est génial ça! [*That's great!*]
—from the *Escalade* textbook

Immediately, in the very first chapter of *Escalade*, the students find them-selves abroad with a backpack and ready to put up at a French youth hostel, or at least this is what the adjacent illustration tells us. The linguistic border is crossed, a new language presented and nationalities asserted. The practice of learning a foreign language is associated with mobility, albeit only mentally when travelling in the textbook.

To begin to study a new language is to approach linguistic and cultural difference and to cross a border into the unknown, be it a language, a culture or a foreign country. It can be seen as more than simply hard work. It can open the door to a pleasant experience, with visions of holidays, travels, encounters with foreigners, beautiful cities, and so on. Borders do not con-stitute extreme or insurmountable limits, but can instead be imagined to be attractive opportunities that stimulate the learner's curiosity: what will one find on the other side? Thus, textbooks offer the chance to discover and mediate cultural representations.

———————

Notes for this section begin on page 83.

Our hypothesis is that despite the curricula's demands for interculturality, furthering of mutual understanding, and discovery of new cultures, French culture is displayed to learners as, to a large extent, knowledge about the French Republic, implicitly reinforcing national borders. The overall aim of this study is to draw attention to these representations in order to ask whether they tend to reinforce the idea of national specificities and European vagueness.

The textbook is regarded here as a part of a system of knowledge production that produces, reproduces and circulates representations, meanings and practices. As stressed by Soysal and Schissler (2005: 7), textbooks 'represent what generations of pupils will learn about their own pasts and futures as well as the histories of others'. This process takes place within a didactic frame of authority and power such that these representations are easily valued as legitimate and relevant. However, the pathway proposed when learning French (or any other modern language) is not automatically intended to lead to the culture of a nation-state or to nationalities. Since the final decades of the twentieth century, education in general and language learning in particular have also been linked to intercultural education. Thus, the teaching state seeks to turn learners into tolerant citizens with minds open to the surrounding world, in which cultural diversity and contrasts increase as a consequence of mobility and a shift of perspective, and where identities are made up of heterogeneous components (Skolverket). The Swedish curriculum explicitly specifies that students who learn foreign languages have to increase their ability to discuss and reflect on living conditions, as well as cultural and societal phenomena and issues, in contexts where the languages are used. In addition, the curriculum states that an international perspective is crucial in a society with frequent contacts across cultural and national borders.

Language textbooks obviously include facts and representations about the territories associated with French. Hence, the aim of this study is to define the cultural content in a corpus of textbooks in order to define how French is presented and how it relates to the surrounding world, so as to understand what may be learnt about France, the French and Europe. Indeed, a starting point here is the conviction that language teaching should not take place in a cultural vacuum. Schlepegrell, Achugar and Oteíza (2004: 67) state that 'no language is ever taught in isolation from content' and therefore it is of major importance, as Risager (2007: 12) points out, that the content communicated be defined. Discourses 'produce subjects and reality' (Wodak et al. 2009: 39), and so the impact of textbooks must not be underestimated – every year, thousands of pupils are affected. In fact, the books carry representations that must be noted and assessed since these may contribute to producing what they show (Bourdieu 1982: 132), especially when communicated in a didactic context of authority (Bourdieu and Passeron 1970: 134; Chappelle 2009). In other words, what incidental understanding about nationalities, borders and Europe may students develop when studying French and using these textbooks?[1]

These textbooks may be seen as 'sites of struggle' (Wodak and Meyer 2009: 10) that convey and reproduce an ideology. According to Wodak et al. (2009: 20), the narrative of a national culture can be linked to a 'narrative of the nation' elaborated upon through 'stories, landscapes, scenarios, historical events, national symbols and national rituals that represent shared experiences and concerns' (ibid.: 23). This can also be found in language textbooks on the pretext of transferring culture. Hence, our focus is on defining the representations and the demarcations of France and French, studying how French is associated with the surrounding world, and trying to understand what may be learnt about France and Europe – since we believe that the content of language teaching (texts, images, examples, exercises) may influence the worldview of learners and their conception of the Other, not to mention themselves.

The corpus that is studied consists of textbooks for the first two stages in three different series. They were all published in the first decade of the twenty-first century and are commonly used in Swedish upper secondary schools. As expected, they include representations linked to French, and accordingly deal with an imaginary world related to the language. This is present in pictures, illustrations, texts and exercises. The corpus is largely limited to written texts.

In order to demarcate representations of France, nations, Europe and borders, utterances that refer to these subjects have been collected and grouped around a 'cultural reference'. This kind of reference can be an explicit allusion to a symbol, a situation, an allusion to a nation or Europe, sometimes circumstantial information in the clause, be it a location in space (*en France, en Europe*), a comparison (*en France comme en Suède*) or obviously pertaining to a main theme, for instance by means of deictics. Methodologically, the analysis is partly realized by drawing on systemic functional linguistics (Halliday 2004; Thompson 2004) that emphasize the use of language (grammar and lexicon) when creating meaning. Since the material collected is rather extensive, a limited number of sentences have been chosen for an analysis that draws on systemic functional grammar. The utterances have been classified according to various themes in order to determine their range. First, we will attempt to determine how the French people are portrayed in the textbooks. Then we will define their territory – 'the national body' (Wodak et al. 2009: 30) – and how it is presented to the learners. The following section is about the French language and its propagation around the world. Finally, a tentative quantitative approach will provide an understanding of how the representations are distributed among the various themes.

'Français, qui êtes-vous?'

Because national identity can be understood as a habitus (in the acceptance of Bourdieu), with associated ideas, representations and attitudes, drawing on Wodak's notion of *Homo Austriacus*, we will now present the *Homo Gallicus*: the 'typical' Frenchman as he is introduced to the pupil. The Swedish learner is supposed to be curious about this *Homo Gallicus*, the Other – hence the chapter heading 'Français, qui êtes-vous?' (French, who are you?). It appears that the average Frenchman works full time, is married, has two children, and prefers to stay in his native country when on holiday. He eats a lot (perhaps too much), buys white bread twice a day at the *boulangerie* and never drinks milk with his meals. In general, French people seem to have rather bad habits: they drink a lot of wine, speak too fast and do not know how to park a car. Their qualities tend to confirm prejudices and stereotypes, or at least simplifications. The French are portrayed not individually, but as a homogeneous entity, with *Monsieur Martin* as the antonomasiac answer to the question 'Français, qui êtes-vous?' (E2: 49). However, generally, the reference is not made by this anthroponym, but is mostly regarded as an anonymous collectivity and a generic plural for the singular: *les Français*, or a synecdochal singular for the plural: *le Français*. What looks like a series of facts is asserted, but this factual knowledge immediately balances on the edge of stereotype: the *Homo Gallicus* is depicted as having a static, timeless identity and the idea of a national habitus that remains. Frenchmen are presented as a homogeneous national category whose specificities are stereotypical: everyday routines become semiotic practices marking a difference but also allowing the learner to identify the Other and to imitate a behaviour – to act, at least to some extent, as if he is part of the group.

  To this end, learning a language also implies learning how to act when you are in the country, which means learning about the behaviours, traditions and beliefs of the French. The practicalities of politeness, daily habits and gastronomy are included, portrayed as valid within the French national borders: *'en France'*. But implicitly, the question of how people behave elsewhere (here, in the teaching country of Sweden) is also posed, especially when the spatial location *en France* is emphasized by means of the position at the head of the clause:

> En France, on dit *bonjour* et *au revoir* quel que soit l'âge. (E1: 8)
> En France, on dit *Bonjour* quand on rencontre quelqu'un ou quand on entre dans un magasin. (MO1: 60)

The French are depicted as rude, uninterested in foreign languages and heavy drinkers (even if their alcohol habits have improved), attached to their *cafés*, gastronomy and culinary traditions. Furthermore, they mainly watch television, especially sports, and do not read the daily newspapers (MO2: 75; G1: 117; G2: 61, 67, 76; E1: 31, 33, 51, 57; E2: 18, 27, 32). French citizens have specific national characteristics, and the iterative pattern is *le Français* or *les Français* as the subject of declarative sentences where facts are presented affirmatively and as incontestable truths. The portrait of the *Homo Gallicus* crystallizes around simplifications that may be hard to grasp for a learner at the beginner's level. Implicitly, the border of what is regarded as non-French, and hence as Swedish, by the authors of the textbooks is posited, and the students are reminded that Swedes drink less and eat healthy breakfasts.

A National Body Anchored in Geography, Time and Emblems

All the textbooks in question display maps, showing France alone or together with Belgium, Luxemburg and Switzerland. The borders are clearly delineated and French territory is located in Europe and the French-speaking world. Learning French implies looking at 'logo maps' (Anderson [1983] 2006: 174) which serve as a visual reference to France's borders – for example, when weather phrases are practised, rivers situated and French regions located within the national boundaries. The learner is constantly reminded that the French language is primarily linked to France, and its importance is recalled constantly, as in the following examples:

> La France tient quelques records dans l'union. (E1: 36)
> Grâce à de bonnes terres ... la France est un des premiers exportateurs mondiaux de produits agricoles et le plus important de l'Union européenne. (E2: 15)
> C'est un grand pays industriel. (G1: 63)

The student learns about the territory and how it is rooted in history. From the very start, France is introduced as a republic with a set of laws or directives that are valid within its borders. The French Republic is clearly defined by its constitution, regarded as a fundamental component of the state, which must be present from the beginning of the learning process. This republic is firmly rooted in the past and in the French Revolution (G1: 83) – the republic appears as timeless and everlasting. The revolution stands out as the foundational event, celebrated every year on 14 July (MO1: 76; G1: 83). Moreover, the border is marked by the law: what is legal on one side of it may be different or even illegal on the other. Hence, we are told about current laws and we come to know that French children must start school at the age of six (G1: 76; E1: 61). Even the structure of the French school day is depicted as being national. In addition, French is of the utmost importance; it can be enhanced (MO1: 9) and closely linked to France, as revealed in headings (MO1: 22) and texts pointing out the emblematic and legal role of French within the republic, as shown in the following excerpt, which encompasses France's national republican symbols:

> La France est une république. ... La langue officielle est le français et le jour de la fête nationale est le 14 juillet. Le drapeau est bleu, blanc, rouge et on l'appelle le drapeau tricolore. Paris est la capitale de la France. ... En France, il y a 22 régions et 96 départements. Le français est la neuvième langue du monde et la langue officielle dans une trentaine de pays du monde entier. (MO1: 22)

Starting out with its constitutional foundation, this excerpt immediately stresses the importance of the language both inside and outside of the republic's boundaries. By means of the conjunction *et* that links two clauses on the same syntactic level, the language is indirectly placed on the same level as the national day, thus becoming a symbol that should be celebrated. But it is also one of the most commonly spoken languages in the world, which makes it worth learning. The statement also clearly reminds us of the French fundamental law, Article 2, stating that 'La langue de la République est le français'. In the same paragraph we find the symbol of the flag, which belongs to the same republic as the national day and the language. The interdiscursivity between the textbooks and the French fundamental law is patent, and recontextualization, which usually involves transformation or adaptation (Wodak and Meyer 2009: 180) to fit into the new context, can hardly be regarded as having taken place here.

Within the first few chapters of a language textbook, we very often find one about the weather, which is confirmed by both *Escalade 1* and *Génial 1*. One might imagine that the weather does not depend on national borders but might present an opportunity for border crossing. Nevertheless, in textbooks, weather is French, and Billig (1995: 116–19) finds that it can belong to the 'homeland-making deixis'. This may still be the case in the context of a language textbook. But we would suggest slightly modifying Billig's terms in order to consider weather as a 'nation-making deixis' instead: it is another opportunity to show a map of France, cite French towns and name French regions.

Geographically, France is introduced as the *Hexagone* (E1: 42; G1: 63) and we find facts about the area, population, main cities, climate, geography – all of which are supposed to pertain to knowledge about the nation and French identity. France is metonymically symbolized by its capital, the political centre of the nation, around which administration, transportation, communication, economy and culture have revolved for several centuries

(Maingueneau 1979: 279–283). In a broad sense, geographical factors are relevant to the citizens of the state within its boundaries and how they perceive their country (Byram 1993: 34–35). In the textbooks, French citizens must also discover their own country, travelling (G1: 113–15) or visiting Paris and its monuments (MO1: 46), and then explaining to the learner what they see as essential to the capital and their feelings about it. Consequently, Paris offers a range of possibilities to all kinds of visitor in every possible field: culture, food, tourism, economy, education, transportation and communication, job opportunities – everything that comes with a democratic nation-state's responsibilities to its citizens. Within the nation, this includes what is offered to those who want to immigrate, as shown below.

At the same time, the foreigner – learner – also becomes aware both of what is within the boundaries of France and of differences, relating them to her (or his) own country and mirroring them (Vajta 2011). How big is her home country's capital? How many people live there? What city is the second biggest? How many people speak her own language, presumably Swedish? So the learner may go mentally back and forth from one country to the other, linguistically alternating between French and Swedish. From her Swedish starting point, (s)he will first notice the flag, the *tricolore*, and *Marianne*, the symbol of the *République* and the national day, the origin of which is situated a long time ago (G1: 83; MO1: 22).

Republican French Crosses the Border

Even though French is the language of the republic, it is not limited to the territory of France but extends beyond its borders. Nevertheless, the worldview of the textbooks depends largely on France as an epicentre, a pivot around which are organized not only the French-speaking world and Europe, but the whole idea of progression in the learning process: the textbooks clearly start out in France and in Paris, mostly saving the overseas peripheries for later. However, they do mention its existence, even if the textbooks have not been updated about some of the terminological modifications made after the French constitutional reform of 2003, when the denomination DOM-TOM was replaced by DROM (Départements et Régions d'Outre-Mer). Thus, La Réunion and la Martinique are both part of France and French *départements*, where 'tout est français', the official language is French, and the currency is the Euro: Europe is brought to the Caribbean and the Indian Ocean, where it has its own history, since 'les Européens se sont installés sur l'île' (E2: 43).

The French language, the emblem of the Republic, is also to be placed in a global context:

Le français est la neuvième langue du monde et la langue officielle dans une trentaine de pays du monde entier. (MO1: 22)
Dans le monde entier on parle français dans 47 pays. Il y a 169 millions de fran-cophones à travers le monde. (G1: 27)

In these examples, the use of the present tense of the verbs *être* and *parler* is easily explained by the fact that they are among the very first verbs to be learnt, due not only to their frequency, but to the role of *parler* as a model for regular verbs of the first group and the use of *être* as an auxiliary: they have to be learnt at the beginning of the process. However, one consequence is a close connection to deontic modality, a linguistic modality that is used to bring about the expression of will, necessity or appropriateness. Thus, all textbooks stress that French is spoken not only in France, but all around the world, emphasizing its utility and making it into a world language, implic-itly comparing it to English. Accordingly, French is the native language of millions of people on all continents, defended by laws and cultural institu-tions and used at international organizations like the United Nations and the European Union. French, we are told, 'est la langue maternelle de 66 millions d'Européens de France, de Belgique, de Suisse, de Luxembourg, de Monaco et d'Andorre' (E2: 8) and 'En Europe, 63 millions de personnes parlent français' (G1: 27): French has become a European language. Further-more, many francophones can be found in the Americas and Africa. France is prepared to share its language with other countries and the myth of *le français, langue universelle* is still strong, even though it takes the shape of an interna-tionally useful language, and one author cannot refrain from overtly interfer-ing with the text by means of a linguistic modality to confirm the advisability of learning French: 'C'est vraiment une bonne idée d'apprendre le français !' (MO1: 22). In this sentence, we observe three different modality markers: the adjective *bonne*, the adverb *vraiment* and the exclamation mark at the end. All three reinforce the interpersonal relationship between the author and the learner, revealing the author's subjectivity, or at least her wish to emphasize the pleasure and benefit of learning French.

France, Europe and Overseas

In Europe, France is 'le plus grand pays après la Russie' (MO1: 148). It is also the biggest country in the EU (E1: 36), a pioneer in high-speed rail (G2: 38), the leading exporter of agricultural products in the EU and one of the world leaders (E2: 15). However, there are some problems since agriculture in Europe has been losing economic significance. Overproduction threatens French agriculture. The textbooks that deal most extensively with these matters are *Escalade 1* and *Escalade 2*, and their message is rather ambiguous.

France and Europe are grouped together and given a heading of their own (*La France et l'Europe*). The text stresses that free movement is possible since there are no longer any borders. Yet linguistic modality refrains from conveying any enthusiasm:

> *Au cours des dernières années*, on a beaucoup parlé de 'l'ouverture' de la France sur l'Europe. Les jeunes *surtout* veulent voir une France *différente* dans une *nouvelle* Europe unie. *Il y en a* qui se *considèrent* plus européens que français et qui *profitent déjà* de la 'libre circulation' entre pays. *Pour eux*, l'Europe est sans 'frontières intérieures'. (E1: 36)

The authors have reduced the values that have been formulated about Europe by using modal expressions (in italics in the excerpt above), allowing the reader to make personal interpretations that may be implicitly understood. The circumstantial *Au cours des dernières années* indicates a period of time that is undefined, but it has not been that way forever – this is something recent, or at least rather new. The adverb *beaucoup* can be understood as 'too much', and the quotation marks around *ouverture* can imply authorial distancing. Furthermore, the adverb *surtout* implies that there are others, probably not *les jeunes*, who are not of the same opinion and probably less interested in a *nouvelle* Europe that will necessarily be *différente* from what they are used to. This is also emphasized by its position in the sentence. *Il y en a* implies that there might be other people who do not consider themselves Europeans, and the verb *se considèrent* can signify that they think so, but the reality may be different: *Pour eux*, Europe is without borders, but that might not be true for everybody. Furthermore, the verb *profitent* can be understood as being negative, at least if it is at the expense of somebody else, and *déjà* may be understood as 'too early' or 'before others who still have to wait'. Finally, the quotation marks around *libre-circulation* and *frontières intérieures* can allude to dissociation by the authors. In fact, the absence of borders is explicitly seen as a primary explanation of a *plaie nationale*, i.e. unemployment, since enterprises freely move into countries where costs are lower (E2: 35).

What is more, two non-European countries return in all textbooks, Morocco and Algeria, both of which are former colonies of France.[2] They are not really shown as independent states, but as dependent upon France, and also appear on a map (G2: 202) as having maintained contact with their former colonizer (E2: 59). The relationship is one of migration from the Maghreb to France, where it is possible to live, study and find a job; the journey in the opposite direction is only for holidays or to see family. Those who have not migrated yet wish to do so if possible because of the higher standard of living in France, and because it is a *très beau pays* (G2: 181). Arrival in Marseille also marks the arrival in Europe. The journey to France is associated with obstacles at the border of the Schengen area, which distinguishes Europeans from non-Europeans but which can be crossed if one is patient: queuing at the border takes much more time if you belong to the group of *autres nationalités*, whereas *tout le monde a passé sans problèmes* at the counter for Europeans, all emphasized by a photograph (MO2: 80, 85). This is presented without any comment or invitation for discussion, thus appearing normal and acceptable. But implicitly we have the question of who belongs to Europe, who is included and who is excluded. Does Europe welcome immigrants at its borders? This is not made clear – but either way they will have to put up with a queue.

The centripetal attractive force is French and it operates in an effective way, entailing immigration and including foreign elements when opportune. When the periphery lies on the other side of the national border and produces a famous French-speaking comic-strip hero (Tintin), there is no mention of the author's Belgian origins: he is implicitly presented as French, just like the Eiffel Tower or Mona Lisa (MO1: 41) – the centripetal attraction of the French and Parisian cultural field is strong and tends through this elliptical to include a successful periphery.

Cultural references are made not only to France, but to other regions, territories and countries in which French is spoken. In order to evaluate the relationships between these French territorial fields of 'Within France', 'Within France but *outre-mer*', 'France and other nations', and 'France and Europe', a tentative quantitative approach has been used to supplement the analysis of the texts, and the occurrences of 'cultural references' have been counted. Cultural references are regarded as the mentioning of national items or emblems (the name of a state or region, language, monuments, flags, works of art, institutions, currency, geography, history, events, etc.) belonging to these fields. This is an arbitrary definition, since the items and occurrences may be of national significance, like the flag, but not necessarily so.

A majority of the references are made to metropolitan France. Among those made to other European countries, Sweden is the most prevalent with half of them, mainly in the context of a comparison between France and Sweden; the remainder are distributed among several different countries. Other European countries appear, but to a lesser extent, even when French-speaking, such as Belgium and Switzerland. Europe is referred to more than any other continent, either in general or in reference to the Euro. But Europe is hardly present as an overall, defined entity. Other continents, and the French-speaking world in general, are almost completely absent, and non-European countries are mentioned only if they are French-speaking. Furthermore, references to other states and regions mostly involve a name or language, but seldom a cultural reference such as in the fields of art or history.

It is understandable that a French textbook would refer to France, and it is there that the dominance of the country clearly shows up. France is by far the most frequent cultural reference, leaving other French-speaking countries or regions in the background. The second biggest entity consists of non-French-speaking European countries, especially Sweden, closely followed by those that are French-speaking but not European. This might be explained by the fact that there are only two French-speaking countries in Europe, – Belgium and Switzerland – whereas there are several non-European ones, including Canada, Morocco, Algeria, and other nations in Africa.

Conclusion

Intercultural education through these language textbooks takes place on a binary French–Swedish axis. Comparisons are made on a national basis, and nationalities are national by definition. Instead of curiosity, the textbooks promote established national borders. Examples of travel and exchange programmes are supposed to enhance the intercultural approach, but 'when one travels, one always ends up in a particular locality, and this locality can be seen as being representative of the target country (national paradigm) or as being one that has a particular identity in itself (going beyond the national paradigm, i.e. denationalisation)' (Risager 2006: 29). In the textbooks, the tourist or student finds him/herself in the national paradigm.

The texts struggle to find a balance between the national and the cultural, not succeeding in differentiating them from one another and finally promoting a French national discourse, with all of its cultural artefacts, emblems, values and beliefs, without any apparent awareness (Vajta 2012). In the texts studied, we discern the elements needed for national identity (Wodak et al. 2009: 25–26): the idea of a 'national spirit' in terms of beliefs, behaviours and traditions, historical and collective memory, anticipation and future orientation (industry, the internet, young people), a 'national body' in terms of geography and landscapes, and a 'nameable beginning', usually the French Revolution (Vajta 2012).

The French national discourse is present in all of its diversity in the Swedish textbooks: language, geography, history, institutions, behaviours and beliefs. The authors probably intend to create meaning by using 'French' content. But symbols, pictures and other information are a selection based on their own mental models, representations, knowledge and ideologies. These choices, evaluated as relevant knowledge for the learner – and not necessarily erroneous, despite being biased – are remembered and reproduced, with the reproduction of the French 'nation' or of this representation of French (Wodak and Meyer 2009: 69) as an obvious consequence. We may observe that if the ideology of a nation-state is to find its way into the educational system of another country, it has to be very well defined and strongly rooted in the consciousness of not only its own citizens but others, thus making confusion between cultural and national possible. Learning the Other is also mirroring the Self, and when textbooks include the national elements of the Other, they also, indirectly and implicitly, further the national elements of the Self, prompting the learner to reproduce the 'us' and to recall his/her intranational sameness with its own national correspondences, be it the flag, the capital, or cultural customs, which will be different but equivalent. By enhancing differences and national stereotypes, the textbooks reconstruct and reproduce a world order in which borders are national and culture is understood as national, leading to the possible consequence that 'nationalist attitudes and stereotypes articulated in discourses accompany and also influence political decision making' (De Cillia, Reisigl and Wodak 1999: 150). This means that the stakes are high and that the issues that follow are not only cultural, but societal and political.

A homogeneous national entity is put forward at the expense of the notion of a more heterogeneous world, which is implicitly disparaged. Understanding and tolerance, the heuristic skills targeted by the Common European Framework of Reference for Languages (CEFR) and demanded by the Swedish curriculum – the 'third stance' referred to by Kramsch (1999) – run the risk of being replaced by accumulated knowledge about emblems and stereotypes and, accordingly, a static and reduced identity whereby the cultural gives way to the national, confusing the two. As Claire Kramsch points out, 'what language learners have to acquire is less an understanding of one other national group than an understanding of "difference" per se' (Kramsch 1993: 350). Even though language textbooks at the beginner's level must simplify, this does not necessarily imply nationalization of the content. The issue of borders, nations and nationalities is an educational one, and it is necessary to reflect over how these notions are transmitted and reproduced. The 'nationalisation of language studies', which Risager (2006: 26–28) situates in the past, has taken a new form. Identities in language textbooks are still displayed in relation to the national borders to which they are supposed to belong according to a tradition that goes back to the nineteenth century, as observed by Risager. The relationship between language and nation is confirmed, and despite the intercultural aims of the past few decades, the 'nationalization of language studies' has not loosened its grip: when you learn French, you must also learn about France. However, French may also be regarded as polycentric, since it is spoken in many countries and on several continents. Even though it is understandable that a textbook in French will try to motivate students by showing and explaining French matters, the ensuing question is whether the incidental knowledge thus presented necessarily has to follow, almost word for word, the French constitution and promote knowledge of France at the expense of other Frenchspeaking countries and regions. Intercultural education aims at building links and understanding differences – not at promoting national and linguistic borders.

Katharina Vajta is senior lecturer in French at the Department of Languages and Literatures at the University of Gothenburg, where she is also Head of Department. Her main research interests are within the fields of sociolinguistics, language and identity, the French-speaking world and intercultural education. She is a member of the steering group for the Centre for European Research at Gothenburg University.

Notes

1. The pedagogic dimension of the textbooks will not be taken into account. It is surely possible to learn French with all of them.
2. Algeria was, in fact, part of France.

References

Anderson, B. (1983) 2006. *Imagined Communities*. London and New York: Verso.
Billig, M. 1995. *Banal Nationalism*. London: Sage.
Bourdieu, P. 1982. *Ce que parler veut dire: L'économie des échanges linguistiques*. Paris: Fayard.
Bourdieu, P., and J.-C. Passeron. 1970. *La reproduction: Éléments pour une théorie du système d'enseignement*. Paris: Les Éditions de Minuit.
Byram, M. 1993. *Germany: Its Representation in Textbooks for Teaching German in Great Britain*. Braunschweig: Georg-Eckert-Institut für Internationale Schulbuchforschung.
CEFR. Common European Framework of Reference for Languages. http://www.coe.int/t/dg4/linguistic/cadre_en.asp
Chapelle, C.A. 2009. 'A Hidden Curriculum in Language Textbooks: Are Beginning Learners of French at U.S. Universities Taught About Canada?', *The Modern Language Journal* 93(2): 139–52.
De Cillia, R., M. Reisigl and R. Wodak. 1999. 'The discursive construction of National Identities', *Discourse Society* 10: 149–73.
Halliday, M.A.K. 2004. *An Introduction to Functional Grammar*. Third edition revised by Christian M.I.M. Matthiessen. London: Arnold.
Kramsch, C. 1993. 'Language Study as Border Study: Experiencing Difference', *European Journal of Education* 28(3): 349–58.
———. 1999. 'Thirdness: The Intercultural Stance', in *Language, Culture and Identity*, ed. T. Vestergaard. Aalborg: Aalborg University Press, pp. 41–58.
Maingueneau, D. 1979. *Les livres d'école de la République 1870–1914*. Paris: Le Sycomore.

Risager, K. 2006. *Language and Culture: Global Flows and Local Complexity*. Clevedon: Multilingual Matters.

———. 2007. *Language and Culture Pedagogy: From a National to a Transnational Paradigm*. Clevedon: Multilingual Matters.

Schleppegrell, M.J., M.Achugar and T. Oteíza. 2004. 'The Grammar of History: Enhancing Content-Based Instruction through a Functional Focus on Language', *TESOL Quarterly* 38(1): 67–93.

Skolverket. Swedish National Agency for Education. http://www.skolverket.se/

Soysal, Y.N., and H. Schissler. 2005. 'Teaching beyond the National Narrative', in *The Nation, Europe, and the World: Textbooks and Curricula in Transition*, ed. Hanna Schissler and Yasemin Nuhoglu Soysal. New York and Oxford: Berghahn Books, pp. 1–9.

Thompson, G. 2004. *Introducing Functional Grammar*. London: Arnold.

Vajta, K. 2011. 'Construction of National Identities in Language Textbooks', in *Identity through a Language Lens*, ed. Kamila Ciepiela. Frankfurt am M.: Peter Lang, pp. 149–158.

———. 2012. 'Le manuel de FLE suédois, véhicule d'un discours sur l'idée de la France', in *Actes du XVIIIe Congrès des Romanistes Scandinaves*, ed. Eva Ahlstedt et al. Gothenburg: Acta Universitatis Gothoburgensis, pp. 747–763. https://gupea.ub.gu.se/handle/2077/30607

Wodak, R., et al. (1999) 2009. *The Discursive Construction of National Identity*. Edinburgh: Edinburgh University Press.

Wodak, R., and M. Meyer. 2009. 'Critical Discourse Analysis: History, Agenda, Theory and Methodology, in *Methods for Critical Discourse Analysis*. London, Sage (2nd revised edition), pp. 1–33.

Textbooks Studied

E1: *Escalade*. 2001. Stockholm, Almqvist & Wiksell / Liber AB.

E2: *Escalade 2*. 2002. Stockholm, Almqvist & Wiksell / Liber AB.

G1: *Génial 1*. 2002. Stockholm, Natur & Kultur.

G2: *Génial 2*. 2003. Stockholm, Natur & Kultur.

MO1: *Mais oui 1*. 2007. Stockholm, Liber AB.

MO2: *Mais oui 2*. 2008. Stockholm, Liber AB.

CHAPTER 5

The Pluricentric Borders of Bavaria

BARBARA LOESTER

Introduction

The boundaries between the concepts of language and dialect have long been debated in linguistic circles and elsewhere. For non-linguists, the language-dialect dichotomy often appears to be much clearer and less blurred, with distinctions based on features such as the number of speakers or the existence of dictionaries and grammar books. However, such characteristics rarely, if ever, coincide with those of descriptive linguists and (socio)linguists who acknowledge that the dichotomy should not be based exclusively on linguistic features (Haugen 1966). Statements, such as Max Weinreich's 'A language is a dialect with an army and a navy' or Auguste Brun's 'A dialect is a language that did not succeed', illustrate the fact that there is more to the 'classification' than accent, words and grammatical structures; social factors play the most important role in differentiating languages and dialects from each other.

A number of such scenarios can generally be found in regions where varieties cross state borders. Germany and Austria are known as German-speaking countries; if we look more closely at the two standard varieties[1] spoken there, differences in pronunciation, vocabulary and, to some extent, grammar become obvious. The southern German federal state of Bavaria appears to act as a transition zone between what is perceived to be German as spoken in Germany and German as spoken in Austria. Such a perception,

---

however, is misleading when we examine the traditional dialect boundaries in the region (cf. Barbour and Stevenson 1990: 76, map 3.4).

The area defined by dialectologists as Bavarian-speaking stretches across the state boundaries of Germany, Austria and Italy. On the German side of the border the speakers are perceived to be speaking a dialect; yet on the Austrian side a variety that is only marginally different is seen as a standard variety. This chapter will explore the concept of German as a pluricentric language, and the implications this has for the disparity in perception by speakers of different varieties of German when it comes to Bavarian. Linguistic, historical and cultural notions are drawn on to explore the concept of a variety that crosses state borders, unites its speakers on a cultural level, separates them on a national level, and yet is perceived very differently when it comes to status.

Pluricentricity: The Power Play between Varieties of the Same Language?

German is one of the languages typically associated with the concept of pluricentricity.[2] Clyne (2004: 296) defines the concept thus:

> The term pluricentric was employed … to denote languages with several inter-acting centres, each providing a national variety with at least some of its own (codified) norms. … In pluricentric languages we see both the relation of language to national identity and the relation of language to power. They are both unifiers and dividers of people in that they enable different nations to communicate in the same language but express their distinctiveness within that language.

As long as an autonomous territory is associated with such a national variety, the chances for its acceptance as a language in its own right are good. For this reason, Austrian German is perceived as a supraregional, standard variety. It varies from Standard German but the differences do not make communication or mutual intelligibility impossible. With regard to the perceived status of the different German varieties, the variety associated with Germany carries the most prestige – German as a foreign language is more often than not taught with a clear focus on the Federal Republic, rather than Austria or Switzerland.

Similar to the layman's perception of the boundaries between language and dialect, the importance of a standard-setting centre gives a language more power. Standards are set via dictionaries, grammars and similar codification instruments; thus it becomes easier – and sometimes more creditable – to label a language as such, provided the speakers can point to such books and related institutions. These associations, in the German-speaking area the *Duden*, tend to be associated with the country of origin.[3] Although an Austrian equivalent (*Österreichisches Wörterbuch*) exists, it is little known outside Austria. Germany acts as the main endonormative centre for the German language; however, Austria's own national standard achieved greater recognition in 1994 when Austria joined the EU and insisted on 'protecting' Austrian-specific terms, mainly of a culinary or agricultural nature, that differed from their Standard German counterparts. The Austrian terms included *Topfen* instead of *Quark* (curd), and *Paradeiser* instead of *Tomaten* (tomatoes). The campaign was also known for its slogan '*Erdäpfelsalat bleibt Erdäpfelsalat*' (Potato salad remains potato salad), as the Austrian German term *Erdapfel* is preferred over the Standard German *Kartoffel* (cf. de Cillia 1998: 78ff.).

Such developments show that Austrian German, while different from Standard German, can achieve recognition and language status; however, the variety associated with Germany tends to overshadow it, based on factors such as speaker numbers and economic superiority. This brings us back to the original dilemma: where does a dialect end and a language begin? Why is the variety of German spoken in Austria regarded as a language while the variety spoken in Bavaria is considered to be merely a dialect, when the two are more closely related to each other than they are to Standard German? Is it really all a question of political autonomy?

Bavaria: In Germany and Outside

Bavaria (*Bayern*) is the largest federal state in Germany; a less well-known fact is that it is also one of the oldest polities in Europe, as its existence was first documented in the sixth century. From a historical perspective, it has often been perceived as a distinct entity within the German-speaking area and its cultural sphere. Within the context of the German federal system, Bavaria is officially known as the Free State of Bavaria (*Freistaat Bayern*). The political area incorporates the regions of Upper Bavaria (*Oberbayern*), Lower Bavaria (*Niederbayern*), the Upper Palatinate (*Oberpfalz*), Swabia (*Schwaben*), and Upper, Middle and Lower Franconia (*Ober-*, *Mittel-* and *Unterfranken*). Collectively, the first three regions are referred to as Old Bavaria (*Altbayern*). To avoid confusion, the term *Altbayern* will be used throughout to denote the Bavarian-speaking area in the Federal Republic of Germany.

The term *Bayern* has a political connotation rather than a cultural or linguistic one as it outlines the area covered by the *Freistaat*. The linguistic region known as *Baiern* (Bavaria) stretches well beyond the political boundaries of the current German federal state; while most of it falls into the linguistic region, Bavarian (*Bairisch*) as a variety is found as far south as Northern Italy. Almost all of Austria is part of this dialect area as well; in addition, there are a number of language islands further afield, mainly in Slovenia and the Balkans. Other isolated communities that still show distinct features of Bavarian can be found in the United States, for example, and are largely due to the migration of religious communities, such as the Hutterites (cf. Lunte 2006; Schabus 2006).

Taking into account this geographical distribution, it reflects the fact that Bavarians are linguistically more closely related to Austrians than to other, Northern German speakers. On a cultural level, a similar picture emerges. We see a community that draws on a shared history, culture, traditions and language varieties, yet is located in two different, independent states; in fact, one of the territories (Austria) is a state in itself, while the other is a federal state of another country (Germany).[4] The (comparatively) homogeneous cultural image has been promoted by various Bavarian politicians as consistent with the visions of a Europe of Regions. Austria, as an independent country, has played its own distinctive role in this discussion about a 'united Europe' and has repeatedly voiced resistance to unifying tendencies that would obliterate the specifically Austro-Bavarian character of the country (cf. de Cillia 1998), both in culture and with respect to the Austrian variety of German, which displays a strong Bavarian influence.

Close relationships often have their own specific problems and it is no different in the case of Germany, *Altbayern* and Austria. While there is little in the way of political conflict nowadays, the cultural and linguistic side displays a different picture. This chapter will discuss how the pluricentric character of the German language brings about a perceived hierarchy between the various national standards. In addition, cultural and linguistic auto- and hetero-stereotypes based on such perceptions play a major role and often paint not only a grim picture, but are used (and misused) for economic reasons, such as the promotion of tourism. In this fashion, negative associations are reinforced, especially in the field of language use and competence – or lack of it. People often perceive speech that differs from the standard as deficient, and can be quick to draw assumptions about speakers' capabilities. Studies in the 1970s and early 1980s explored the academic achievement of children and concluded that speaking a dialect was directly mirrored in poorer achievement (cf. Ammon 1972, 1978, 1983; Reitmajer 1979). From the late 1980s onwards, the linguistic tenor had changed considerably, moving away from what sounded like a general condemnation of dialect use among many non-linguists, towards a more balanced view or even outright support of dialect use in education alongside the standard variety (Ammon and Kellermeier 1997). Public opinion, however, has remained largely unchanged. One result of these attitudes is the generally more negative perception of Bavarian identity – this applies to the self-perception of Bavarian speakers and to how other Standard German speakers see them.

Historical and Political Background to the Linguistic Situation of Bavarian

In order to understand the position of Bavarian, a brief look at the development of the German language and its standards in general is beneficial. Germany did not emerge as a unified country until the late nineteenth century, and Austria became a state only in 1919. These circumstances partially explain the relatively high prestige of some dialects, such as *Altbairisch* or various Austrian regional varieties, in contrast to other countries.

It is worthwhile to note that manuscripts exist in early forms of German ('proto-German') that date to before the tenth and eleventh centuries; although Latin largely replaces the vernacular after this time, we can still observe a degree of functional bilingualism (Keller 1978: 243). The ruling dynasty, the Hohenstaufen – often referred to as the Staufer – is closely associated with the rise and fall of the medieval German Empire (1154–1250), starting with Frederick I, better known as Barbarossa (1152–1190) (Schulze 1998: 17f.). The heartland of the ruling Hohenstaufen dynasty was situated in Franconia and Swabia; therefore, the main influences on the written varieties at the time were Frankish and Alemannic. The southern and western parts of the German Empire led the movement towards a more standardized language. After 1250, an approximation to a 'standard' German, imposed by the Hohenstaufen, disintegrated into regional written varieties that were shaped by the writing conventions of chancelleries in the various areas. It is, therefore, possible to regard German as a written language that displays many regional features (Keller 1978: 72ff., 240ff.; König 2007: 75ff.). From the extant manuscripts, it is clear that a strong writing tradition had been established in the south (including Bavaria and Austria), which was to shape the future of written German as a whole.

The German language in the Middle Ages can be classified as pluricentric, largely due to the power shifts between the various houses and dynasties that governed the Holy Roman Empire. In the fourteenth century, under Ludwig the Bavarian (1313–1347), the chancery language of the empire was strongly influenced by Bavarian; it is even possible to speak of a Bavarian standard language for a few decades. In this respect, the linguistic situation was similar to that of the twelfth and thirteenth centuries under the Staufer rule, where manuscripts and official documents reflect a strong southern influence. The writing and literary tradition that had been established in the Bavarian region during the Middle Ages did not continue. In the following centuries, power shifted towards Prague, where East Central German traits were incorporated, and in the sixteenth century these still prevailed, although *Meissnisch* (the variety spoken in the Meissen area of Saxony) was beginning to gain influence. Establishing chanceries and printing presses all over the country helped to create more linguistic uniformity; however, regional variations were still to be found around these printing centres.

Keller identifies centres throughout the southern part of the territory: for the Austro-Bavarian print area, Vienna, Munich and Ingolstadt were the focal points. Other noteworthy printing centres in southern German-speaking areas were Zurich, for the Swiss varieties, and Tübingen, Ulm and Augsburg in the Swabian area. The varieties connected to the printing houses eventually replaced the earlier norm-setting chancery varieties. At roughly the same time, it can be observed that the southern varieties started to lose out due to their geographical position on the German dialect continuum. Central German dialects have the distinct advantage of being closer to both the northern and the southern varieties, as they are reasonably levelled and have fewer distinctly northern or southern dialectal features; thus, they are easier to understand for people from the far ends of the country. Similar to the developments in the south, the North German varieties also saw a decline in status. The emerging standard based on Central German was increasingly adopted in the north of Germany, not only in print but also in speech. By adopting a largely levelled variety, the market for printers expanded geographically. Martin Luther's translation of the New Testament into German was not the first of its kind but it was the most accessible version, making use of the Central German idiom and helping to establish a variety of the language that was understood throughout the German-speaking area. On the other hand, during early modern times, a number of universities, mainly in the south, were established and helped to spread the southern varieties, or rather some of its features, further north as students came to the south to study and eventually returned home to the central and northern parts of the country (Keller 1978: 336ff.; König 2007: 91ff.).

With the emergence and establishment of a standard, the regional varieties and their literatures were becoming increasingly marginalized. A small revival of vernacular prose can be charted in the late nineteenth and early twentieth centuries, linked to prominent writers such as Franz von Kobell, Lena Christ, Ludwig Thoma and Oskar Maria Graf. To this day, however, their writing remains very much a niche area of interest. As the invention of movable type and the printing press helped to establish writing conventions, they would assist in establishing a unified standard. With the publication of the first *Duden: Rechtschreibung der Deutschen Sprache* in 1880, Standard German orthography became codified, followed in 1898 by Theodor Sieb's *Deutsche Aussprache* which focused on pronunciation (Ammon 1995: 326f.). The Austrian equivalent of the former, the *Österreichisches Wörterbuch,* was not published until 1951, before that the German codification applied exclusively (Ammon 1995: 137). As we can see throughout the development of

Standard German, what once was a heavily influenced Southern variety in the Middle Ages turned into a Central and partially Northern-influenced standard. Such an evolution sheds light on the emerging conflict of the various national standards of German.

Bavarian-speaking Areas

The most profound difference when discussing Bavaria is revealed when using the adjectives *bayerisch* and *bairisch*. Similarly, when it comes to people, it makes a vast difference whether someone talks about *Bayern* or *Baiern*, as not all of them are Germans. As both variants of each word are homophones, context reveals the intended meaning in speech only. *Bayern* and *bayerisch* refer to the German federal state. *Bairisch* designates the language and culture of the Bavarians (*Baiern*), and the associated cultural region extends well beyond the political area of the Free State and the Bavarians (*Bayern*) who live there. The area in which Bavarian (*Bairisch*) is spoken covers *Altbayern* and most of Austria. The Austrian federal state of Vorarlberg, bordering on Switzerland, is excluded as it is part of the Alemannic dialect area (cf. Barbour and Stevenson 1990: 76, map 3.4). Similarly, Swabia and Franconia, although part of the Free State, belong to the Alemannic and Franconian dialect areas, respectively. Franconian is classified as *Ostfränkisch* (East Franconian dialect); the dialect spoken around the area of Aschaffenburg in the north-west is *Rheinfränkisch*; and in the far north, around Ludwigsstadt, one can even encounter Thuringian (Aman 1986: 189; Zehetner 1985: 16). As the dialect spans such a large area, it can ultimately be divided into three distinct branches – Northern, Central and Southern Bavarian (*Nordbairisch*, *Mittelbairisch* and *Südbairisch*). These, in turn, can be subdivided into various regional and local varieties (cf. Zehetner 1997: 7; König 2007: 230f.).[5]

The varieties most relevant for the Free State and Austria are those of Central Bavarian, found between the Danube and Isar rivers and along the Danube Valley from Straubing to the Czech Republic. Central Bavarian is the most progressive of the three Bavarian branches as its focal points are Munich and Vienna, which serve as centres for innovation. It has been claimed that the Munich variety has all but vanished, at least among young people (Kratzer 2010). Irrespective of the metropolitan influences, the dialect area as such is characterized by its rural nature, with a strong emphasis on farming. The Danube plays a vital part in the region's transport links, which means that the Central Bavarian dialect alongside the river has always been the one most prone to change, having to accommodate native speakers and traders alike. Many of the cultural centres, due to their commercial power, are located in or within easy reach of the Danube Valley: Regensburg,

Ingolstadt, Landshut, Passau, Tegernsee and Freising, as well as the Austrian cities of Salzburg, Linz and St Pölten (Zehetner 1985: 60).

Southern Bavarian is not spoken in the *Freistaat* at all, but in Austria. It is largely confined to Upper and Lower Austria, Tyrol, Carinthia, Styria and the southern part of the Burgenland. Parts of Northern Italy (*Südtirol*) also lie in the Southern Bavarian dialect area. Zehetner concludes: '*Baiern leben ja nicht nur im Freistaat Bayern, sondern auch in Österreich und Südtirol. Aber nicht in ganz Bayern spricht man bairisch*' [Bavarians do not only live in the Free State of Bavaria but also in Austria and South Tyrol. Bavarian, however, is not spoken in all parts of (the Free State of) Bavaria] (Zehetner 1985: 16). A mock spoken standard, *Edelbairisch* (noble or distinguished Bavarian), can be identified, but it is generally treated with contempt as it appears to be snobbish or spoken by would-be Bavarians; similarly, what is often perceived by outsiders as a standardized spoken Bavarian variety exists but is profoundly influenced by Munich speech, as the major television and radio stations are based in the capital:

> Außenstehende glauben oft, es gäbe eine bayerische Staatssprache. Zwar existiert etwas wie eine 'bayerische Koiné' münchnerischer Prägung, die auch im Rundfunk, im Bayerischen Fernsehen und in der Werbung ihren Platz hat – aber dies ist nicht 'das Bayerische'! Es ist ein im wesentlichen nur lautlich dem oberbayerisch-münchnerischen Dialektklang angenähertes Hochdeutsch. (Zehetner 1997: 6)
> [Outsiders often think there is a national Bavarian language. Something like a 'Bavarian koiné' of Munich origin does, in fact, exist; it has its place on radio, Bavarian television and in advertising – but this is not 'the Bavarian language'! It is simply Standard German with distinct phonological influence from the Upper Bavarian and Munich dialects.]

The mass media, mainly television, have been a great leveller when it comes to language; they are possibly as influential as the printing press in the Middle Ages, if not more so. As with the Bavarian case of Munich-influenced idiom being the most prestigious, Moosmüller (1990) charts similar developments in Austria. The spoken varieties associated with Vienna and Salzburg appear to be the most acceptable and best suited to develop into or be adapted to a supraregional Standard Austrian.

Pluricentricity and its Problems: The Status of Bavarian and Standard Austrian German

German, like English, is classified as a pluricentric language; the term initially used by Kloss (1978) illustrates the fact that nations can use largely the same language, which can express cultural connections as well as incorporate national differences, thus creating national varieties, such as Standard

Swiss German or Austrian German (Clyne 2004: 296). In our context, this means that what is correct in Austrian German, and therefore correct in the perception of *Altbairisch* speakers in Germany, is not necessarily correct in Standard (German) German. Examples of such overlapping features are the preference of Bavarians for the use of the perfect tense instead of the imperfect (Bavarian: '*ich bin in die Stadt gegangen*' vs. Standard German: '*ich ging in die Stadt*'; 'I went to town'), and the use of different copula when forming the perfect (Standard German uses '*er hat gesessen*' as opposed to Austrian German (and Bavarian) '*er ist gesessen*'; 'he sat down') (cf. Clyne 2004: 296).

The major difference between the Bavarian spoken in Germany and in Austria is that it has been acknowledged by its own speakers as well as other Germans to be 'only' a regional variety within Germany, whereas Austrian German serves as the official language of the country. Standard (German) German and Standard Austrian German are mutually intelligible; however, the latter incorporates distinct Bavarian lexical, syntactic and phonetic features (cf. Ammon 1995; Pfrehm 2010). It would be easy to assume that Austrian German is fully accepted as a standard throughout the German-speaking world as being on par with (German) German; however, this is not always the case.[6] Clyne has drawn up a ten-point list outlining the differences between dominant and non-dominant or, as he labels them, 'other', varieties in pluricentric language situations (Clyne 1995: 22). It should be mentioned, though, that Northern Germans often struggle to understand speakers of Bavarian dialects; this perceived unintelligibility has given rise to some of the stereotypes discussed in the following section.

Assuming a folk linguistic perspective, dominant nations have a tendency to dismiss other national varieties as 'trivial', and often equate these differences with regional variation, thus demoting non-dominant varieties to the level of dialects. Linguistic research, resulting in grammars and dictionaries of the non-dominant varieties (e.g. *Österreichisches Wörterbuch*), shows that the latter possess a grammatical structure that differs somewhat from the dominant standard grammar of the language. In addition, the situation is complicated by the dominant nations having assumed that variation occurs only at the spoken level. Due to these differences, the dialects are sometimes perceived to be a 'corrupt' version of the dominant standard and the speakers are perceived as unable to speak 'correctly'. Such assumptions tie in with the perception of dialect as a purely oral medium. In the case of Germany and Austria, such a difference in prestige between the standards can be observed and may subsequently affect Bavaria as well. To a large extent, Bavarians and Austrians take great pride in using the vernacular and assign it a vital role in their identity construction; dialect symbolizes home, and this sentiment resurfaces with a number of other references to associated keywords, such as honesty, feeling whole, being at ease and being part of the community (Loester 2009: 143, 154ff.).[7]

As pointed out earlier, the Bavarian-speaking area, both in Germany and Austria, is predominantly rural, and even metropolitan centres, such as Munich, rarely influence this perception. A shared language and a considerable number of shared cultural traditions make the alpine region appear to outsiders as a homogenous area. Speakers of a Bavarian variety, irrespective of whether they are German or Austrian, are regarded by standard German speakers as conservative country folk. The image of Bavarians (and to a significant extent Austrians) as beer-swilling, Lederhosen-wearing simpletons can be traced back as far as travelogues from the seventeenth century, and is not an invention of modern tourism marketing (cf. Gockerell 1980); however, it has largely been maintained by that sector. The picture of unspoilt, uncorrupted country dwellers has come back to haunt the present people. While the image of an unspoilt landscape and its population appears desirable, the very same image conjures up a picture of an uncivilized, backward region; Bavaria maintained its agricultural sector well into the twentieth century, thus fuelling the perception longer than other regions. The same holds true for the associated dialect – while the rural variety is deemed 'pure' and 'genuine', it is also regarded as 'common' and 'uneducated', thus creating a conflict situation. In this scenario, a split becomes obvious. While the social identity as a Bavarian can be regarded as positive due to its association with an unspoilt environment, the linguistic identity is regarded as negative due to its rural associations: '*Der Bauer, der in die Stadt kommt, ist plötzlich nicht mehr der Exote mit dem positive konnotierten Dialekt, sondern der auch wegen seiner Sprache belächelte Provinzler*' [The farmer who comes into town is all of a sudden not the exotic being with a positively connoted dialect anymore but, based also on his language, the ridiculed provincial] (Moosmüller 1990: 106).

At the same time, most Austrians are far from keen on being regarded as Germans; being a *Piefke* (a derogatory term for a German, based on the same surname; cf. Godeysen 2010) is far from desirable, even though they share a language: '*Der Piefke sei gar kein Herr, sondern ein Gattungsbegriff, erklärte er: eine Allegorie, in der ein Österreicher den teutonischen Großkotz, seinen Stechschritt, sein Säbelrasseln und den Kasernenhofton imaginiere, also den Deutschen schlechthin*' [The Piefke is not a gentleman but a generic term, he explained: an allegory, in which the Austrian imagines the Teutonic flash git, his goose-stepping, his sabre-rattling and the sergeant-major voice – in short, the German par excellence] (Riedl 2007). In this description of 'the German par excellence', the Old Bavarian recognizes 'the Prussian' – the very same image of the (Northern) German under a different name. The conflict between north and south in Germany has been a long-standing one, continuing to the present day; the Kingdom of Bavaria joined the German Empire only in 1870–71 and was effectively ruled by the Kingdom of Prussia, thus emphasizing the North–South divide, which had already been established linguistically with the rise of Central German Standard by means of Luther's bible translation. Stereotypically, Bavarians perceived (and often still do) Northern Germans as Prussians, with the same attributes that Austrians associate with the *Piefke*. While both Bavarian-speaking groups scorn the same stereotype, the state border turns Bavarians into the scorned ones when viewed from the Austrian perspective. Cultural proximity is overruled by political borders.[8] As we can see, both the dominant and the non-dominant German-speaking groups have very strong culturally and historically determined stereotypes of each other, which are reflected in judgements about each other's varieties.

The question as to why Bavarian and Austrian German are less prestigious than 'German' German still remains. As Clyne (2004: 296) states, the varieties are geographically contiguous, unlike the various national standards for English (e.g. British and American). Geographical distance might make it easier to establish differing norms; thus Austrian German, like Swiss German, will always struggle against the hegemony of Standard German. In addition, Germany is the largest of all German-speaking countries and has the largest number of German speakers, which simply makes it a more prominent variety. Historical reasons also play a role in the desire to have a different standard not only recognized but fully accepted as a means of differentiation, thus creating distance from Germany (Ammon 2006: 1767):

> Austrian identity is, in contrast, clearly 'German' in some sense or other; Austria is, and sees itself as, a German-speaking country, and yet, since the Second World War, a majority of Austrians have come to accept a distinct Austrian identity, distinct from that of Germany ... The fact that there has never been a state uniting all German-speakers, and that many of them in the past and in the present have not desired such a state, makes the case for postulating a common national identity linking speakers of the language difficult to argue. (Barbour 2000: 159)

Maybe the European Charter for Regional and Minority Languages will eventually come to the aid of *Altbairisch* and thus also strengthen the position of Austrian German. Germany ratified the charter in 1998 and included, as expected, Sorbian, a West Slavic language, like Czech and Slovak. Also recognized among other minority languages was Low German. A conference of northern German federal states had suggested including Danish and Frisian in the charter, and these recommendations were eventually accepted. Anthony Rowley, editor-in-chief of the Bavarian dictionary (*Bairisches Wörterbuch*), advocates a regional language status for Bavarian. According to him, Bavarian meets the following criteria set by the charter: first, it is spoken in a particular region of the nation by members of that country who are fewer in number than the overall population (Part 1, Article 1a); second, Bavarian differs from the official language. The third criterion is somewhat trickier to prove: languages that are neither dialects of the official language nor the language of immigrant groups can also be accepted under the charter (Rowley 1999: 9–10).

All dialects, including Standard German, are dialects of German from a legal point of view; however, Rowley argues that, like Low German, Bavarian is a German dialect but not derived from modern Standard German, the country's official language. He points out the historical pedigree and development to support his argument (Rowley 2011: 306). It is the same line of reasoning that has been used to classify Galician, Venetian and Scots as languages under the charter. Obviously, the question that needs to be answered is: 'Where does a dialect end and a language start?' (Haugen 1966). Such a decision is not easy to arrive at; in the case of Low German, it was argued that, historically, it was (and is) a language, which had been used in the Middle Ages as a written medium. The same applies to Bavarian; hence the criteria for the recognition of it as a minority language are fulfilled by analogy.

Grammars, dictionaries and a certain degree of standardization are often regarded as the indicators of a full-fledged language – Bavarian can prove its language status on the grounds of the first two, and a wealth of literature to go with it. Austrian German, with its close links to *Altbairisch*, provides support to the argument for standardization – if a particular feature is classified as being standard in one country why should it not be so in the neighbouring one? Rowley (1999: 9–10) quotes Hinderling, who claims that Bavarian qualifies because its grammatical features are considerably different from Standard German: '*Der Abstand Bairisch – Hochdeutsch ist größer als der zwischen Dänisch und Norwegisch oder Tschechisch und Slowakisch*' [The *Abstand* between Bavarian and Standard German is larger than the one between Danish and Norwegian or between Czech and Slovak]. However, to this day, Bavarian has not been accepted as a minority language in Germany, and Austrian German has yet to gain more prestige.[9]

Conclusion

'This consciousness of community is, then, encapsulated in perception of its boundaries, boundaries which are themselves largely constituted by people in interaction' (Cohen 1985: 13).

Language is a prime means of interaction and can be used to reinforce similarities and differences, as is the case with Bavarians, Austrians and other German speakers in their communities. Historical developments, such as the long-shared bond of the Holy Roman Empire, and linguistic developments, such as the late codification of Austrian German, have left enduring marks on the Bavarian varieties and the associated standards. While the language has brought and kept the Bavarians and Austrians together on a cultural level, historical processes, such as the collapse of the Habsburg monarchy and the establishment of the German Empire, have forced them apart.

Linguistically as well as culturally, the southern state boundary of Germany, separating Bavaria and Austria, exists mainly on maps. The more distinctive dividing line is between Northern and Southern Germans, between the *Piefkes* or 'Prussians' and Bavarian speakers. Regional varieties help to maintain this border in the sense that they are one of the seminal features not only to express identity but in being identity markers in themselves. On the other hand, this distance between Standard German and the non-dominant varieties, such as Austrian German (and Bavarian), is maintained by social stereotypes based on an urban–rural divide that, to a large extent, no longer exists. Absolute number of speakers, economic power and the size of the state, in conjunction with perceived power by way of language status, help to retain the status quo among the national standards of German.

It remains to be seen what future political developments, such as a potential 'Europe of Regions', bring for non-dominant varieties of German, irrespective of whether they are regarded 'only' as dialects by speakers and non-speakers alike or whether they are assigned the status of national languages. While the mass media, mobility and education undoubtedly have a mainly negative influence on the retention or survival of non-standard varieties, such as Bavarian, the much proclaimed death of dialects, prophesied for decades, has still not occurred. As long as speakers associate crucial elements of their lives with their language, such as a strong attachment to home and positive associations with their culture, linguistic varieties that serve as markers of identity and cultural borders will remain.

Barbara Loester is senior lecturer in English linguistics at the University of Winchester, UK. Her research focuses on minority and regional languages in Europe, with a particular interest in Germanic varieties, language policies and identity construction. She has published on language attitudes, and identity construction of Scots and Bavarian speakers.

Notes

1. In linguistics, the term 'national variety' generally refers to the variety spoken in a particular country, e.g. Australian English in Australia or New Zealand English in New Zealand.

2. English is also classified as a pluricentric language, with British English and American English as the two main standard 'providers'.

3. In the English-speaking world, we see similar associations; the *Oxford English Dictionary* is associated with British English, while *Merriam Webster's* is closely connected to American English.

4. Söhrman discusses the role of Austria as one of the dominant states in the Balkans in Chapter 6 of this volume.

5. While the use of dialect in contemporary society is generally perceived to be declining, the actual dialect boundaries as reflected in Map 3.4 in Barbour and Stevenson (1990: 76) have hardly changed.

6. Fehlen discusses how Luxembourgish has struggled with similar problems in Chapter 7; see also Trudgill (2004) and Millar (2005).

7. See also Järlehed's discussion of the Basque language and identity in Chapter 9.

8. Comparatively few academic studies about this phenomenon exist, and evidence tends to be anecdotal; Gockerell's analyses (1974; 1980) appear to be the only ones that attempt a scholarly debate. Public opinion polls are published regularly but mainly deal with the stereotypes and perceptions of dialects.

9. In his discussion of the linguistic situation of Italy, Tamburelli (2014) offers a quantitive approach to the language–dialect divide. Based on methods from speech recognition he uses the intelligibility criterion to establish where boundaries between langages and dialects could be set.

References

Aman, R. 1986. *Bayrisch-Österreichisches Schimpfwörterbuch*. Munich: Goldmann.

Ammon, U. 1972. 'Dialekt als sprachliche Barriere: Eine Pilotstudie über Schwierigkeiten von Dialektsprechern im Schulaufsatz', *Muttersprache* 82: 224–37.

———. 1978. *Schulschwierigkeiten von Dialektsprechern: Empirische Untersuchung sprachabhängiger Schulleistungen und des Schüler- und Lehrerbewusstseins mit sprachdidaktischen Hinweisen*. Weinheim and Basel: Beltz.

———. 1983. 'Soziale Bewertung des Dialekt-Sprechers: Vor- und Nachteile in Schule, Beruf und Gesellschaft', in W. Besch et al. (eds), *Dialektologie: Ein Handbuch zur deutschen und allgemeinen Dialektforschung*, Vol. 2. Berlin and New York: de Gruyter, pp. 1500–10.

———. 1995. *Die deutsche Sprache in Deutschland, Österreich und der Schweiz*. Berlin: de Gruyter.

———. 2006. 'Die deutschsprachigen Länder/The German-speaking Countries', in U. Ammon et al. (eds), *Sociolinguistics: An International Handbook of the Science of Language and Society*, Vol. 3. 2nd completely revised and extended edition. Berlin: de Gruyter, pp. 1765–72.

Ammon, U., and B. Kellermeier. 1997. 'Dialekt als Sprachbarriere passé? 25 Jahre danach: Versuch eines Diskussions-Erweckungsküsschens', *Deutsche Sprache* 1: 21–38.

Barbour, S. 2000. 'Germany, Austria, Switzerland, Luxembourg: The Total Coincidence of Nations and Speech Communities', in S. Barbour and C. Carmichael (eds), *Language and Nationalism in Europe*. Oxford: Oxford University Press, pp. 151–67.

Barbour, S., and P. Stevenson. 1990. *Variation in German: A Critical Approach to German Sociolinguistics*. Cambridge: Cambridge University Press.

Clyne, M. 1995. *The German Language in a Changing Europe*. Cambridge: Cambridge University Press.

———. 2004. 'Pluricentric Language/Plurizentrische Sprache', in U. Ammon et al. (eds), *Sociolinguistics: An International Handbook of the Science of Language and Society*, Vol. 1. 2nd completely revised and extended edition. Berlin: de Gruyter, pp. 296–300.

Cohen, A. 1985. *The Symbolic Construction of Community*. London: Routledge.

de Cillia, R. 1998. *Burenwurscht bleibt Burenwurscht: Sprachenpolitik und gesellschaftliche Mehrsprachigkeit in Österreich*. Klagenfurt/Celovec: Drava.

Gockerell, N. 1974. *Das Bayernbild in der Literarischen und 'Wissenschaftlichen' Wertung durch fünf Jahrhunderte*. Munich: Herbert Utz Verlag.

———. 1980. *Die Bayern: Land und Leute in Reisebeschreibungen aus vier Jahrhunderten*. Zurich and Freiburg im Breisgau: Atlantis Verlag.

Godeysen, H. 2010. *Piefke: Kulturgeschichte einer Beschimpfung*. Wien-Klosterneuburg: Edition Va Bene.

Haugen, E. 1966. 'Dialect, Language, Nation', *American Anthropologist* 68(4): 922–35.

Keller, R.E. 1978. *The German Language*. London: Faber and Faber.

Kloss, H. 1978. *Die Entwicklung Neuer Germanischer Kultursprachen seit 1800*. Düsseldorf: Pädagogischer Verlag Schwann.

König, W. 2007. *dtv-Atlas zur Deutschen Sprache*. 16th edition. Munich: Deutscher Taschenbuch Verlag.

Kratzer, H. 2010. 'Geij Bou, dassd fei schee schmaadzd!', *Süddeutsche Zeitung*, 19 May. Retrieved 28 February 2017 from http://www.sueddeutsche.de/kultur/dialekt-geij-bou-dassd-fei-schee-schmaadzd-1.892735.

Loester, B. 2009. 'A Contrastive Study of Language Attitudes and Identity Construction in the North-East of Scotland and Bavaria', Ph.D. thesis. Aberdeen: University of Aberdeen.

Lunte, G. 2006. 'Besondere Dialektmerkmale der bairisch-deutschböhmischen Mundart von Ellis, Kansas, USA', in N. Berend and E. Knipf-Komlósi (eds), *Sprachinselwelten: The World of Language Islands*. Frankfurt am Main: Peter Lang, pp. 237–57.

Millar, R.M. 2005. *Language, Nation and Power: An Introduction*. Basingstoke: Palgrave Macmillan.

Moosmüller, S. 1990. 'Einschätzung von Sprachvarietäten in Österreich', *International Journal of the Sociology of Language* 83: 105–20.

Pfrehm, J. 2010. 'The Role of Age in Austrians' Perceptions of the Frequency of Use and Likeability of Lexical Teutonisms and Austriacisms', *Folia Linguistica* 44(2): 439–70.

Reitmajer, V. 1979. *Der Einfluss des Dialekts auf die standardsprachlichen Leistungen von bayerischen Schülern in Vorschule, Grundschule und Gymnasium*. Marburg: N.G. Elwert.

Riedl, J. 2007. 'Der ewige Piefke', *Die Zeit Online*, 23 August. Retrieved 28 February 2017 from http://www.zeit.de/2007/35/Piefke-Invasion.

Rowley, A. 1999. 'Bairisch und die Europäische Charta der Regional- und Minderheitssprachen.' Förderverein Bairische Sprache und Dialekte e.V., *Rundbrief* 29: 9–10.

Rowley, A. 2011. 'Bavarian: Successful Dialect or Failed Language?' in J.A. Fishman and O. García (eds), *Language and Ethnic Identity. The Success-Failure Continuum in Language and Ethnic Identity Efforts*. Oxford: Oxford University Press, pp. 299–309.

Schabus, W. 2006. 'Südbairische Elemente in der deutschen Mundart der Hutterer', in N. Berend and E. Knipf-Komlósi (eds), *Sprachinselwelten – The World of Language Islands*. Frankfurt am Main: Peter Lang, pp. 273–99.

Schulze, H. 1998. *Kleine Deutsche Geschichte*. Munich: Verlag C.H. Beck.

Tamburelli, M. 2014. 'Uncovering the "Hidden" Multilingualism of Europe: An Italian Case Study', *Journal of Multilingual and Multicultural Development* 35(3): 252–70.

Trudgill, P. 2004. 'Glocalisation and the Ausbau Sociolinguistics of Modern Europe', in A. Duszak and U. Okulska (eds), *Speaking from the Margin: Global English from a European Perspective*. Frankfurt am Main: Peter Lang, pp. 35–49.

Zehetner, L. 1985. *Das Bairische Dialektbuch*. Munich: Verlag C.H. Beck.

———. 1997. *Bairisches Deutsch: Lexikon der deutschen Sprache in Altbayern*. Munich: Heinrich Hugendubel Verlag.

CHAPTER 6

The Influence of Imagined Linguistic Performances

INGMAR SÖHRMAN

> 1. On ne parle jamais qu'une seule langue.
> 2. On ne parle jamais une seule langue.
> —Jacques Dérrida, *Le monolinguisme de l'autre*

Derrida's words ring true. We do not know other languages as well as we believe we do – but we think we do. On the other hand, we live in a plurilinguistic world and, as it turns out, linguistic and political borders coincide more seldom than we are led to believe, given the ubiquity of the old Romantic idea of 'one language, one people, and one nation' promoted by nationalistic, or rather state-focused, political forces of very different brands (communists, socialists, liberals and conservatives), reflecting the ambition of creating a 'modern' homogeneous state without minority complications.

The idea that a common language is that which constitutes a nationality and thereby establishes nation-state borders is often used as the principle argument for territorial claims, as has recently been the case in the complicated annexation of Crimea, and Russian claims on eastern Ukraine. An example of this is when Russian nationalist politician and writer Edward Limonov claimed in an interview that the people living in these parts of the world are Russians since Russian is the language mainly spoken in these regions, as is the case in Crimea, and the population is thereby Russian, and furthermore those regions belonged to Russia for a long time before being

Notes for this section begin on page 113.

transferred to Ukraine during the Soviet era (Fernández 2014: 3). Language cannot be the only argument for belonging to a country. The linguistic situation is often very complicated, and very few countries are monolingual. This, however, does not mean that linguistic and cultural minorities are not entitled to support and respect.

Still, this monolingual nationalist vision constitutes a considerable communicative problem within plurilingual states, and it affects the information and analyses that we receive and believe in much more than we would like to think. Languages are often used to set the cultural standards that determine who belongs to a certain society.

As a consequence of this sociolinguistic reality within a milieu where modern media such as the internet have led to a need for ever-faster information, speed has become – or so it seems – more important than the deep knowledge and intent to be objective, which require reflection and more thorough study. Analysts and journalists do not stand a chance of grasping the reality outside their own competence in a particular field, as they have no time to enhance their language or history skills, including recent political and economic developments, even if they want to, and they do not have the time to consult specialists due to the pressure to produce information quickly.

There is an ongoing discussion about declining trust in journalists and the media, which has led to promotion of 'lighter news' such as the Eurovision Song Contest (Gelotte 2012: 2). This is sometimes seen as lack of respect for the audience, mostly due to economic reality and the pressure to produce news immediately without time to check what is really true and valid. Thus, superficiality becomes more evident when journalists have to cover vast linguistically and politically heterogeneous areas. Many of them are forced to obtain information in a language they know, often English, or interview only people who speak English, even in countries like France and Germany, and these interviewees might not be the ideal sources of adequate information on a specific topic or situation, but are still chosen because they speak English. It is imperative to recognize that linguistic, cultural and political limits often obscure and blur the transmission of correct information and the sources on which we base our ideas and decisions. A typical situation is one where things are mixed up, such as when Crown Prince Haakon is presented as the son of Queen Margarethe, although she is the queen of Denmark, and he is the son of King Harald of Norway (Constenla 2014: 72). This kind of mistake diminishes the credibility of the rest of the information given.

There are still, however, quite a few analysts and journalists who speak 'strange' languages (in a globalized world pretty much anything other than English), and they must be highly regarded, but many are simply sent to an unfamiliar part of the world with little or no time for preparation. They are hardly to blame for this state of affairs, but the result can be disastrous for the credibility or objectivity of the information they communicate.

As has been pointed out above, in most countries there are groups of people whose mother tongue is not the official or majority language, but the speakers of this majority language often take it for granted that their language is spoken by all citizens, as this is, often even officially, the common vernacular of all the citizens of that particular country. If people who belong to a majority speak another language, it is usually an international one like English or Spanish, and not necessarily one spoken by a minority within their own country (cf. Söhrman 2004). These minority languages tend to be reduced to a regional, local or family issue. However the political rhetoric often pretends that it is more of an equal and plurilinguistic situation. In most parts of Europe and in the Americas, we encounter the predominant assumption that at least politicians and people in the tourist industry speak a foreign, or rather *the* foreign, language (i.e. English). This is a very simplistic view that colours our understanding and reception of information from other parts of the world in various ways without our noticing or consenting to it.

I would therefore suggest two hypotheses that show how the idea of stable borders makes us believe in imagined linguistic performances (or practices) that crash head-on with linguistic (and political) realities:

> 1. Most people perceive the state borders of today as stable, corresponding to one particular linguistic community.
> 2. The presumption is that the use of English or some other 'international language', like Spanish or Russian, in interviews 'abroad' is always functional, but this idea limits, and sets a border to, our view of what is going on in the world (and thus our perception of contemporary society).

Today, when the world has shrunk mentally due to modern means of communication, and we can travel anywhere in a few hours, the simplicity of speed has made us believe in quick overviews and shallow perspectives on that which constitutes very complex realities. Thus, we suffer unconsciously from the loss of a more nuanced reflection of the world. To many people, the world appears limited to a 'frozen' moment of history that is relevant to their presuppositions of what constitutes their own national history. Thus, today's borders erroneously appear to be final, everlasting and true.

The purpose of this chapter is to discuss how mental 'linguistic borders' prevent us from getting adequate and objective information from countries where the languages normally spoken are not very familiar to us – in other words, most countries. That way we are unconsciously led to believe in half-truths and nationalistic myths.

We and the Others

WE are not always WE, as a feeling of exclusion can make people feel that they are the OTHERS. For instance, the Romanian feeling of being forgotten is not only self-pity. Ever since the Second World War, Romania has been left to its own devices by the West, and the interest shown has been little. Just as the previously existing *leyenda negra* (black legend) targeting Spain hurt the Spanish reputation for so long that Spaniards internalized parts of 'everybody is against us and describe us as the bad ones', there was a black legend concerning Romania as well (Watts 2010: 660–64), a feeling of being purposely abandoned and excluded, and thus WE were the OTHERS.

Thus the OTHERS are also a WE, which can be difficult to admit and accept. French anthropologist Marc Augé, when insisting on the exchange of roles (I – Other), adds the idea of *non-lieux* (non-places), which is an ambiguous space that is supposed to exist between 'here' and 'there' and thereby it is outside the 'real world' as it has none of the characteristics of the real place. It is something in between and thus outside the real world. There is no sense of belonging anywhere, and when the OTHERS is located in one of the non-places they are reduced to oblivion being outside and thus insignificant (Augé 1985, 1986, 1989). Prejudices often seem to be taken for granted for no reason at all, merely on the basis of misconceptions and myths. The concept indicates that the dichotomy of WE and the OTHERS is simplistic and not corresponding to reality but to a narrow interpretation of a much more complicated and partly evasive reality, and this has an impact on the information and interpretations that we receive.

Since it is often hard to appraise information from secondary sources, many people try to improve their information base by conducting interviews in English. This could in itself be a good thing. However, this means that the information source is restricted to people who know English. Whether they are representative of the country, the culture and the prevailing ideas and opinions within it is, of course, a completely different thing.

> What are the implications of a state of affairs in which the choice of who represents one side is shaped to a significant degree by self-selected representatives of the other? The play of identities that this social structure affords enables maximum flexibility and deniability, as well as the opportunity to *reduce account-ability* by bodies, procedures, and structures on both sides. (Wedel 1998: 193)

The linguistic level of these 'representatives' – that is to say, their comprehension and active knowledge of English – might influence the message that the interviewer receives. Besides, there is always some kind of collegial understanding, which means that journalists tend to trust other journalists without really knowing anything about the reality or how much their colleagues really know. The scandal about ex-President Iliescu's feigned KGB affiliation, produced by the scandal-focused paper *Ziua*, was a big issue in the West precisely because Western journalists believed their colleagues without checking with anybody else. This piece of information turned out to be entirely bogus.

An Old World in New Clothes

It is evident that the fall of Communism created a 'brave new world' in the former Soviet bloc where many of these concepts, earlier disregarded, came to play a decisive role, and not only there. Religious and linguistic realities, as well as nationalistic feelings, have come to challenge geopolitical borders. Take for instance the notion of *Els països catalans* (the Catalan countries), a concept that unites parts of France and Spain (and Italy), and 'Scots English' (cf. Grant and Murison 1931–76, which is presented by more nationalistic activists as a linguistic variety in its own right, and different from Scottish English. Is the division of Bosnian, Croatian and Serbian a linguistic, cultural, religious or ethnic one (Mønnesland 1995: 77–92)? Are people who speak Hungarian in Transylvania 'Hungarians' or 'Hungarian-speaking Romanians'? What are the implications of these notions and what are the political and ideological consequences. Will Spain and the UK split up? And will a new language be coined in Scotland?

Christopher Pountain (2000) has pointed out three different kinds of linguistic frontier that can enlighten us on our way to understanding the complexity of this problem:

> *(1) Natural microfrontiers* between very closely related lects (language varieties), which exist between communities (indeed, at maximum resolution, between every speaker), an example of which would be the speech of La Coruña as opposed to the speech of El Ferrol (both situated in Galicia, north-west Spain).
> *(2) Natural macrofrontiers* between distantly related or unrelated languages (e.g. the frontier between Basque and Navarro-Aragonese (a Romance variety) and Spanish. Basque is not related to any spoken language in Europe today).
> *(3) Artificial macrofrontiers* between imposed or agreed standards (e.g. the Spanish–Portuguese border, which is more of a linguistic transition than a well-perceived linguistic boundary; or the formal border imposed but hardly distinguishable between Moldovan and Romanian).

Artificial macrofrontiers are tricky as they differentiate between acknowledged linguistic standards, however vague they might seem. In this last category we might include the boundary between standard Norwegian (*bokmål*) and standard Swedish, which are closer than many acknowledge; Norwegian and Swedish varieties are close to the standard linguistic varieties. This is also the case in many places in Europe (and elsewhere) such as between Bulgarian and Macedonian, and between Romanian and Moldovan, both of which are precariously weak linguistic frontiers indeed, but they could also be seen, at least partially, as examples of the first case. They could be seen as representing what is a minority (versus a majority in a neighbouring country). Is it then a minority in relation to a local, regional or national majority, and does it have a majority position on any level (Söhrman 2009)? Therefore, in order to create a stable mental and ideological reality with historically motivated and well-established borders, there seems to be a tendency to freeze a certain moment in history as THE moment when a certain (your own) nation is created (ibid.), and this moment overshadows any other historical event, thus completely disregarding all other times when this place might have been crucial to the founding of another nation. Both Albanians and Serbs can claim Kosovo as their homeland, but at different times, and the Hungarians and Romanians discuss who first populated Transylvania after all Dacians and Roman authorities allegedly left that region (Ludanyi 2011). It often seems that to many it is impossible to grasp the idea of a plurinational historical reality and heritage that would imply the equality and shared rights of several national, ethnic and linguistic communities. This leads to a tricky question: How do 'cultural superstitions' and beliefs create and influence the politics and idea of the 'true' reality of our modern world? And who transmits these beliefs – and to what purpose? It is quite obvious that political agendas are involved, and that personal and/or ideological ambitions are behind the promotion of these ideas.

An Example: The Balkans

In order to illustrate this complex reality and make it more comprehensible, we need a good example, and there are many. We will look at the Balkans, Romania in particular, with reference to other similar or divergent situations in Europe.

In the contemporary environment (scientific border-crossing and interdisciplinary), it is often more fruitful to talk about areas than countries, a term we use since we are educated to see the world in regions that are limited by geopolitical borders. However, the broader idea of a transnational area that is based on a cultural, linguistic, historical or religious unity of some kind does, of course, fit this idea of border-crossing extremely well as a focus for study, and the Balkans are a prototypical example.

The historical experience of all the countries is a long struggle for preservation and creation of autonomy, culture (Cuche 2010) and language. It is a true crossroads. After many centuries of migration waves, both before and after it was held by the Roman Empire, the territory became a stage for armed conflict between three superpowers with interests in the region: Austria, Russia and the Ottoman Empire. Their interests were the expansion and strengthening of their own spheres of influence. While the empires dedicated themselves to this task, the peoples living in the area struggled to maintain their cultures, religions and languages, often from minority positions, and the Balkan reality is still a hodgepodge (cf. Svanberg and Söhrman 1996).

However, the Balkans have attracted a lot of attention, especially lately, after the fall of Communism and the civil wars in ex-Yugoslavia in the 1990s. These wars served to confirm old prejudices concerning blood feuds, violence and banditry as 'traditional' behaviour in south-eastern Europe. This corroborates the idea of the Balkans as being alien (THE OTHERS) in relation to Western Europe, supporting statements such as, 'You cannot understand Balkan mentality. People there are different from us'. This idea has been, and often still is, repeated as an explanation of why there was war in a Europe that had lived in peace for almost three generations. This stigmatizing concept of the 'bloodthirsty Balkan peoples' has seriously damaged the image of the Balkans, limited their possibilities, and almost provided justification for ruthlessly ambitious politicians in their hunger for power.

'Our estimation of a nation is tied in with our capacity to identify with it, to project ourselves in it' (Bruckner 1986: 80), and after the fall of Communism there was a strong sentiment in the 'West' to integrate what had earlier been Central Europe – Poland, Hungary and Czechoslovakia – while Romania and Bulgaria, being Orthodox and not really Central European, were presumed as not only more different, but as culturally and sentimentally oriented towards the East (Wedel 1998: 19–20).

Interest in the Balkans is by no means new. Still, it has to be emphasized that the idea of Balkan culture and history is largely obscured by various romantic ideas. In the Gothic novels of the nineteenth century, we find mythical vampires, bandits and operetta principalities (*Tintin* and *The Prisoner of Zenda* can serve as examples), where violence and romantic adventures occur. Romantic adventurers like Lord Byron, and also pretentious Balkan kings (King Zog of Albania, for instance) and other royalty, have confirmed this picture. The oriental connection became more apparent during the interwar period, when economy and politics sometimes took on a small-scale 'bazaar' mentality. The Orient Express was the very essence of the Balkans as a gateway to the mysterious and romantic Orient.

Even the Communist postwar period had its share of romantic ideas. Although they were completely different and attracted a different public, Yugoslavian independence and openness set an example for many non-Moscow Communists and socialists. The same goes for Albania, though this country, according to many 'believers', had turned into a socialist dream – independent and extremely strict in its application of Communism. Very few people had a realistic understanding or genuine knowledge about the Balkans.

There is an understandable, but also deplorable, mental border that simplifies what is far away, and this tendency to simplify seems to increase logarithmically. However, the more a region seems different (language, culture and religion), the sooner the logarithmic distance increases. The United States, for example, is much better known in Europe than neighbouring countries like Morocco, Algeria or Turkey.

Specialists on Eastern Europe and Communism focused mainly on the Soviet Union and Central European Communist countries; they mainly knew Russian, not the other languages, and based their information on Russian sources. This was even more obvious in Northern and South Western Europe, where the Balkans seemed very far away, at least mentally. The prevailing concept was of 'Communist Eastern Europe', thus concealing the idea of the Balkans. This politically motivated notion has thus obscured the considerable linguistic, cultural and religious differences within what was once considered Eastern Europe.

The Balkans – Central or Eastern Europe?

Ingmar Karlsson (1999), among others, has shown another mental anomaly in the division of Europe due to recent political developments: the line that divides Europe into two equally big parts goes from northern Finland to Greece, thus changing the idea of what is actually Central Europe. Mentally, its more western location is due to an erroneous idea of a western localization of Central Europe (originally *Mitteleuropa*) with Germany and Berlin at the centre, and this image has had a great impact on the idea of Europe ever since the First World War.

The struggle between the two superpowers after the Second World War redirected the interest of many researchers to the core regions and thereby possibly exaggerating the division of Europe – the importance of the 'iron curtain', as Churchill labelled it. With an East–West (Communist–Free World) perspective, the complexity of both parts reduced the interest in the smaller countries and regions, and their specific situations and problems. This fact has of course led to certain discrimination against the Balkans, and this discrimination has had clear linguistic implications.

This predominant focus on Eastern Europe and the Soviet Union left the Balkans in the hands of Russian specialists and, in the best case, Slavists – or more correctly, journalists and analysts who knew one or two Slavic languages and societies. Thus, they came to monopolize the whole of Eastern Europe, including the Communist Balkans, leaving Greece to others. To be fair, it should be pointed out that there were few alternatives to sending these journalists and using these analysts; this was the hard economic and cultural reality.

Informational and Linguistic Shortcomings

The whole idea of studying a vast area and its interaction instead of just one country that can be a very recent construct seems fruitful. This serves very well for a better and deeper understanding of contemporary Eastern and South Eastern Europe. This perspective is thus a major advantage, and offers a much better and more realistic view of political, cultural and linguistic interdependence. The main disadvantage is that experts on areas tend to be experts on one country, which means that they know the language spoken by the majority of that country and perhaps some others related to this language. In the Balkan case, this has not always been very fruitful, as will be explained later. What has happened, due to the fact that the Balkans have been considered to be part of Eastern Europe, is that analysts dealing with this part of the world have mostly known Slavic languages. This fact has marginalized the non-Slavic countries of the region – Hungary (close to the Balkans), Romania, Albania and, to a lesser extent, Greece, which, for political and tourist reasons, has been better treated.

When someone does not know a language and wants to do something that is connected to a particular culture that person is forced to use translations and translators or, as is often the case, simply rely on secondary sources that provide information in a language s/he knows. These secondary sources are not always well informed and certainly not necessarily as objective as they may seem to be. They might represent one party's interpretation of the reality, which, of course, is normally the case with primary sources as well. The difference is that when you look into primary sources you are careful to take this into consideration, comparing various statements and points of view in order to develop what is supposedly a balanced view. A secondary source is in itself often considered a balanced view for no reason at all. It can or might be – and, in fact, often is – a highly partisan view, even developing its arguments by combining other views with the author's (A) to the extent that A is quoting B to strengthen A's view, when B is not presenting new material but actually quoting A. Thus, A may fictitiously come to quote him/herself, even without knowing it, thus adding false credibility to a statement. At the time of Radio Free Europe, this happened on several occasions (personal experience). This is said without disregarding the long and extremely valuable research that was carried out at the broadcast station in Munich and elsewhere, or the symbol of hope it gave to so many for so long when such symbols were rare indeed.

Another problem arises for journalists and researchers who deal with Balkan countries in the post-Communist period of online archives that provide original documents and English translations when the translation or parts of it are censored for some reason without any indication that text has been left out. Censorship can, of course, obscure a text in the presented 'original' without changing the language, although it seems easier to do so in translations of other translations, thus obscuring the original message, as well as when the text has been tampered with (Watts, forthcoming).

A striking example is the English 'translation' of certain Romanian proposals to the Warsaw Pact. For political and, it seems, anti-Romanian purposes, Warsaw Pact 'translations' of the Romanian originals were presented, although a footnote says it is a summary, but there is no mention of the changes or omissions, as can be seen in the following example (and there are many more):

> English version of the Romanian original (which was never published outside the meeting until recently):
>
> Establish a 'PCC[1] of the European socialist countries that is not linked to the Warsaw Pact – which has a *military aim* – but ensures multilateral cooperation of our parties and states *in the political and economic domains*'
>
> The 'modified' and published translation:
>
> Establish a 'PCC of the European socialist countries that is not linked to the Warsaw Pact – which has **purely** *military aims* – but ensures multilateral cooperation of our parties and states *in the political and **military spheres***'
>
> (Romanian Proposal for Warsaw Pact Reform: Letter of the CC of the Romanian Communist Party, 8 July 1988, PHP; cf. Chapter 15 in Watts, forthcoming)

Thus it is by no means unreasonable to ask for a critical eye on the use of secondary sources, as well as to admit limitations as to the knowledge of the countries whose languages are not known to the informer. We could use the word 'relativism' in the sense of a 'relative' interest and therefore a more 'relative' idea of what could be considered the truth. It can certainly be argued that a researcher cannot dedicate very much time to learning more languages just to be able to read original documents and talk directly to people in the country in question, but some kind of decent self-restraint would not seem too much to ask. This is even more important now that the recently acquired freedom of speech in many of these countries has resulted in rumour mongering in the press (and of course social media) without any checking at all. This is obviously often the case in the Balkans.

The negative and unfavourable reputation of Romania in Western mass media can partly be explained by the lack of knowledge of Romanian and thereby also of Romanian culture and history. This is turned into a vague concept of the incomprehensible and oriental culture and history of the Balkans.

Washington's and certainly Western Europe's interest in Eastern Europe has been – and still is – focused on the former Soviet Union, now the Russian Federation, for obvious political reasons. This has led to a situation where there are many good experts not only on the various societies, but on Russian and, as an understandable consequence, other Slavic languages. The East European countries with non-Slavic languages have thus been cast aside, with the obvious exception of the former DDR (which can be said to be the most ignored or the main point of Western attention, depending on one's perspective). Albania, Hungary and Romania have long been the linguistic outsiders of Europe. These countries are 'small and insignificant' in many researchers' eyes. Nevertheless, Romania is an interesting example since it has sometimes been seen as good and at other times as bad. This frequent change of political view in the eyes of most Westerners complicates the analyses. Romanian independence in foreign policy in the 1960s was favoured and praised, and Romanian tourism flourished. Then the West became aware of Ceauşescu's repressive policies, and things turned negative before the revolution. That event was perceived as the people's and the Hungarian minority's uprising. Later on, there arose doubts about whether the new regime was truly democratic and whether the revolution was instigated by an elite within the Communist Party itself. A lack of efficiency was interpreted as a lack of intent. The mere fact that power changed due to election results and that power was given up peacefully by President Iliescu have added to Romania's democratic credibility, and, along with Bulgaria, it is now a member of the European Union, but with restrictions (non-Schengen, etc.). Problems related to corruption, political intent and capability have thrown Romania into Europe's backyard once more. Italy has tried to diminish Romania's EU status by stopping Romanians from migrating to Italy, and to a certain extent, there and elsewhere in Europe, Romanians have been considered 'Gypsies' (Roma). With this derogatory label, dusty old racist arguments have returned to the political stage. The fact is that Romanians, who speak a Romance language, can often learn Italian or Spanish quickly and are thus integrated into society more rapidly. But in economically difficult times, immigrants are no longer welcome, and any excuse will often serve to single them out.

Reduced Focus

Another issue that might have to do with not knowing the language, and lacking interest in the country and its development as a consequence, is the narrow focus on a single topic, such as the plight of children in orphanages and on the streets of Romania. In and of itself, it is a good thing to focus on mistreatment and abuse, especially when suffered by those least able to combat it on their own. And this, of course, is one of journalism's main goals. But a narrow focus on a single topic conveys a completely false impression of what is actually happening in the country if it is not connected with more diversified information, even when the information is correct per se. What is even worse is that countries from which little is reported are not taken seriously, so it does not seem to really matter that the image given is false, as long as it is selling newspapers. Many have provided sensationalist descriptions of situations that they had essentially already decided upon before arriving in the country. The spreading of false information has resulted; and, without going into detail, the main point is that there does not seem to be any real interest in showing the true picture of countries that are fairly unknown. In Romania's case, and in the case of all the Balkan states, we could consider the almost total lack of basic knowledge in the rest of Europe outside the Balkans. Many people cannot distinguish between Bucharest and Budapest, nor do they know whether Bulgaria is situated north or south of Romania. So when it comes to more sophisticated things, knowledge is obviously more based on bits and pieces that happen to have passed before the eyes and ears of 'Western' readers and listeners.

The Albanian case is perhaps even worse since Albanian is not closely linked to any language family, although it is an Indo-European language. Who then is supposed to take an interest in the language and follow the press, books, and so on, and undertake regular talks with ordinary people in Albania?

The common historical experience of the Balkan countries has of course also led to a certain number of cultural and linguistic influences and similarities. There has been a long discussion about how this sharing of certain features in grammar and vocabulary should be seen. Without going further into this discussion, it seems reasonable to accept the existence of a Balkan *Sprachbund*, but this should not be overestimated (Söhrman 2012). Knowing one country and one language does not provide the necessary base for interpreting what is going on in neighbouring states.

This marginalization of Hungary, Romania and Albania due to linguistic (and sociocultural) ignorance, and the impossibility of natural and spontaneous communication with the inhabitants of these countries, also applies to the Slavic-speaking countries. They have fallen into the trap of often being taken care of by people with 'semi-knowledge' – people who know Russian, Russia and Eastern Europe but with very vague ideas of the various Balkan cultures. Therefore South Eastern Europe has been reduced to the backyard of Eastern Europe rather than being seen as an area rich in culture and languages that just happens to have shared the experience of Communist dictatorships with Eastern Europe, but which differs considerably from these countries, as they differ substantially from one another.

Scholars often use the metaphor of a gate or a door in order to describe what a language is. The image is striking since this is what actually happens when you learn a foreign language and start using it in the country where it is spoken. Where you were virtually locked out before, you have now become a more or less integrated part. The study of the language has, in itself, provided you with the cultural background. The struggle with the grammar and the vocabulary has given you the means to use the language and to get to know people who speak it. It is without doubt the entrance to a new and exciting world, and this of course is true for any language.

Nevertheless, not only the mother tongue but also other languages can be seen as parts of our identity and this is what helps us to relate to other peoples; but it is also often seen as a golden key to everything, every interpretation of a representation of any culture (Norman Manea from a seminar at the Gothenburg Book Fair, 28 September 2012).

The discussion and examples confirm the assumptions made at the beginning of this chapter. However, it is seldom said that not knowing a language is anathema, i.e. the non-understanding of a certain culture and the country where the language is spoken. And, of course, there is the question of whether a reporter can report anything of value about a locality and events within it without knowing the language. This lack of knowledge might be seen as some kind of laziness. Perhaps it is more correctly viewed as an effect of the need for quick and not necessarily correct information due to the haste of getting 'there' first and publishing it in an easily read and quickly digestible way, but one that makes it, of course, quickly forgotten. This kind of transgression of cultural and linguistic borders leads to disinformation and questions the whole range of the value of 'news'. Today's society has the advantage and disadvantage of various media and near-speed-of-light dissemination of news and (dis)information. This could also be seen as a possible 'death of a discipline' (Spivak 2003). Nevertheless, it should be stressed that it must be seen and used as a motivation for the promotion and spread of the Balkan languages and other lesser-known languages and cultures. This not only applies to language students but to many others who need knowledge about these societies and cultures in their future professions, and especially for the sake of the democratic right of people to obtain news that is as objectively accurate as possible.

Ingmar Söhrman is Professor Emeritus of Romance Languages at the University of Gothenburg. Among his publications is *Diachronic and Typical*

Perspectives on Verbs (2013, with Folke Josephson), and he has written on syntax, semantics, cultural contacts and nation-building in the Romance world.

Note

1. The PCC was the Political Consultative Committee (or Council), the leading body of the Warsaw Pact, in which all party leaders were members. If it was a PCC meeting then the party leaders were there.

References

Augé, Marc. 1985. *Traversée du Luxembourg* [Traversing Luxembourg Gardens]. Paris: Hachette.
————. 1986. *Un ethnologue dans le métro* [An ethnologist on the metro]. Paris: Hachette.
————. 1989. *Domaines et Châteaux* [Domains and castles]. Paris: Seuil.
Bruckner, Pascal. 1986. *The Tears of the White Man: Compassion as Contempt*. New York: Free Press.
Constenla, Tereixa. 2014. 'Cuando las mujeres reinen en Europa', *El País semanal* 1969, 22 June, pp. 72–74.
Cuche, Denys. (1996) 2010. *La notion de culture dans les sciences sociales*. Paris: La Découverte.
Dérrida, Jacques. 1996. *Le monolinguisme de l'autre*. Paris: Galilé.
Fernández, Rodrigo. 2014. 'Ucrania debería haber sido generosa y haber devuelto lo que se le dio'. *El País*, n° 13,512, 30 June, p. 3.
Gelotte, Gert. 2012 'Misstrodda journalister', *Göteborgs-Posten*, 6 May, p. 2.
Grant, William, and David Murison (eds). 1931–76. *The Scottish National Dictionary*, 10 vols.
Karlsson, Ingmar. 1999. 'Central Europe's Boundaries, Yesterday, Today and Tomorrow'. Lecture given at 'Colloque Frontières', University of Strasbourg, 12–14 November 1999 http://www.abisf.com/pdf/CentralEuropesboundariesyesterday,todayandtomorrow. (retrieved 10 March 2017)
Ludanyi, Andrew. 2011. 'The Legacy of Transylvania in Romanian and Hungarian Historiography', in Tibor Frank and Frank Hadler (eds), *Disputed Territories and Shared Pasts: Overlapping National Histories in Modern Europe*. Houndmills, Basingstoke: Palgrave Macmillan, pp. 247–72.
Mønnesland, Svein. 1995. 'Finns det ett slaviskt språk – bosniska?', in Sven Gustavsson and Ingvar Svanberg (eds), *Bosnier: En flyktinggrupp I Sverige och dess bakgrund*. Uppsala: Uppsala Multiethnic Papers 35, pp. 77–92.
Pountain, Christopher. 2000. 'Frontiers, Political and Linguistic'. http://www.cus.cam. ac.uk/~cjp16/arts/frontiers.htm (retrieved 23 June 2014).
Söhrmann, Ingmar. 2004. 'Intercultural Communication or Parallel Cultures? The Swiss Example with Special Regard to the Rhaeto-Romance Situation', in J. Allwood and B. Dorriots (eds), Intercultural Communication at Work. Papers in Anthropological Linguistics 29, Gothenburg, pp. 65–80.
————. 2009. 'Where, When and What is a Language', in Mats Andrén et al. (eds), *Cultural Identities and National Borders*. Proceedings from the CERGU Conference 7–8 June 2007, pp. 15–34.
————. 2012. 'Balkanisms in Modern Romanian', in Thede Kahl (ed.), *Balkanismen heute – Balkanisms Today – Balkanizmi segodnja*. Vienna: LIT Verlag, pp. 299–306.
Spivak, Gayatri Chakravorty. 2003. *Death of a Discipline*. New York: Columbia University Press.

Svanberg, Ingvar, and Ingmar Söhrman. 1996. *Balkan:Folk och länder i krig och fred*. Stockholm: Arena.

Watts, Larry. 2010. *With Friends Like These: The Soviet Bloc's Clandestine War against Romania*. Bucharest: Editura Militară.

———. Forthcoming. *Extorting Peace: Romania, the Struggle within the Warsaw Pact and the End of the Cold War*.

Wedel, Janiner R. 1998. *Collision and Collusion: The Strange Case of Western Aid to Eastern Europe 1989–1998*. New York: St Martin's Press.

Part III

MENTAL SPACES AND BARRIERS

CHAPTER 7

Mental Barriers Replacing Nation–State Borders

FERNAND FEHLEN

Luxembourg likes to present itself as the model pupil of Europe, and its persistent enthusiasm for the European project is in contrast to the success of the Far Right and Eurosceptic parties in the 2014 European Parliamentary elections. But a closer look at the second smallest Member State shows that a rise in nationalism and a re-ethnicization of social relationships is taking place, challenging the discourse of Europeanness and openness that has dominated since the 1950s.

The search for a national identity in this small country was profoundly influenced by its location at the Romance–Germanic language border, a delineation regarded in the nineteenth and first half of the twentieth century not only as the meeting point of the two language areas, but a cultural border separating two quarrelling civilizations. It has often been stated that French and German cultures differ in their concept of nationhood and citizenship: a state-centred, assimilationist understanding of nationhood in France and an ethnocultural, differentialist understanding of nationhood in Germany. These differing understandings of nationhood are embodied in distinct legal doctrines, often referred to as *jus soli* and *jus sanguini*, and are generating two kinds of nationalism: 'civic nationalism, characterized as liberal, voluntarist, universalist and inclusive; and ethnic nationalism, described as illiberal, ascriptive, particularist and exclusive. These are seen as resting on two understandings of nationhood: common citizenship in the first case and common ethnicity in the second' (Brubaker 1999: 56).

Notes for this section begin on page 125.

Brubaker (1994) and Gosewinkel (2004) showed that the two paradigms are present in both countries. So referring to the ethnocultural paradigm as 'German' and the civic as 'French' is a simplification, but has the advantage of showing the dilemma Luxembourgish élites faced. Offering an ethnocultural ('thick') or a civic ('thin') definition of their identity[1] often went hand in hand with sympathy for one neighbour or the other, or at least proximity to its discursive context. Bridging the cultural border, Luxembourg's élites invented their identity and language by drawing on these two paradigms of nationhood.

Invention of the Luxembourg Nation and Language

The Grand Duchy of Luxembourg was created in 1815 when the Congress of Vienna reorganized Europe after the defeat of Napoleon and became one of the member states of the Germanic Confederation, a loosely knit association of thirty-nine German states that lasted until 1866. It covered most of the territory of the former Duchy of Luxembourg, and its inhabitants were divided into two linguistic communities, one belonging to the Romance sphere, the other the Germanic area. Nobody was concerned about the language border; as in the *ancien régime*, neither the points of view nor the vernacular of the subjects were taken into account.

Because the king of the Netherlands was appointed grand duke of Luxembourg, the fate of the young state was linked to the history of the United Kingdom of the Netherlands. After the Belgian Revolution of 1830 and the secession of the southern provinces, Luxembourg became part of the newly established Kingdom of Belgium for nine years, until the revolution was definitively settled by a realignment of the boundaries of 1815. The idea of the romantic nation that emerged out of German intellectual circles in the early nineteenth century had made its way to the negotiating table. Thus, the Austrian and Prussian plenipotentiaries insisted on keeping the area 'in which the German language and customs had been preserved' as a part of the Germanic Confederation; they were, however, willing to cede the Walloon part, which was not considered a real loss because 'the Walloons would never become Germans' (cited in Stengers 1989: 5–29 [author's translation]). The Grand Duchy was split in two: the 'province of Luxembourg' became part of Belgium, and the smaller and truncated, German-speaking Grand Duchy remained an independent state. But calling it a German-speaking country is a simplification. As a matter of fact, its population spoke a German dialect they called 'Luxembourger German', while dialectologists referred to it as 'Moselle Franconian'. Sermons and hymns were the only times they heard standard German. The elite preferred French, and the administration

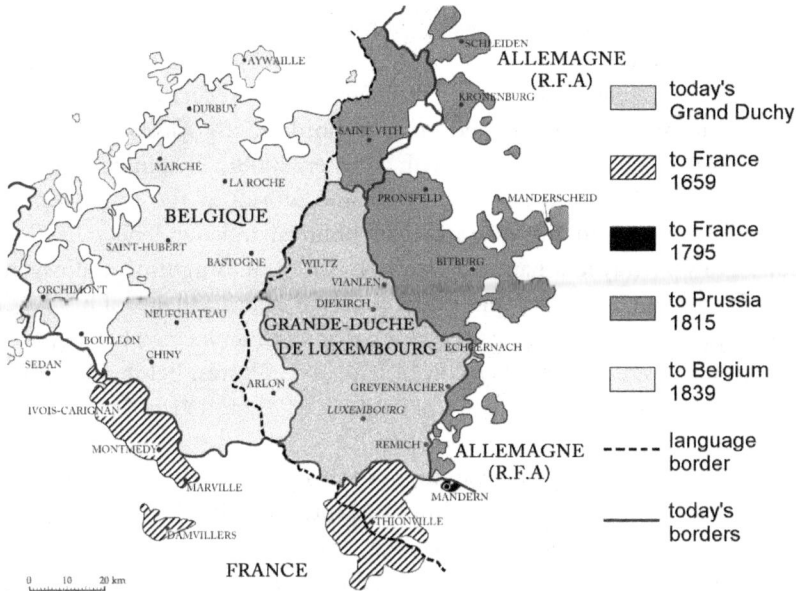

Figure 7.1 Partitions of the former Duchy of Luxembourg (source: Watelet 1989, modified by the author).

used both languages. The Constitution of 1848 mandated the equality of French and German, and all pupils had to learn both languages in school.

In the mid nineteenth century, as the government began constructing its institutions within the new national borders, which have remained unchanged up to the present, Luxembourg's politicians, thinkers and poets tried to define their national identity. Two main schools of thought can be discerned: a search for an ethnolinguistic essence rooted in ancient history, and an attempt to make the best of the arbitrary national boundaries by transcending the German–French dichotomy.

Hobsbawm's maxim that 'languages multiply with states; not the other way round' (Hobsbawm 1992: 63) is borne out by Luxembourg's history. 'Luxembourger German' was to become a language because it gradually assumed the functions of a language in the small state, thus being a prototypical example of what Kloss (1967: 29–41) called an 'Ausbau language' – a language that exists by extension or construction. The true engine of Luxembourgish nationalism was the threat of German imperialism. As the principal argument for annexation was the proximity of the Luxembourgish and German languages, Luxembourgers had to emphasize the independence of their language to claim political autonomy; linguistic patriotism thus became the central element of national identity. Nevertheless, the 'German'

ethnic conception of citizenship gained currency and found its expression in
an understandable but fruitless search for a national essence, deeply rooted
in the Middle Ages.

In the early twentieth century, Luxembourg intellectuals invented an
original concept that transcended cultural borders, the *Mischkultur* (mixed
culture) (Batty Weber 1909, cited in Conter 2008), imagining a double
membership in the Romance and Germanic worlds as the foundation of
a specific identity and the guarantee of political independence. In 1911,
Nicolas Ries portrayed a national character based on 'linguistic and psychic
dualism', embodied in a 'complex soul, forged by the accidents of history …
A border people, bilingual since the beginning of time, located between two
great nations – or suffocated by both – and two cultures, belonging neither
to one nor to the other' (Ries 1911, cited in Esch 1912: 114 [author's
translation]).

Given that Luxembourg was supposed to be a borderland and bridge
between two cultures, some Luxembourg intellectuals felt that they were,
in a somewhat megalomaniacal manner, invested with a mission of cultural mediator between their great neighbours. At best it was a 'one-way
bridge' (Trausch 1988), bringing French culture to Germany, as some
Luxembourgish journalists, authors and translators gained a certain degree
of notoriety in Germany. While the concept of *Mischkultur* is not explicitly used today, it remains deeply rooted in popular belief, which portrays
Luxembourg culture as a mixture of the best its two neighbouring cultures
have to offer. The sophistication of French cuisine combined with German
generosity is one of the most common stereotypes about Luxembourg.

After the Second World War, the threat of German annexation no
longer existed. Luxembourg's independence was definitively assured. The
conflict between the two big neighbouring countries was eliminated by
French–German reconciliation. On the one hand, there was no longer a
political need to foster a cultural identity through a common unique language. On the other hand, Luxembourgish had evolved as a language, at least
in most oral domains, while it still lacked functionalities in written domains
where it was outstripped by German for ordinary use and French for formal
use. The constitutional article that placed German and French on an equal
footing was suppressed. In 1984, a law was passed declaring Luxembourgish
to be the national language (*Loi du 24 février 1984 sur le régime des langues*).
Apart from this symbolic gesture, the law provided no particular planning
measures in favour of Luxembourgish and ratified French as the legislative
language. French, German and Luxembourgish were all to be accepted as
languages of administration.

Nevertheless, political debates over the definition of Luxembourg's
national identity flare up now and again, mostly in relation to language

issues. Partisans of a 'thick' identity insist on fluency in the Luxembourgish language as a requirement for citizenship and participation in social life, while supporters of a 'thin' identity insist on trilingualism and the French language as the lingua franca of Luxembourg society and its economy. Both aspects have some basis; the overemphasis of one point of views leads to the simplification of a complex linguistic configuration that Nico Weber described as follows: 'French holds the country together, triglossia keeps it going and *Letzebuergesch* [Luxembourgish] sets it apart' (Weber 2000: 88).

Luxembourg, a Bridge between European Communities

Like its two neighbours, Luxembourg benefited from a *Wirtschaftswunder* (economic boom) that brought mass consumption and a new international culture. Questions of ethnic identity were no longer on the agenda, and Luxembourg's self-conception needed a new foundation.

Ever since the late nineteenth century, the economy of the Grand Duchy had been dominated by the export-oriented steel industry. Participation in the European Coal and Steel Community, which was established in 1951, and the European Economic Community that followed in 1957 was a sterling opportunity for the small, export-oriented country. Since then it has become a forerunner and a model pupil of European integration. The European institutions that were established in its capital and the many financial and banking institutions that have taken root since the 1980s have transformed the formerly sleepy provincial town of Luxembourg into a cosmopolitan city. The political élites who were the bearers of this transformation developed a new discourse of Europeanness and in-betweenness that could draw on the old *Mischkultur* concept. National history was rewritten, placing Luxembourg's 'natural European vocation' at the centre of a new master narrative beginning with the Lotharingia (Kingdom of Lothar), created by the Treaty of Meerssen in 870 C.E. when the former Carolingian Empire was partitioned (Majerus 2007).

Especially in the early days of the European Union, Luxembourg politicians could play the role of facilitators; they included Gaston Thorn, Jacques Santer and recently Jean-Claude Juncker, three prime ministers who became presidents of the EU Commission. Their real and sometimes imagined achievements are presented by domestic media as a confirmation 'that Luxembourg manages to impose itself in Europe as soon as its leaders establish a bridge between the nations that have been closest to it, starting with the Franco-German couple. This art of building bridges between cultures is a mission that Luxembourg is glad to take on' (Moyse 2007).

In mainstream discourse, borders are no longer perceived as limitations. This reflects the political and economic reality, as the well-being of the state depends on a globalized economy and the presence of numerous EU institutions. Tolerance, cosmopolitanism and the valorization of cultural diversity are the main ingredients of a discourse that presents the traditional multilingualism of Luxembourg as a precondition for economic growth and consequently the well-being of the country. Openness and the integration of 'all people living and working in the country' have been declared the raison d'etat. This discourse is also embodied in the name of 'Schengen', a tiny wine-making village on the banks of the Moselle River, where France, Germany and Luxembourg meet. It is eponymous of the Schengen area, a symbol of unrestricted travel in Europe.

Building on the image of 'Luxembourg as borderland and bridge', the country is presented as the 'heart' or 'green heart' of Europe. One recent example of many comes from the pavilion at the Shanghai Expo 2010, where the 'world's only Grand Duchy' was described as 'open, diverse and dynamic':

> Luxembourg lies on the divide between Romanic and Germanic Europe and borrows traditions from both sides. It is often said that the Luxembourgers enjoy fine French food ... in German proportions! Luxembourg is called the Green Heart of Europe because of its fertile green countryside and its strategic location in the heart of Western Europe. ... The competitiveness of the Luxembourg economy is to a large extent ensured by the competences, the cross-border thinking, the mobility and the cosmopolitan nature of its workforce. (Jeannot Krecké, Ministry of the Economy and Foreign Trade, cited in Embassy of Luxembourg in Beijing, 2010)

In its extreme form, this discourse tends to dilute the Grand Duchy's distinctiveness and national territory through what Péporté et al. call a centrifugal strategy: 'Increasing border transaction flows and crossborder commuter numbers have led to a reinterpretation of state borders, previously represented as delimitations of a specific cultural space or area of communication. In the context of European regionalization processes, borderlands are proclaimed "test beds for the construction of Europe"' (Péporté et al. 2010: 196).

This discursive strategy is backed by the EU regional policy, the Interreg programme to stimulate cross-border cooperation. One of the eligible regions is the 'Greater Region', which overlaps Belgium, Germany, France and Luxembourg and is inhabited by eleven million people. The Grand Duchy is only a small part of it (4 per cent of its inhabitants and territory), but it is the engine that drives its economy and the only subspace that is expected to grow in the next few decades. The topos of the Greater Region assumes only minor status in the political discourse of France, Germany and

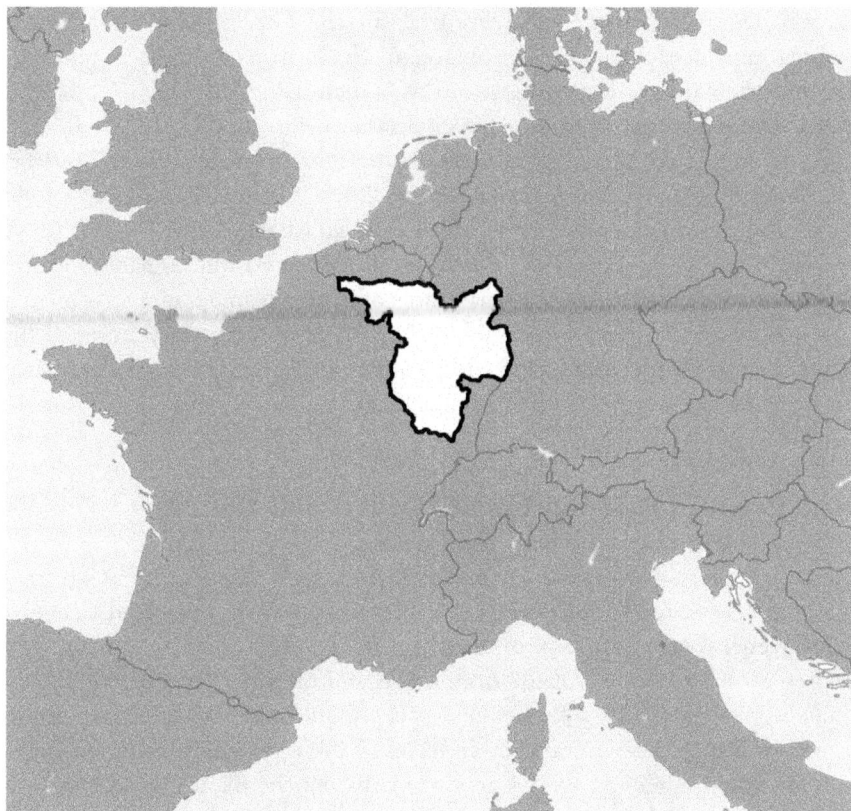

Figure 7.2 The Greater Region without inner borders. (Adapted from map by TUBS via Wikimedia Commons, CC BY-SA 3.0; based on IPSE 2010: 199).

Belgium, but it is emphasized in Luxembourg. Some of its promoters consider it to be a 'new *Heemecht*' (homeland), and describe the Grand Duchy as 'the navel of this region'.[2]

The process of amalgamating Luxembourg and the Greater Region climaxed in 2007 when Luxembourg was designated the European Capital of Culture. Although this programme is intended for cities, the Luxembourg government persuaded the EU to include the entire country, as well as the Greater Region. Many cultural events were organized to celebrate the Greater Region and Luxembourg City as its virtual capital. This mingling strategy is also embodied in maps of the Greater Region by no longer showing its inner borders, which are in fact national borders (see Figure 7.2).

The following two examples, which stem from projects sponsored by the European Capital of Culture 2007, show attempts at making the Greater Region more consistent. (1) There is no individual or collective identity without a proper denomination, but all attempts to find a suitable name have failed. The authors of a book about the Greater Region propose, rather immodestly, the German name *Reich der Mitte* (Middle Kingdom), the historic name of Lotharingia, or the French name *le berceau de la civilisation moderne* (the cradle of modern civilization). Finally they conclude: 'the *centre at the edge* might yet prove to be the most appropriate title, as it reflects the unwritten transnational history of the Great Region and the way of life of the border inhabitants' (Loges, Mendgen and Langen 2007: 212). (2) A movie entitled *The Epic of the Great Region* presents a questionable historic narrative to prove that the Christian roots of Europe can be traced as far back as 600 C.E. in the Greater Region, when an Irish missionary mingled his Christian faith with local Celtic and Druidic rites, giving birth to an original doctrine that competed with the official Catholicism.

The Eventful Relationship of Borders and Cultures

In recent years, the Grand Duchy of Luxembourg has experienced rapid growth. Its resident population has increased by nearly one-third over the past twenty years, and its workforce by 90 per cent. Non-nationals now represent 45.3 per cent of the population and 68.3 per cent in the city of Luxembourg, as well as 71.1 per cent of the workforce.[3] While Luxembourg is one of the wealthiest countries in terms of GDP per capita, new inequalities are emerging along with a new gap between the majority, who benefit from the economic boom, and the minority, who suffer unemployment and high rental prices. These social and economic changes have posed a challenge to cultural identity, and given rise to a discursive dichotomy. The official modernist discourse promoted by government agencies through national branding is opposed by a retrograde, ethnocultural discourse. Nevertheless, compared to the rise of nationalism and the re-ethnicization of social relationships in other European countries, the social climate in Luxembourg is open despite the steadily growing immigrant population. This shows that xenophobia, or at least its public expression, is not automatically linked to the presence of immigrants. Xenophobia manifests in Luxembourg in a highly euphemistic discourse, taking folkloristic forms, such as enthusiasm for medieval symbols of grandeur (Fehlen 2008). This does not mean that it has no influence on political decision making, however, as the passing of the new law on citizenship in 2008 reveals.

   Although the modernist forces had an overwhelming majority in Parliament, it took five years of quarrelling to find a compromise between openness and restrictiveness. The 2008 law promotes openness by (1) dual citizenship – i.e. new Luxembourgers are not obliged to renounce their original citizenship, and (2) the reintroduction of the double *ius soli*, which had been suppressed in 1940. The restrictive aspects are the raising of minimum residence before naturalization and the adoption of a test in spoken Luxembourgish (Scuto 2013: 11). Thus, the demands made by linguistic patriots since the late 1930s have been met. Moreover, re-ethnicization *strictu sensu* is embodied in Article 29, which provides that descendants of a Luxembourgish forebear can automatically recover their citizenship under certain circumstances. As a result, a new category of ethnic Luxembourgers abroad has been created, comparable to the concept of *Volksdeutsche* (ethnic Germans).

This overview of the Grand Duchy's history reveals the eventful relationship of borders and culture over the past two centuries. Under the ancien régime, boundaries had a purely dynastic function, but, with the advent of a romantic conception that amalgamated language and ancestry to define a Volk or a nation, borders acquired a cultural dimension. This concept shaped the drawing of the boundaries of the modern Luxembourg state in 1839. To protect the political independence of the small state, its elites invented a cultural identity embodied in a language of its own and a history rooted in the first millennium. This movement culminated in the 1930s with the assertion of a Luxembourgishness (*Luxemburgertum*),[4] which did not prevent Nazi Germany from overrunning the amateurishly fortified borders of the Grand Duchy. Nowadays a modernist discourse of Europeanness and openness is hegemonic in public opinion, but opposed by a retrograde discourse, centred on the national language as a means of affirming identity. At least for a large minority of Luxembourgers, the fading influence of nation-state borders in recent decades is giving way to new mental borders embodied in language ideology, as the young national language represents the last bastion in protecting a national identity.

Fernand Fehlen retired in 2015 as senior lecturer at the University of Luxembourg. He is a pioneer in Luxembourg studies; his publications include *Die Luxemburger Mehrsprachigkeit: Ergebnisse einer Volkszählung* (Bielefeld: transcript 2016, with Andreas Heinz), and 'Luxembourgish: A Success Story? A Small National Language in a Multilingual Country', in *Handbook of Language and Ethnic Identity* (Oxford University Press, with Sabine Ehrhart).

Notes

    1. See Chapter 1 by Linda Berg concerning various forms of identification.
    2. The two formulations were used in a parliamentary discussion reported by Péporté et al. (2010: 221).

3. Figures for 2013 and 2014 according to the Statistical Office: http://www.statistiques. public.lu/en/index.html; the population bureau of Luxembourg-City http://www.vdl.lu/ vdl_multimedia/Publications/La+ville/Etat+de+la+population+au+31_12_2012.pdf and the Inspection Générale de la Sécurité Sociale, http://www.mss.public.lu/

4. This was a replication of the concept of Germanness (*Deutschtum*), somehow a helpless takeover of the enemy's ideology to beat him at his own game.

References

Primary Sources

Embassy of Luxembourg in Beijing. 2010. 'Shanghai 2010: Zoom into Luxembourg!' http://www.luxembourgexposhanghai.com/introduction-au-luxembourg (accessed March 2011).

Esch, M. 1912. 'A la lisière de la Germanie', *Revue Bleue: Revue politique et littéraire* 113–17 and 148–51.

IPSE (Identités Politiques Sociétés Espaces) (ed.). 2010. *Doing Identity in Luxembourg: Subjective Appropriations – Institutional Attributions – Socio-Cultural Milieus*, Bielefeld: transcript.

Loges, K., E. Mendgen and A. Langen. 2007. *Im Reich der Mitte: Le berceau de la civilisation européenne*. Saarbrücken and Konstanz: Hartung-Gorre.

Moyse, L. 2007. 'Luxembourg: A Bridge between European Communities', in *La Voix du Luxembourg*, 15 March [translation: Eurotopics] http://www.eurotopics.net/en/dienste/medienindex/media_articles/archiv_article/ARTICLE15320-Luxembourg-a-bridge-between-European-communities (accessed October 2011).

Ries, N. 1911. *Essai d'une psychologie du peuple luxembourgeois*. Diekirch: J. Schroell.

Secondary Sources

Brubaker, R. 1994. *Citizenship and Nationhood in France and Germany*. Cambridge, MA and London: Harvard University Press.

———. 1999. 'The Manichean Myth: Rethinking the Distinction between "Civic" and "Ethnic" Nationalism', in H. Kriesi (ed.), *Nation and National Identity: The European Experience in Perspective*. Zurich: Ruegger, pp. 55–71.

Conter, C.D. 2008. 'Mischkultur', in S. Kmec et al. (eds), *Lieux de mémoire au Luxembourg. Usages du passé et construction nationale*. Luxembourg: Éditions Saint-Paul, pp. 23–28.

Fehlen, F. 2008. 'A New National Flag For Luxembourg: Struggling over Identity in a Small Multilingual Society', in M. Andrén et al. (eds), *Cultural Identities and Cultural Borders*. Gothenburg: University of Gothenburg, pp. 67–84.

Gosewinkel, D. 2004. *Einbürgern und Ausschließen: Die Nationalisierung der Staatsangehörigkeit vom Deutschen Bund bis zur Bundesrepublik Deutschland*. Göttingen: Vandenhoeck & Ruprecht.

Hobsbawm, E. 1992. *Nations and Nationalism since 1780: Programme, Myth, Reality*. Cambridge: Cambridge University Press.

Kloss, H. 1967. 'Abstand Languages and Ausbau Languages', *Anthropological Linguistics* 9: 29–41.

Majerus, B. 2007. 'Le petit Européen parfait: L'Europe, le Luxembourg et la construction nationale', in N. Beaupré, C. Moine and É. François (eds), *L'Europe de Versailles à Maastricht*. Paris: Éditions Seli Arslan: pp. 223–35.

Péporté, P., et al. 2010. *Inventing Luxembourg: Representations of the Past, Space and Language from the Nineteenth to the Twenty-First Century*. Leiden: Brill.

Scuto, D. 2013. 'Country Report Luxembourg'. EUDO Citizenship Observatory, URL http://eudo-citizenship.eu/docs/CountryReports/Luxembourg.pdf (accessed June 2014).

Stengers, J. 1989. 'Les changements de nationalité en Europe occidentale et le cas du Luxembourg', *Hémecht* 41(1): 5–29.

Trausch, G. 1988. 'Un créneau étroit entre l'Allemagne et la France: le Luxembourg à la recherche d'une conscience nationale (1839–1945)', in H. Dyserinck and K. Syndram (eds), *Europa und das nationale Selbstverständnis: imagologische Probleme in Literatur, Kunst und Kultur des 19. und 20. Jahrhunderts*. Bonn: Bouvier, pp. 381–411.

Watelet, M. 1989. *Luxembourg en cartes et plans*. Tielt: Lannoo.

Weber, N. 2000. 'Universe under the Microscope: The Complex Linguistic Situation of Luxembourg', in K. Deprez and T. Du Plessis (eds), *Multilingualism and Government: Belgium, Luxembourg, Switzerland, former Yugoslavia*. Pretoria: Van Schaik, pp. 82–90.

CHAPTER 8

Crossing Borders and Redefining Oneself

The Treacherous Life of Aino Kallas

KATARINA LEPPÄNEN

The idea of cultural borders forms imaginative and creative mental spaces for thinking about identity and otherness. Whether cultural borders are thought of as following linguistic, national, territorial or other officially drawn lines on political maps, or only as states of mind, their consequences and meanings are unpredictable.

Historically and geopolitically, the Gulf of Finland, with Finland to the north, Russia to the east and Estonia to the south, has been a region not only of wars but also vigorous cultural and national negotiations. The cultural histories of Finland and Estonia must always be interpreted in relation to current and previous powers. The representation of a national 'us' has, furthermore, been articulated in relation to, but not always against, inner others who could be interpreted as residue of foreign dominance.

An analysis of the work of Finnish writer Aino Kallas, née Krohn (1878–1956) shows how multiple dimensions of belonging build on the tension between language, nationality and identification but nevertheless offset the longing for oversimplified unity. The written and printed word, more specifically the novel, has been identified as paramount to the establishment of the modern nation-state (Anderson (1983) 2006; Moretti 1998). This chapter works with life writing as a textual site for negotiating national belonging during the turbulent first few decades of the twentieth century. The fundamental questions are as follows. How does Kallas choose to depict her loyalties? What aspects are given meaning: culture, language or official citizenship? What limitations did she encounter? I will argue that nationalism can also be articulated without invoking sharp distinctions between nations, languages or cultures. Kallas did not write anything that could be defined as an autobiography in the narrow sense of the word. Her diaries were minimally edited, and three books published in the 1940s and 1950s are reflections on past times and people with autobiographical elements rather than autobiography per se.[1] Because the various genres involve differing author/ reader expectations, the term 'life writing' may be better suited to describe the material. Life writing brings together autobiography, biography and diaries. Furthermore, life writing is 'interest[ed] in alterity, self expression and subjectivity. In being a practice that exceeds the purely literary (if there is such a thing), life writing assumes the possibility of dialogue, the communicable nature of experience, and – most obviously – the link between personal experience and public context' (McCooey 2004: viii).

Life writing is a broader term than memoir or autobiography; as a field of study, it understands 'subjectivity and its writings as profoundly "relational". Our sense of self and our narratives of selfhood are productions of complex relations, transactions and performances' (McCooey 2004: viii–iv). The question of the self in relation to the nation and culture can be read in terms of the articulation of 'complex cultural experiences rather than mere illustrations of archetypes' (Ommundsen 2004: 101).

Borders are places of negotiation, conflict and security. Franco Moretti, who has examined the construction of borders in European literature, concludes that internal and external borders are tropes for fundamentally different stories. In contrast to external borders, which are sites of adventure, internal borders 'work differently, and focus on a theme which is far less flamboyant than adventure, but much more disturbing: *treason*' (Moretti 1998: 37). Like the heroes of historical novels who turn traitors as they cross internal borders, the crossing of cultural borders often amounts to treachery. And accusations of treachery played an important role in Kallas's navigation between different self-representations. Her movement between different languages and nations occasionally placed her in a literary/cultural no man's land. There were times when Kallas was considered neither a Finnish nor an Estonian author. She was excluded from a Russian anthology on Finnish authors because her themes were Estonian. Estonian critics question her ability to present the true Estonian soul because she was not 'really' Estonian; and the Baltic Germans regarded her as a dangerous agitator for Estonian interests. Not only did this affect her personally but it also had serious consequences when it came to receiving grants and other financial support for her creative endeavours.

The chapter will proceed in the following manner. First, the frame within which Kallas presents herself is described, along with additional biographical information. After that, three episodes in Kallas's life provide a springboard for discussing what the changing spatial and national locations meant to Kallas. The first example concerns leaving Finland and Finnishness in the late nineteenth century, the second example deals with her entry into Estonian culture in the early twentieth century, and the third example relates the scandal caused by her first play in the 1930s. Ideas surrounding treason and disloyalty will be in focus.

From Young Laurel-wreath Binder to Mature Playwright

Kallas crossed many linguistic and national borders during her lifetime. Even though almost all the movement was voluntary – caused by cultural ideology, marriage and her husband's work – it was emotionally and intellectually wrenching at times. Kallas was born in Finland, then a Russian Grand Duchy.[2] Her father Julius Krohn descended from a large family, which had been dispersed throughout Europe. He became a professor of folklore and was the first one to adopt Finnish as the language of a linguistically non-Finnish family. Kallas's mother Maria (Minna) Lindroos was Krohn's second wife and the headmistress of a girls' school. Kallas's siblings were well-educated members of the cultural elite. Kaarle Krohn was a professor of Finnish and comparative folklore, and Ilmari Krohn was a church musician and university instructor in music theory. Her sisters Aune Krohn and Helmi Krohn (married names Setälä) pursued literary careers and were involved in the Finnish movement by publishing and participating in Finnish language education for girls.[3] She married an Estonian by the name of Oskar Kallas, soon to receive his PhD in folklore, and lived with him in St Petersburg, Tartu (then in Russia, later Estonia), Finland and Great Britain. From 1944 to 1952, she lived in exile in Sweden, where Oskar died. Once stability had been restored after the war she returned to Finland, Estonia having become inaccessible under Soviet occupation.

From a very young age, Kallas devoted her time to creative writing. Translating, and editing the works of male family members, as well as writing on their own behalf, was an informal literary and nationalist pursuit of all the sisters, among whom Kallas attained the greatest national and international renown (Leskelä-Kärki 2006: 105; Leskelä-Kärki et al. 2009). She also contributed to several literary journals as a critic and author.

The very first page of Kallas's diary depicts her as a young girl situated in a culture marked by linguistic conflict. The entry recounts that three Finnish-minded candidates of philosophy approached her in 1897 and asked her to be their laurel-wreath binder for the upcoming promotion party at the University of Helsinki (Kallas 1952: 7–10). The honour was traditionally extended to the daughter of a professor. The selection of Kallas was thought to be ensured by the fact that there was a majority of Finnish-minded members among the candidates. However, at the last moment eight Swedish-minded candidates registered and the choice fell to the Swedish binder. The episode weaves together all ingredients of the late nineteenth-century quarrel between the Fennoman and the Svecoman movements. The Fennoman movement was a cultural effort to enhance the status of Finnish as the language of both learning and culture, while the Svecomans argued for the importance of Swedish. Both, however, were strongly against the use of Russian.

It is telling that Kallas starts the story of her life with this episode, which vividly and personally reflects a cultural conflict, by placing herself in the midst of the events on the Finnish side. The fact that she edited and published the diaries in exile makes her portrayal of national belonging highly interesting. She was well aware that her Finnishness had been questioned ever since she decided to marry an Estonian man, as well as the probability that her future home would have to be Finland. Her diaries, which cover 1897–1931 and were published in the 1950s, and memoirs (many of which were reprints and reworks of newspaper columns) trace her personal reflections about the numerous movements across cultural borders, such as language and the inner borders of the Russian Empire. The question of belonging, both as a professional author and as a human being, required continuous attention and reflection.

Identifying Selves and Articulating Belonging

A 'Change of Sides'

'I had a black moment yesterday', Kallas writes in her diary on 10 February 1900. She had met the husband of her sister Helmi, Eemil Nestor Setälä, a professor of Finnish and literature at Helsinki University, who had scorned her for marrying a foreigner.

> I had a long conversation with Eemil Setälä yesterday. 'You are lost to us', he said. 'You have abandoned your nationality. And a person who does that will always be broken down, her personality cannot remain intact. You have not even tried to hold on to your Finnishness, but let it go, complying with the wishes of a man. And the Estonians, what are they? A dying people, the work they are doing there is nothing but honourable fighting before defeat. And if you had children, what school would you put them in?' I remembered what Oskar had once said and replied: 'Probably a Russian school'. Eemil flared up: 'A Russian school! Your children, Julius Krohn's grandchildren, is that your national loyalty!? So that is what our women are like, they can throw away their national loyalty like a worn-out garment, and that is why we are oppressed! And you will be wed in German – I will hardly come to your wedding in that case'. [Kallas explains that she has done what she sees as her duty as the wife

of an Estonian man] Eemil was agitated: 'Men don't have the right to demand
any such thing; if I were in his place I would let you speak Finnish and raise
my children in Finland. Because if you want to make them Estonian then you
can bring them up as peasants or craftsmen from the beginning, as there is no
Estonia culture'. (Kallas 1952: 213)

Kallas was grappling with related issues in her diaries, and only a few
months earlier she proudly declared: 'So, I was to become an Estonian
woman, the wife of an Estonian man and a daughter of Estonia. There are
no two ways about it. It's all or nothing.' (Kallas 1952: 205). Aino Krohn
was to disappear, she reasoned, but Aino Suonio, the literary alias she borrowed from her father, would live on. Writing in Finnish would give her
the opportunity to 'be something to my previous home country too, the
country of my birth; it will make my change of nationality much easier'.

The adversary in the example, Setälä, forced Kallas into a position of
either/or without leaving any space for positive formation of new identifications. Setälä's resignation is a consequence of his Finnish nationalism, which
valued Finland higher than what he regarded as uncultured Estonia. Perhaps
the most scathing claim was that Estonia had no culture but consisted solely
of peasants and craftsmen. This is a sore point in the self-image of the aspir-
ing Estonian intelligentsia, of which Kallas and her husband were a part. The
Estonians were trying to establish an Estonian cultural scene with literary
societies, theatres, and music festivals. But Setälä's criticism of Kallas's disloyalty was by no means a given stance, even for an ardent nationalist.[4] Kaarle
Krohn, Kallas's brother, who belonged to the same Finnish-minded circles
as Setälä, appreciated her husband, introduced her to him and accepted the
relationship from the start. Kaarle Krohn appreciated Oskar Kallas's devotion
to the science of folklore, Estonia, the Estonian people and Estonia's struggle for independence, which was parallel to the one in which Krohn was
active in Finland. They shared nationalist sentiments and convictions, simply
working for the status and independence of different states.

Becoming Estonian did not require giving up being Finnish, as Kallas
reflected on the co-existence of various aliases, and her choice to adapt to
Estonianness is even less surprising considering her father's choice of Finnish
as the family's language instead of Russian or Swedish (though he raised his
children to be multilingual in the manner common to the upper classes).
Kallas was well aware of, and wrote about, the mixed-bloodedness of her
father's family, and called herself a nationalist 'by education' rather than
emotion or birth.[5]

Replanting?

In January 1907, Kallas was sharply reproached by her Estonian friend
Gustav Suits, an author and literary critic. At her request he commented

on her manuscript *Ants Raudjalg* in a personal letter, and later reviewed the book. He concluded that she failed to 'deal with issues taken from our lives' and would always remain 'a "stranger" in our lives'. Attempting to write Estonian historical novels was a risky project for someone 'not born from Estonian soil, but only replanted there' (quoted in Laitinen 1973: 98). He went on to detail her shortcomings: her language did not have a homely melody because it was too perfect, and she 'lacks the intimate and instinctive knowledge of our people and circumstances' (ibid.: 99).

Her diary reiterates her answer to Suits and tries to define her relationship to Estonia: 'Up until a year ago I thought that I would certainly be at home here. That was a mistake' (Kallas 1953: 63). Suits challenged her writing for not being Estonian enough. To this Kallas retorts that her aim was to unravel humanity's eternal and universal questions set in a national context, suggesting that the primary purpose in choosing themes for the novels from Estonian history was neither to claim to be Estonian nor to depict the nation as such (ibid.: 60–63). Thus the Estonian national setting was only one possible space in which universally human themes could be explored. While arguing that the themes were universal in some sense, she also viewed them from a different angle: 'In Finland I could hardly have empathized with reality even to the extent I have in Estonia, where the strangeness of circumstances opened my eyes' (ibid.: 62). Kallas points here to the privilege of being a stranger and the experience of being an outsider, which made it possible to perceive elements of everyday life that were hidden from someone all too familiar with the culture. However, in contributing to the national awakening of a new nation, the choice of Estonian settings was not completely arbitrary.

Kallas became part of the Noor-Eesti [Young Estonia] nationalist and cultural movement in the early twentieth century, and contributed to strengthening the very Estonian culture that Setälä had dismissed. After spending time in St Petersburg, where her husband finished his doctoral thesis, the family moved to Tartu, then a Russian province. He was already established in the cultural revivalist movement, the Tartu Renaissance, and Kallas soon followed but chose a somewhat different path. The publication of *Ants Raudjalg* and the subsequent discussion coincided with Kallas's shift from realism to symbolism, impressionism, new realism and archaic chronicles, suggesting that her national reorientation had spilled over to the literary arena (Laitinen 1973: 105).

Typically she found commonality with others who were reinventing their heritage, the circle of the Noor-Eesti movement. She took part in their activities, including literary salons, intellectual exchanges and the attempt to create a truly European–Estonian cultural scene. The group was not reluctant to incorporate modern European, and even Russian, influences

into their writing. They were not simply trying to recover the heritage of
the Estonian people, but to place Estonia in the European cultural tradition.
Thus, the Estonian identity they were constructing was a forward-looking,
innovative (as opposed to retrospective) movement. This did not mean that
they were not also scouring Estonian history for stories, but Kallas charac-
teristically experimented with modernistic style rather than realism when
inspired by old chronicles. Suits, who had been critical of her ability to represent true Estonianness, writes about Noor-Eesti:

> What buoys up and exalts humanity is education. Our slogan is: More culture!
> More European culture! Let us remain Estonians, but let us become Europeans
> too. We want to discover the ideas and forms towards which we are impelled
> by our national spirit, character and needs on the one hand, and by European
> culture on the other. (Suits, cited in Matthews 1950: 118)

Firmly emphasizing national spirit and character, Suits nonetheless
looks to Europe for a common culture, this European outlook distinguishing Noor-Eesti from the nationalism of the Tartu Renaissance, which had
emphasized the Estonian peasant culture. The European cultural horizon
attracted Kallas, which is evident from her lists and her comments about
having read all the great European literature.

Her 1918 book-length survey of the Noor-Eesti movement and its
leading members does not include herself and never uses the word 'us'
(Kallas 1918). She describes the group as consisting of young Estonian men
affected by the 1905 revolution and its aftermath. The main purpose is to
emphasize how much European influences can enrich the national literature and how well the Noor-Eesti writers managed to remould European
impulses into Estonian ones. Those involved in revolutionary/nationalist
activities had to leave Tartu, several of them ending up in Finland as students
at Helsinki University and later working in Finland or Estonia as language
instructors, and such like. During the political turmoil of 1905, when the
Russian Empire was torn by revolutionary sentiments, Kallas was not part
of the Estonian group as such. The unrest led to greater autonomy and a
Finnish parliament, while the Estonians experienced stricter Russian control.
Paradoxically this allowed Estonian nationalists to flee to Finland, even
though both areas were still part of the Russian Empire.

The point here, of course, is not to pigeonhole Kallas as part of
one nationalist movement or another, but to point out that she found a
group that offered her an artistic home but still left her on the periphery.
Gender, age and political persuasion certainly played a role here. Kallas
was slightly older than the others. She and Hella Wuolijoki, an Estonian
author and political figure who had settled in Finland, were the only
active women.[6]

Treason – Again!

The Kallas family spent 1918–34 abroad on diplomatic missions in Helsinki and London. Having left a relatively new independent nation in the midst of an active cultural revival in 1918, they returned to a country split by internal political quarrels, settling in the rival town of Tallinn rather than Tartu, her husband's home and the base of the Noor-Eesti movement (Raud (1953) 1991; Kriss 2006: 28–39). The situation was complicated by the changing nationalist atmosphere in Estonia. In 1933, Konstantin Päts came to power, proclaimed a state of emergency, closed the parliament, outlawed all political parties and censored the press in an attempt to neutralize the extreme right-wing paramilitaries ('Vapsid'). Jaan Tõnnisson, a friend and ally of the Kallases who had led the parliament before Päts, resigned and turned over *Postimees*, which had been the newspaper of the Tartu Renaissance, to new leadership. The 'time of silence' in Estonia had begun (Raun 1987: 74–80).

In 1935, Kallas's nationalist loyalties and historical truthfulness came under attack in the reception of her first play, *Mare ja hänen poikansa* (Mare and Her Son). The new regime vigilantly censored cultural expressions that could be interpreted as opposed to nationalism. The debate had obvious political undertones. The play was an adaptation of an Estonian folktale, *Imant and His Mother*, but shifted the focus from the son to the mother. The year is 1343 in Livland. Imant and three hundred fellow peasants are planning a raid against the Baltic German oppressors in the castle. His mother Mare has raised her sons to hate the Germans – she has already lost six sons to the cause and reveals the plot to the lord of the castle in a desperate attempt to save her last son. Imant is captured and all his co-conspirators are killed. When he discovers her betrayal, he throws himself off the castle wall and dies. Mare returns home and is stoned to death by the villagers.

The play premiered in Helsinki in October 1935 and received mediocre reviews. In November, it opened in Tallinn, immediately attracting the attention of nationalists. Their criticism was not directed at Kallas's depiction of the nation: the play is obviously a plea for the peasants against their oppressors. The problem is that Mare's betrayal overshadows Imant's heroic deeds. Kallas had altered the original tale by changing Mare's social status from an 'old woman' to a 'chieftain's wife'. Loyalty to the nation should trump familial emotions, critics argued, and Mare's actions were 'depressingly profane' (Rasmus Kangrol-Pool, cited in Laitinen 1995: 353). The criticism quickly turned against Kallas as a foreign writer 'who could of course write what she wanted', but it was an insult to the Estonian people and nation. However, Kallas found support among friends, critics and nationalists who emphasized that the play was a historical tragedy not to be confused with contemporary conditions. Her Estonianness was also proclaimed with reference to her contribution to the nation as the ambassador's wife. The last words in the debate, supporting Kallas, were from the same Gustav Suits who had questioned her ability to depict the truly Estonian aspects of daily life almost twenty years earlier.

Comparing the situation in 1935 to the criticism made by Suits in 1907, a striking difference can be seen in the sharp, non-negotiable tone. No room for resistance remained, attempts at self-identification seemed useless. The limits of identification can be tied to the changing character of Estonian nationalism. Internal politics had stagnated in the 1930s, turning inwards in order to protect internal borders. Given the political situation, this should not have come as a surprise. When President Päts outlawed political parties other than his own in an attempt to strangle extreme right-wing nationalists, it was obvious that the common horizon of an independent Estonian nation had been replaced by quarrels over the true interpretation of the nation.

Gender, Identification and Belonging

Thus far, the analysis has focused on challenges to Kallas's artistic production and life choices. The picture Kallas presents in her diaries is of a continuous dialogue with her contemporaries, friends, family and colleagues, as well as with science of heredity and concepts of blood, nation and peoplehood. In this last section, I will describe theoretical tools that can be used to analyse Kallas's experiences as conveyed in her life writing. The subheadings of Gender/Nation, Identification and Belonging should not be understood as different aspects of Kallas's identity, but as various dimensions of her experiences that reinforce each other.[7]

Gender/Nation

Nira Yuval-Davis has studied gender relations in national projects in terms of women as reproducers of both nation and citizenship, showing that different rules applied to men's and women's loyalties and behaviour (Yuval-Davis 1997: 3). Women in their role as mothers passed on traditions and culture, and their achievements were most often perceived as secondary to those of male war heroes (Cusack 2000). The position of the married woman was especially precarious because she was subordinated to her husband with respect to nationality as well. A woman was expected to be loyal to her husband's nation, and automatically lost her nationality if different from his (Leppänen 2009). This was obvious in Setälä's anger, which clearly related to Kallas's alleged betrayal of her role as a mother of the nation in both a symbolic and concrete sense.

The Setälä example highlights the problem of changing loyalties between nations, but gender also mattered within the various groups. Kallas's ambivalence about belonging to the Noor-Eesti group was a recurring topic in her life writing. As a member of the board, her full participation seemed obvious, and this 1912 diary note supports such an interpretation: 'Do I finally feel connected to a group of people, no matter how small, and not just to individual people, as I have felt so far?' (Kallas 1953: 281). Her memoir of 1946 returned to the men of Noor-Eesti and the 'great insatiable hunger for life and knowledge that burned in these young people's veins', and noted that she knew that 'regardless of her pronounced femininity' she had the ability to participate in 'this kind of sincere, honest working community' (Kallas 1946: 258–59). Thus, being a female author required reflection about gender expectations for participating in an artistic collective (Laitinen 1973: 119).[8] In this example, community and femininity were understood to be incompatible, and the connection between the Noor-Eesti young men and Kallas was special.[9] Therefore, there could be no 'us', and she places herself in a marginal position, choosing not to identify with them.

Another fact that testifies to the tendency to view women's loyalties and politics as different from men's is the fact that those who retained close contact with the leading figures of both the Postimees/Tartu Renaissance and the Noor-Eesti group were two women: Kallas and Hella Wuolijoki. Even after Gustav Suits's public criticism of Jaan Tõnnisson's reformist cultural politics and the widening gap between the two groups, Kallas and Wuolijoki moved in both circles (Tuomioja 2010: 70).

Identification

Indeterminacy can be problematic regarding both gender and nationalism. Judith Butler argues in *Who Sings the Nation-State?* that there is 'a certain tension produced between modes of being or mental states, temporary or provincial constellations of mind of one kind or another, and juridical and military complexes that govern how and where we may move, associate, work and speak' (Butler and Spivak 2007: 4). This is why 'national identity' is a powerful concept. It is a device for inclusion and exclusion of people, as well as a technology that shapes ways of states of being and mentality. Caught between various identifications, Kallas laconically observes that a 'person has her own human value independent of parties and citizenship' (Kallas 1953: 63). As early as 1908, at the time of the dispute with Suits over *Ants Raudjalg*, she writes that she no longer dreamed of being either one or the other but imagined belonging at another level, 'so if I could choose freely now, I would no longer ask for roots in Finland or Estonia, but in the larger community of humanity in which we can all take root and grow'.

An obvious approach to Kallas's change of nationality and her movement between countries would be to analyse it in terms of fluid identity.
But as Brubaker and Cooper have argued, identity as an analytical tool is
so widely applied to a variety of phenomena that it has 'been driven out
of its wits by overuse' (W.J.M. Mackenzie, cited in Brubaker and Cooper
2000: 3). Brubaker and Cooper are primarily occupied with identity as an
analytical category; however, my interest is in the limitations on discussing
intellectual and emotional complexity encouraged implicitly or explicitly by
the concept of identity.[10] Self-perception and self-representation understood
as a phenomenon or problem of identity, dealing with hierarchical and conflicting loyalties, fails to capture the complexity of a life such as Kallas's. A
person's identity depicted as primary, secondary, layered, or even verging on
pathological conditions like 'loss of identity' are insufficient to capture the
flexibility and fluent nature of multiple belongings.

Some problems of the identity approach become evident if Kallas's life
and writing are interpreted in terms of 'identity crisis' (Kurvet-Käosaar 2011:
94) or insecure national identity. Based on the entries in her diaries, it is clear
that she envisaged a change – she was going from being a Finnish woman to
an Estonian one. Her Estonianness was not to replace her Finnishness, but
was more like an additional aspect. It is fully reasonable to see Kallas as not
having one national or linguistic identity that underwent a crisis and was
replaced by another identity. First, I would argue that the initial identity is
not one, but includes many conflicting and fluctuating loyalties and feelings
– for example, the 'mixed bloodedness' of her ancestry (see also Olesk 2011:
169). Second, based on what we read in Kallas's diaries, her identity was not
in crisis. The problem was that her ideas about what she could be or write
were not recognized as valid or feasible.

Belonging

The claim that people do not have solid and singular identities does not mean
that it is easy to respond to the kinds of challenges described above. On the
contrary, many letters to Kallas's family and friends, as well as her diaries,
relate feelings of loss, homelessness and the difficulty of being a stranger. If
identity does not express anything that is essentially given, every challenge
requires a (re)positioning of oneself in relation to people, politics and territory. For that reason, I am most interested in understanding identification
in relation to recognition and articulation. Identification can be articulated
in a public or political context in which identity is less interesting than possible recognition or misrecognition of it. As her diaries show, Kallas initially
thought about becoming a 'daughter of Estonia'. The idea was part of a young
woman's romantic understanding of her role as a wife, in line with cultural
expectations for those of her social standing. Her desire may also have been

connected to, although not entirely explained by, the explicit condemnation she experienced in Finland for having married a foreigner and the absence of recognition as a Finnish author. Questions like these have existential dimensions. One problem for Kallas was the idea that a person's value was viewed as inextricable from clear-cut identification with a single nation.

Later in life, as she moved in the diplomatic circles of the UK and the United States, her diaries refer to many possible friends and enemies. Her observations about the '*corps diplomatique*' (Kallas 1955) are sometimes hilarious, depicting dinners and soirees at which Nordic and Baltic diplomats mingled with their Soviet, German and Polish colleagues. But her loyalties were complicated to say the least. She could not at times deal with the Finnish representative, she writes, because he was Swedish-minded, while she had no trouble with the Swede, who nevertheless represented a country that had occupied both Finnish and Estonian territory!

Ernesto Laclau defines some of the prerequisites of a nationalist movement that allows for identification without requiring origins, contingency rather than predefined alliances, and solidarity between various national struggles without requiring sameness. He argues that the strength of nationalism is that it creates an empty signifier, which arises out of the need to name an object that is both impossible and necessary (Laclau 2005: 76). Nationalism has to be able to encompass all difference in order to pursue a single goal. What unites a nationalist movement is not a shared identity, but a willingness to let nationality take priority over all internal differences (social class, gender, political affiliation, geographic origin, language). That is why its uniting force dwells in its promise as a horizon, something to strive for, rather than a ground (an imagined original identity) to build on. Laclau's perspective is informative because it focuses on the fundamental characteristics of a movement rather than the identities of its members. This is crucial to understanding the interplay between acceptance and rejection of a person who moves between various national self-identification. My interpretation is that at the turn of the twentieth century, ethnic nationality played only a small part in the nationalist movement of this geopolitical area, whereas the foundation of independent states was seen as very important. Kallas embodied various types of national and cultural identification, and her persona became a battleground of cultural conflict. The more closed the practice of nationalism became, as empires crumbled and nation-states emerged, the less room there was for the kind of solidarity nationalism to which Kallas was devoted.

★

Where do negotiations of belonging take place? In the case of Kallas, it is obvious that questions of belonging, home and loyalty were conveyed directly and indirectly through her writing, both public and private. Furthermore, her literary production reflected aspects of her true belonging. In this sense, she was what she wrote.

Katarina Leppänen is senior lecturer in history of ideas, University of Gothenburg, Sweden. The book *Elin Wägner's Alarm Clock: Ecofeminist Theory in the Interwar Era* (Lexington Books 2008) was her doctoral thesis. The chapter in this volume is part of a project on national identity in the Nordic–Baltic region.

Notes

This chapter is part of a project entitled, 'Articulation and Representation of National Identity in Estonia and Finland in 1900–1940: Theoretical Readings of Aino Kallas and Hella Wuolijoki'.

1. Kai Laitinen has compared the original diaries to those that have been published (Laitinen 1973: 126–47)

2. Recently a generation of feminist researchers has produced a number of new and different readings of Kallas's work; see Kurvet-Käosaar (2006), Leskelä-Kärki (2006) and Melkas (2006) for theses. These researchers are also involved in a number of anthologies, *Aino Kallas: Negotiations with Modernity*. For years, Kai Laitinen's thesis from 1973 and its sequel in 1997 dominated the field.

3. In her dissertation, Maarit Leskelä-Kärki (2006) has analysed the participation of the three sisters in the Fennoman movement.

4. I use the term nationalist in a broad sense as pertaining to anyone who advocates, speaks for, writes in favour of, or is otherwise engaged politically or culturally in enhancing the standing of a nation or state. As used here, the term does not say anything about claims made in the name of the nation.

5. Leena Kurvet-Käosaar (2011) has shown that Kallas was inspired by contemporary theories of blood, race and the inherited characteristics of various peoples; see also Olesk 2011: 169.

6. Wuolijoki was a young political activist in Tartu when Kallas moved there; see Tuomioja 2006.

7. This is of course a point argued most strongly by theorists in the field of intersectional studies; see, e.g., Lykke 2010.

8. Later research has placed her in the group. Both the great works of Estonian literary history from the Soviet period and later Finnish researcher Kai Laitinen include her among the central figures of the movement.

9. The difficulty of combining motherhood and creative work is the topic of many entries in Kallas's diaries; it is also mentioned in most studies on her life and writing.

10. Even self-identified contructivist theorists reify the blunt understanding of identity by meshing 'contructivist language and essentialist argumentation' (Brubaker and Cooper 2000: 6).

References

Anderson, B. (1983) 2006. *Imagined Communities: Reflections on the Origin and Spread of Nationalism.* London: Verso.

Brubaker, R., and F. Cooper. 2000. 'Beyond "Identity"', *Theory and Society* 1: 1–47.

Butler, J., and C. Spivak. 2007. *Who Sings the Nation-State? Language, Politics, Belonging.* London: Seagull.

Cusack, T. 2000. 'Janus and Gender: Women and the Nation's Backward Look', *Nations and Nationalism* 4: 541–56.

Kallas, A. 1918. *Nuori-Viro. Muotokuvia ja suuntaviivoja.* Helsinki: Otava.

———. 1946. *Uusia kanssavaeltajia ja ohikulkijoita.* Helsinki: Otava.

———. 1952. *Päiväkirja vuosilta 1897–1906.* Helsinki: Otava.

———. 1953. *Päiväkirja vuosilta 1907–1915.* Helsinki: Otava.

———. 1955. *Päiväkirja vuosilta 1922–1926.* Helsinki: Otava.

Klinge, M. 1993. *The Finnish Tradition: Essays on Structures and Identities in the North of Europe.* Helsinki: SHS.

Kriss, A.T. 2006. 'The Tartu/Tallinn Dialectic in Estonian Letters and Culture', in M. Cornis-Pope and J. Neubauer (eds), *History of the Literary Cultures of East-Central Europe: Junctures and Disjunctures in the 19th and 20th Centuries*, Vol. 2. Amsterdam: John Benjamins Publishing Company, pp. 28–39.

Kurvet-Käosaar, L. 2006. *Embodied Subjectivity in the Diaries of Virginia Woolf, Aino Kallas and Anais Nin.* Tartu: Tartu University Press.

———. 2011. '"The Vitality of Primeval Peasant Blood": The Hereditary Potential of Estonians in the Work of Aino Kallas', in L. Kurvet-Käosaar and L. Rojola (eds), *Aino Kallas: Negotiations with Modernity.* Helsinki: SLS, pp. 94–113.

Laclau, E. 2005. *On Populist Reason.* London: Verso.

Laitinen, K. 1973. *Aino Kallas 1897–1921. Tutkimus hänen tuotantonsa päälinjoista ja taustasta.* Helsinki: Otava.

———. 1978. *Aino Kallaksen maailmaa. Kuusi tutkielmaa Aino Kallaksen vaiheilta.* Helsinki: Otava.

———. 1995. *Aino Kallaksen mestarivuodet. Tutkimus hänen tuotantonsa päälinjoista ja taustasta 1922–1956.* Helsinki: Otava.

Leppänen, K. 2009. 'The Conflicting Interests of Women's Organizations and the League of Nations on the Question of Married Women's Nationality in the 1930s', *NORA – Nordic Journal of Feminist and Gender Research* 4: 240–55.

Leskelä-Kärki, M. 2006. *Kirjoittaen maailmassa. Krohnin sisaret ja kirjallinen elämä.* Helsinki: SKS.

Leskelä-Kärki, M., K. Melkas and R. Hapuli. 2009. *Aino Kallas. Tulkintoja elämästä ja tuotannosta.* Helsinki: SKS.

Lykke, N. 2010. *Feminist Studies: A Guide to Intersectional Theory, Methodology and Writing.* New York: Routledge.

Matthews, W.K. 1950. 'The Background and Poetry of Gustav Suits: A Study in Estonian Symbolism', *American Slavic and East European Review* 2: 116-127.

McCooey, D. 2004. 'Editorial: Life Writing and the Public Sphere', *Life Writing* 2: vii–xi.

Melkas, K. 2006. *Historia, halu ja tiedon käärme Aino Kallaksen tuotannossa.* Helsinki: SKS.

Moretti, F. 1998. *Atlas of the European Novel, 1800–1900.* London: Verso.

Olesk, S. 2011. 'Aino Kallas on the Boundaries of Finland, Estonia and the World', in L. Kurvet-Käosaar and L. Rojola (eds), *Aino Kallas: Negotiations with Modernity.* Helsinki: SKS, pp. 165–83.

Ommundsen, W. 2004. 'Floating Lives: Cultural Citizenship and the Limits of Diaspora', *Life Writing* 2: 101–21.

Raud, M. (1953) 1991. *Kaks suurt: Jaan Tõnisson, Konstantin Päts ja nende ajastus.* Toronto: Orto.

Raun, T. 1987. *Estonia and the Estonians.* Stanford, CA: Hoover Institution Press.

Tuomioja, E. 2006. *Häivähdys punaista: Hella Wuolijoki ja hänen sisarensa Salme Pekkala vallan-kumouksen palveluksessa.* Helsinki: Tammi.

———. 2010. *Jaan Tõnisson ja Viron itsenäisyys.* Helsinki: Tammi.

Yuval-Davis, N. 1997. *Gender and Nation.* London: Sage.

CHAPTER 9

Evolving Symbolic Divides in Basque Language Promotion Logos

JOHAN JÄRLEHED

This chapter deals with the cultural bordering of a Basque language community. It is not just about a communicative barrier between people who
speak the Basque language (Euskara) and people who do not. Fed by a
long, complex and conflicting relationship between language and identity
(Järlehed 2008), both the external and the internal borders of the Basque
language community are continuously being renegotiated and re-presented
in terms of linguistic, cultural and ideological belonging. The theoretical
approach developed in this chapter is consistent with the shift in border
studies from 'treating the concept of the border as a territorially fixed,
static line ... [to] thinking of it in terms of a series of *practices*' (Parker and
Vaughan-Williams 2009: 586). The chapter looks at some of the practices
that are involved in the yearly festivities of the Basque medium schools, the
Ikastolen Egunak. In particular, it presents a diachronic visual analysis of the
logos used to promote the events.

   In response to the increased competition for attention that characterizes
communication in contemporary society, the logo – with its (ideally) simple
and clear graphic design – has become central to the production, manifesta-
tion and exchange of symbolic capital (Lury 2004). Consequently, it also
serves as a site for ideological contestation and reflects contemporary bordering practices in public space (Chmielewska 2005). In this study I suggest
that the *Ikastolen Egunak* logos and the yearly festivities that they announce
should be seen as part of an ongoing bordering practice conditioned both by

local cultural and political history, and by global tendencies of change. With the aim of identifying and critically engaging with the principal transformations in the imagining and bordering of the represented Basque language community, I will try to answer the following questions:

- Along which symbolic divides (urban/rural, etc.) are the visual identity displays of the Basque language community constructed?
- How and why do these symbolic divides evolve?

As mentioned below, events similar to the ones announced by these logos are also performed by other European linguistic minorities, thus underscoring the importance of studying them since they can inform us of more general tendencies in the formation of cultural borders and identities in Europe. Moreover, and as explained in more detail below, *Ikastolen Egunak* logos constitute a relevant object of study because of the centrality of Euskara and Basque medium schools in the formation of the Basque national identity, and also because, contrary to most other logos that construct identity with coherent and limited visual resources, they rely on visual variety for their construction of a Basque language community.

The analysis is based on a corpus containing 169 images produced by the five local divisions of the Federation of Basque Medium Schools (*Ikastolen Elkartea*).[1] It is a sort of umbrella organization; five of the seven 'historical Basque territories' (see Figure 9.1) have their own association, and each of them organizes a yearly fundraising and consciousness-raising event in order to support and promote the Basque language: *Ibilaldia* (march) in Bizkaia, *Araba Euskaraz* (Araba in Basque) in Araba, *Kilometroak* (kilometres) in Gipuzkoa, *Nafarroa Oinez* (Navarre on foot) in Nafarroa, and *Herri Urrats* (people's march) in Iparralde.[2] Since the corpus includes all of the logos ever produced for these events, it covers the period from 1977, when the first one appeared, to 2014.[3]

The first part of the chapter consists of a description and contextualization of Ikastolen Egunak, stressing the long and conflicting relationship between the Basque language and identity, and connecting this relationship to the sociopolitical role of the Basque medium schools. The second part is dedicated to a discussion of the findings, pointing out both constants and changes in the imagining and bordering of the Basque language community. In the concluding remarks, I draw attention to the ways in which the evolution of the analysed symbolic divides might impinge on further re-bordering of the Basque language community.

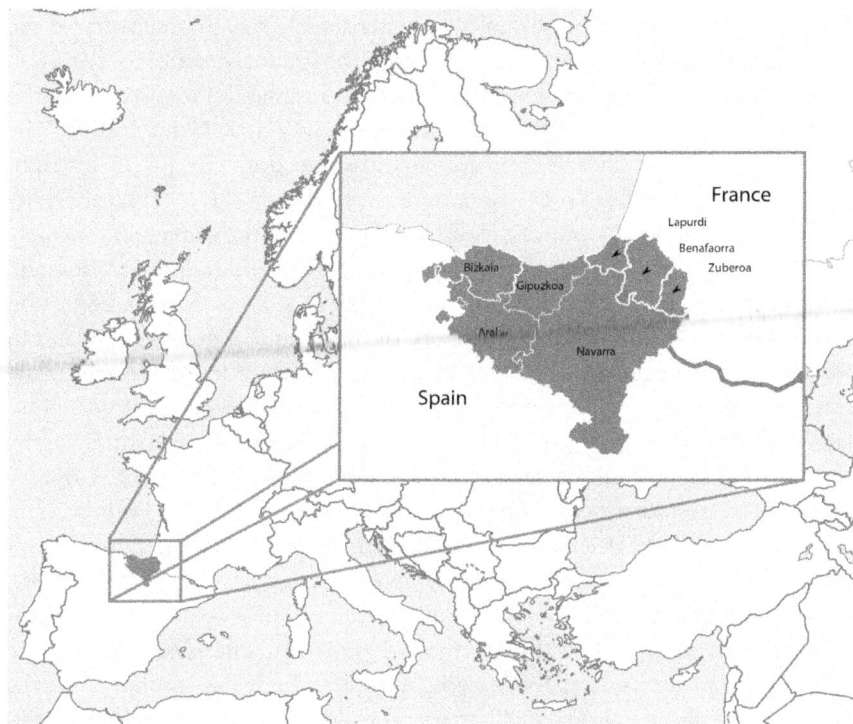

Figure 9.1 Map of the Basque Country, showing the seven historical territories, the Spanish–French border, and the autonomous communities of the Basque Country and Navarre.

By Gabriel Trisca [CC BY-SA 3.0 (http://creativecommons.org/licenses/by-sa/3.0)], via Wikimedia Commons.

Sociopolitical Role of the Basque Medium Schools

Various authors have stressed the central importance of the Basque medium schools (*ikastolas*) for the revitalization of Euskara. Partly thanks to their work, the process of decline that Euskara was undergoing during most of the twentieth century was partially reversed. However, during the first decades of their existence – the 1950s and 1960s – the *ikastolas* served principally as a symbol of resistance to Franco's repression of the Basque language, culture and identity (Joly 2004: 79). Wide – and later conflicting – sectors of Basque society consequently came to see them as 'the mythical stronghold of Basque identity' (Tejerina Montaña 1996: 229). But as Pérez-Agote (2006: 114) points out, political persecution of the Basque language did not only lead to an increased symbolic valuing of Euskara, 'which enhanced its capacity to symbolize both social solidarity and ethnic difference ... A further consequence, even less predictable and intentional, was the recovery of the language's communicative function through the gradual creation of *ikastolas*'.

Following the Spanish transition to democracy and the legalization of the *ikastolas* in the Spanish-Basque territories, their unifying role diminished. The main cause was the increasing fragmentation that both Basque nationalism and the Basque language movement underwent during the 1980s, principally due to institutionalization of the least radical sectors of the movement, namely the creation of the Basque government, the autonomous administration and the Basque education system. Until the creation in 1983 of the new education system in the Autonomous Community of the Basque Country, and later in the Basque-speaking parts of Navarre as well, Euskara had no place in the Basque public schools but only in the *ikastolas*. Since 1983, however, more and more children have had Euskara as the language of instruction in the Basque schools, both in the Autonomous Community of the Basque Country and in Navarre (Azurmendi, Bachoc and Zabaleta 2001: 243). Furthermore, during the last two decades, the Basque government and the autonomous administration have made several attempts to integrate the private *ikastolas* into the public education system – so far with limited success – and to dissociate Euskara from politics (Pérez-Agote 2006: 122). The latter is resonating in the general motivation for learning Basque which has 'shifted from the politically symbolic to the socially practical realm' (ibid: 126). In other words, people today tend to express more utilitarian and communicative reasons for learning Basque than before. Taken together, and even though the majority of the *ikastolas* have remained independent, these changes condition the recruitment grounds for the *ikastolas* and arguably influence their capacity for fundraising, consciousness raising, and community building during the yearly festivities, as well as the way they design their logos.

Ikastolen Egunak: Ritual Festivities for Language Promotion, Community Building and Bordering

The annual celebration of Ikastolen Egunak mobilizes tens of thousands of people who come together for a day and walk five to six kilometres. Their contribution is important for both economic and symbolic reasons. Every participant pays an optional amount of money for each kilometre and for the various attractions along the route: bars, food stalls, concerts, dancing, improvised verse and clowns, artisanal displays, books and records. The money goes to the local ikastola that organized the event. The fact that the participants come from all around the Basque Country testifies to the solidarity between the speakers, and serves to increase it. Furthermore, the sheer presence of so many people at one spot, all moving in the same direction for the same reason, is important because it creates feelings of belonging and strengthens the community. At the same time, the events also contribute to the continuous bordering of the Basque language community, both along the lines of language loyalty (differentiating 'us' – the friends of Euskara – from 'them' – the indifferent or hostile rest), and of those other features that best define Basque culture and identity.

This process of community building and bordering takes place then and there among the participants, as well as ahead of time through the preparatory work of the organizers and the media and personal projections, and afterwards through the symbolic resonance of the festivities in the media and the participants' retellings. The logos that I analyse are involved in each phase of this process – before announcing the event, during the event as visual backdrop, and afterwards as symbols that come to represent the experience of those who were there and those who were not there, thereby reminding them of the border between the former and the latter.

For a better understanding of these festivities and their cultural status and function, we can compare them with *Korrika* (Running), a much bigger and more sporting event that was created in 1980 by the nationalist left-wing organization AEK and has been celebrated for two weeks every other year.[4] Groups of people (friends, colleagues, etc.) buy a kilometre and run a relay race during which they pass a baton called *el testigo* (the witness) on to the next group along the route. It is always laid out in a way that covers all seven historical Basque territories. In her influential study of *Korrika*, del Valle (1994: xii) describes it as 'a metaphor of Basque unity' and 'a ritual for ethnic identity'. However, Douglass (1998: 83) has commented that this is a divided unity or a unity shared by only one sector of Basque society, 'the radical Basque left'. Non-Basque speakers and people who support moderate right-wing nationalism rarely participate, and the Basque government withholds financial support. Hence, as Douglass says, 'while *Korrika* seeks to transcend symbolically the internal [administrative and geographic] boundaries within the Basque Country, ironically it underscores and enhances [sociolinguistic and ideological] divisions within Basque society' (ibid.).

Nevertheless, rituals are spaces of rupture with daily routines and order, pointing to alternatives and facilitating collective visions and dreams. This also holds true for *Ikastolen Egunak*, which intends to create, for one day and in one place, the specific Basque-speaking ambience that the organizers desire for every day of the year and in the entire *Euskal Herria* (Apaolaza Beraza 1993: 59). In this sense, they also create spaces of rupture, Basque-speaking voices in overwhelmingly Spanish- and French-speaking surroundings. As pointed out by Apaolaza Beraza, they are festive and symbolic actions articulating political claims (ibid.: 55). Yet, as I will show in the remainder of this chapter, the way these claims are visually and linguistically framed also contributes to the outer and inner bordering of the Basque language community.

Euskara as a Marker of Continuity and Difference

The analysis of the logos reveals two constants. First, of all the common markers of Basque identity or Basqueness, only one, Euskara, is represented throughout the whole corpus during the period studied. The other markers of Basqueness are used only for shorter periods, mostly during the first few years. This finding seems to confirm the observation of Apaolaza Beraza (1993: 58) in his study of the *Araba Euskaraz* in the 1980s, that these events were more unifying than *Korrika* as they tended to dissociate Basque nationalism from the Basque language. To the organizers and participants in *Korrika*, being an *abertzale* (left-wing Basque nationalist) also implied being a *euskaltzale* (friend of the Basque language) and vice versa. As I will show below, the logos of the earlier *Ikastolen Egunak* display a similar ideological association through the use of symbols that refer overtly to Basque nationalism. But the disappearance of such symbols during the 1990s indicates a shift towards a language community whose borders less clearly depend on the divide between nationalists and others.

It is not strange that the Basque language is used to communicate within the Basque language community, but in addition to this functional value, Euskara also has an important symbolic value. Euskara is still a minority language in Basque society, one that is not understood by the majority, and hence functions as an efficient border marker between the community of *euskaldunak* (those who possess Euskara) and the *erdaldunak* (those who do not possess Euskara). As a consequence of this diglossic situation, one might expect Basque language promotion campaigns to be bilingual so as to also reach potential Basque learners and eventually enlarge the Basque-speaking community. However, in an earlier study of the visual promotion of Euskara from 1970 to 2001, I observed the contrary and concluded that the campaigns were essentially auto-referential, directed to and constructed by a Basque-speaking public (Järlehed 2008: 294, 327). The almost exclusive use of Euskara in *Ikastolen Egunak* logos underscores their auto-referential character and reaffirms the border between the *euskaldun* and *erdaldun* communities.

Variety as a Tactic of Inclusion

The second constant that can be observed in the logos is that they are characterized by variety. What varies is more the design than the represented content; all the logos include the name, place and date of the event, in most cases in Euskara; most of them also include a slogan and a symbol, tending however to vary from year to year. In this sense, they depart from one of the central functions of a logo, namely to serve as an easily recognizable identifier of the social actor that has designed it and to strengthen its identity and public image (see Lury 2004). However, one of the major challenges for the organizers of *Ikastolen Egunak* is how to mobilize and unite people who are marked by differing geographic, cultural, historical, political and social dividing lines. Variety emerges as an effective tactic to enhance the dynamics of the events and make them more inclusive. This interpretation is in line with Urla's argument that the popular sector of the Basque language movement often uses variety and bricolage as 'tactical resources' for enhancing the credibility of their claims among their audience (Urla 2012: 173). The lack of coherence articulated by the logos is also represented by the divergent and often homemade-looking designs of the websites for the various events[5] and the local *ikastolas*.[6] This reflects the relatively horizontal structure and democratic working methods of the *ikastolas* in contrast with the more coherent and standardized public image of the Basque institutions as the result of top–down design processes influenced by corporate and management philosophy (see Urla 2012).

This discussion also has to be related to the shift from popular mobilization and collective idealism to institutionalization and individualism that characterized the Basque language sector during the 1980s and 1990s. As del Valle (1994: 68) observed, the organizers of *Korrika*, AEK, who represent the most popular sector of the Basque language community, try to show that it is 'the people who own the language', not the institutions. At the same time, since the mid-1980s the institutions have taken over much of the work and responsibility for the Basque language (Tejerina Montaña 1996). There are also critical voices who claim that it is time to focus on individuals; they are the real 'owners' of Euskara, responsible for its use, transmission, status and future (Azurmendi, Bachoc and Zabaleta 2001). The increased variety and decontextualization (see below) that can be observed in the logos of the *Ikastolen Egunak* starting in the mid-1990s are definitely responding to this shift and representing the Basque language community as less marked by collectivity and more by individuality, thereby opening up the borders of the community.

Stylization of Traditional Basque Iconography

Returning briefly to the issue of language, the analysis reveals that while all the logos of *Kilometroak* and *Herri Urrats* are monolingual (Basque), some

KiLOMETROAK'81

ARRASATE - VRRIAK 4

IKASTOLEN
IBILALDIA
1
URRILA-OCTUBRE
1978

BIZKAIKO   CAJA DE AHORRO
AURREZKI KUTXA   VIZCAINA

Figures 9.2 and 9.3 Traditional nationalist graphic repertoire in early logos (*Ibilaldia* 1978, *Kilometroak* 1981).

of the earlier logos of *Nafarroa Oinez*, *Araba Euskaraz* and *Ibilaldia* are also bilingual (Basque and Spanish). This pattern corresponds well with the linguistic map, which shows that in the 1980s Gipuzkoa and the inner parts of Iparralde had the highest density of Basque speakers. Accordingly, the organizers of the early *Ikastolen Egunak* targeted a community that was not always held together by shared linguistic practice, but perhaps more so by shared aesthetic and ideological values. This is suggested by the recurrent use of a traditional nationalist graphic repertoire, such as the Basque flag, and its red, green and white colours,[7] the prototypical Basque farmhouse (*baserri*), the Gernika oak leaf, and the rustic Basque lettering[8] (see Figure 9.2).

In the course of the last few decades, however, the various elements of the traditional Basque graphic repertoire have undergone a process of abstraction and stylization. For example, whereas the *baserri* that appears in the logo of *Ibilaldia* in 1982 is detailed and contextualized, the later ones are highly stylized and decontextualized. As Coupland (2007: 154) explains, stylization introduces 'new and dissonant identities and values' into an existing situational frame and social context, therefore requiring 'an acculturated audience' to be perceived. Furthermore, stylization often involves the ideological process of 'erasure', which is the simplification of 'one pattern of meaning associations' and the elision of 'one part of the meaning complex' (ibid.: 22–23). This not only makes the stylized symbols, like the oak leaf and *baserri*, less recognizable to the foreign eye, but renders them less authentic, in the sense that their meaning is less socially contentious and culturally marked.

The Persistence of Basque as a Rural Language

In a wider study of the visual promotion of the Basque language during the last three decades of the twentieth century, I observed a clear movement from a predominantly rural to a predominantly urban setting (Järlehed 2008: 290). However, the more limited analysis of the *Ikastolen Egunak* logos shows a Basque language community clearly rooted in the countryside. Only two of the 169 logos contain figurative elements that situate the event in an urban context (see I-1982 and I-2001). Even though many of the logos display a setting that is neither rural nor urban, but abstract (e.g. K-1983, AE-2010, I-1998), the general picture is of a Basque language and Basque language community that is rurally anchored. It might be argued that this predominance of the rural is a consequence of the events having been celebrated mainly in the countryside, but many of them take place in urban settings and the majority of the participants are urbanites. The rural–urban divide, central to most nationalism, is thereby upheld through the visual neglect of urban life.

Cultural and Political Decontextualization

However, this rural anchoring is paralleled, and perhaps undermined, by a tendency towards a decontextualized representation of difference. Traditional and sometimes obsolete markers of Basqueness like the Basque lettering and colours, as well as traditional Basque nationalist symbols such as the oak leaf, the *baserri* and the *lauburu* (a four-pointed cross, see K-1977) disappeared almost completely from the logos during the 1990s. Difference is instead constructed with stylized local symbols stripped of political antagonisms. This can be illustrated with the many marine symbols that appear in the logos of Ibilaldia during the last decade (the crab in 2002, the whale in 2003 and the octopus in 2011; see Figure 9.3), and the wine leafs and grapes represented in the logos of *Araba Euskaraz* in 1989, 1999, 2003, 2004 and 2008. Through these references to local economic history – for centuries the sea was crucial to the industrial and economic development of Bizkaia, where *Ibilaldia* is organized and viniculture has long been an important part of Araba's economy – these logos clearly contribute to the construction of distinct local visual identities.

Figures 9.4 and 9.5 Stylized local symbols free from nationalist connotations (*Ibilaldia* 2002, 2003).

Discussion and Concluding Remarks

The 169 logos designed for the *Ikastolen Egunak* that were celebrated from 1977 to 2014 constitute a rich source for discussing both constants and changes in the imagining and bordering of the Basque language community. While most of the symbolic divides that have been discussed in this chapter have evolved, two have remained constant and reiterated during the thirty-seven years of celebration of the *Ikastolen Egunak*. This first divide is between the Basque-speaking and the non–Basque-speaking communities, reaffirmed through the constant and exclusive use of Euskara. Although the principal reason for the monolingualism of the logos is their auto-referential function, this practice indirectly but efficiently excludes all non–Basque speakers and thus contributes to establishing monolingual voices within the officially bilingual Basque public space. The second divide represented as constant is between rural and urban society, the latter being totally absent. This brings up a long-standing discussion within the Basque language movement about the necessity to adapt Euskara – especially its image – to urban life. Leading proponents of the *ikastolas*, like Xabier Garagorri, state that Euskara is 'an urban phenomenon', a fact that should inform the revitalization effort.[9] This study points to a gap between the goals and the concrete practice of the Basque medium schools.

By upholding these two divides, the Basque medium schools' yearly celebrations might be criticized for underscoring and enhancing divisions within Basque, similarly to the way *Korrika* does. However, we have also seen that the *Ikastolen Egunak* logos contribute in several ways to transcendence and dissolution of the *inner* borders of the Basque language community. The disappearance during the 1980s of traditional Basque nationalist iconography suggests the possibility of being Basque-speaking and supporting Euskara without having to be a Basque nationalist. This neutralization of the Basque nationalist/non–Basque nationalist divide follows from the institutionalization and normalization of important parts of Basque politics on the one hand, and the institutionalization and professionalization of the Basque language movement on the other. Also related to this is the ideological erasure implied by the stylization of politically charged symbols and identity displays in the logos, which can be explained by important changes to the recruitment grounds of the *ikastolas* in the 1980s and 1990s. It corresponds with the waning of their unifying role and the shift in motivation for learning Basque, which has become less symbolic and more pragmatic. This also leads to a more open image of the Basque language community, and arguably contributes to weakening its *outer* borders.

The analysis revealed a clear trajectory towards a more fragmented depiction of the Basque Country, by which the traditional nationalist and cultural

Basque symbols that reaffirmed the 'hegemonic narrative of Euskal Herria' (Mansvelt Beck 2006) during the 1980s give way to more local identity displays. This shift articulates a complex re-bordering of the imagined territory of the Basque language community, downplaying the outer borders while some of the inner ones are highlighted. However, the tendency towards decontextualization points in another direction, towards a downplaying of the most localized identity displays. This paradoxical situation is arguably the result of the interference caused by the local development of Basque society and politics on the one hand, and wider global, economic, technological and political changes on the other. In particular, I would argue that the visual stylization and generalization that can be observed in the *Ikastolen Egunak* logos rely on a more all-encompassing tendency towards cultural commodification. Similar to images in widespread contemporary visual genres like advertising and corporate identity displays, they tend to 'not represent actual places or events and they do not document or bear witness, but they symbolically represent marketable concepts and moods such as 'contentment' and 'freedom' (Machin 2004: 316). That way the *Ikastolen Egunak* logos also bear witness to 'an ideologically pre-structured world which is in harmony with consumerism' (ibid.).

These findings suggest that the visual identity work of the *ikastolas* has taken the step from modernity to postmodernity in the sense expressed by Bauman (1996: 18): 'If the *modern* "problem of identity" was how to construct an identity and keep it solid and stable, the *post-modern* "problem of identity" is primarily how to avoid fixation and keep the options open'. The analysed logos also appear to move towards the representation of what Appadurai calls a 'postnational imaginary'. According to Mattern (2008: 493–94), this concept is 'more diverse, more fluid, more ad hoc, more provisional, less coherent, less organized' than the 'multinational' or the 'international', and may therefore overcome 'the incapacity of the nation-state to tolerate diversity'. Perhaps the great formal variety of the *Ikastolen Egunak* logos – arguably the result of an inclusive tactic – and symbolic diversification can serve to counter the generalization brought by consumerism and the occasional reactionary articulation of a rural and linguistically closed community.

Johan Järlehed is senior lecturer in Spanish at the Department of Languages and Literatures at the University of Gothenburg, Sweden. Formerly deputy director of the Centre for European Research (CERGU), he has published on topics like minority languages and nationalism, authenticity and tourism, and typographic landscapes in international journals such as *Social Semiotics*. He has also won important research grants, including from the Swedish Research Council.

Notes

1. All the logos can be seen on the *Ikastolen Elkartea* webpage (www.ikastola.net), under *Ikastolen egunak* in the menu to the left. The individual logos that appear in this text are reproduced by kind permission of the organizers of *Araba Euskaraz, Herri Urrats, Ibilaldia, Kilometroak,* and *Nafarroa Oinez*.

2. Iparralde or the French Basque Country consists of three 'historical Basque territories': Lapurdi, Nafarroa Behera, and Zuberoa. Due to much weaker institutional support and popular mobilization in favour of the Basque language than on the Spanish side of the border, and a less clearly expressed differential identity of each one of the three territories, the Basque language schools are organized by the same association in all three: *Seaska* (cradle in Basque).

3. The first of these festivities – *Kilometroak* – was organized in 1977. In 1980, the first *Ibilaldia* was celebrated, and the first *Araba Euskaraz* and *Nafarroa Oinez* followed in 1981. The first *Herri Urrats* was held in 1984. Between 1977 and 1988, forty-three festivities took place. Since the mid-1980s, five have been celebrated each year, totalling 169 by 2014.

4. In recent years, Korrika has also inspired similar language promotional events in Mallorca, Valencia, the Catalan Countries (*Correllengua*) and Galicia (*Correlingua*), in Brittany (*Ar Redadeg,* 'The Race') and Ireland (*Rith,* 'Running'). The events dealt with in this chapter should be understood as a relatively new but important ritual that has been developed and practised in various parts of Europe by specific language movements, and whose influence on the formation of cultural borders and identities merits additional studies.

5. http://www.arabaEuskaraz.net/, http://www.herriurrats.com/, http://www.ibilaldia.net/, http://www.kilometroak.net/, http://www.nafarroaoinez.net/.

6. See, for example: http://www.bastidaikastola.net/, http://www.beasaingoikastola.com/, http://gure-ikastola.org/, http://www.andramariikastola.net/.

7. The Basque flag was used in the logos of *Herri Urrats* in 1993 and 1994, and *Ibilaldia* and *Kilometroak* in 1997. The Basque colours are predominant in the logos of *Araba Euskaraz* in 1981–83 and 1991, *Herri Urrats* in 1984–88 and 1992–95, *Kilometroak* in 1978, 1983–89 and 1992, *Ibilaldia* in 1978, 1984, 1986–87 and 1989, and *Nafarroa Oinez* in 1987.

8. See K-1981, NO-1982–83 and 1988–90. For a more detailed account of vernacular Basque lettering, see Järlehed 2012 and 2015.

9. I interviewed Xabier Garagorri in San Sebastián on 26 June 2003 when he was representing the Federation of the Ikastolas in Guipúzcoa.

References

Apaolaza Beraza, Joxe Miguel. 1993. '"Araba Euskaraz": Acción simbólica de cáracter étnico', in J.M. Apaolaza Beraza (ed.), *Lengua, etnicidad y nacionalismo: su concreción en Salvatierra.* Barcelona: Anthropos, pp. 55–61.

Azurmendi, M.-J., E. Bachoc and F. Zabaleta. 2001. 'Reversing Language Shift: The Case of Basque', in J. Fishman (ed.), *Can Threatened Languages be Saved? Reversing Language Shift, Revisited: A 21st Century Perspective.* Clevedon: Multilingual Matters, pp. 234–59.

Bauman, Zygmunt. 1996. 'From Pilgrim to Tourist – or a Short History of Identity', in S. Hall and P. du Gay (eds), *Questions of Cultural Identity.* London and New Dehli: Sage, pp. 40–68.

Chmielewska, Ella. 2005. 'Logos or the Resonance of Branding', *Space and Culture* 8(4): 356–80.

Coupland, Nikolas. 2007. *Style: Language Variation and Identity.* Cambridge: Cambridge University Press.

Douglass, William A. 1998. 'A Western Perspective on an Eastern Interpretation of Where North Meets South: Pyrenean Borderland Cultures', in T. Wilson and H. Donnan (eds), *Border Identities: Nation and State at International Frontiers*. Cambridge: Cambridge University Press, pp. 62–95.

Järlehed, Johan. 2008. *Euskaraz: Lengua e identidad en los textos multimodales de promoción del euskara, 1970–2001*. Gothenburg: Göteborgs universitet.

———. 2012. 'La letra vasca: Tradición inventada, nacionalismo y mercantilización en el paisaje lingüístico de Euskal Herria'. In: Fernández Ulloa (ed.) *Ideology, Politics and Demands in Spanish Language, Literature and Film* (334-357). Newcastle upon Tyne: Cambridge Scholars Publishing.

———. 2015. 'Ideological framing of vernacular type choices in the Galician and Basque semiotic landscape', in *Typographic Landscaping: Creativity, Ideology, and Movement*, ed. J. Järlehed and A. Jaworski [Special Issue], *Social Semiotics* 25(2): 165–99.

Joly, Lionel. 2004. 'La cause basque et l'euskara', *Mots. Langue(s) et nationalisme(s)* 74: 73–90.

Lury, Celia. 2004. *Brands: The Logos of Global Economy*. London and New York: Routledge.

Machin, David. 2004. 'Building the World's Visual Language: The Increasing Global Importance of Image Banks in Corporate Media', *Visual Communication* 3(3): 316–36.

Mansvelt Beck, Jan. 2006. 'Geopolitical Imaginations of the Basque Homeland', *Geopolitics* 11(3): 507–28.

Mattern, Shannon. 2008. 'Font of a Nation: Creating a National Graphic Identity for Qatar', *Public Culture* 20(3): 479–96.

Parker, Noel, and Nick Vaughan-Williams. 2009. 'Lines in the Sand? Towards an Agenda for Critical Border Studies', *Geopolitics* 14(3): 582–87.

Pérez-Agote, Alfonso. 2006. *The Social Roots of Basque Nationalism*. Reno: University of Nevada Press.

Tejerina Montaña, Benjamín. 1996. 'Language and Basque Nationalism: Collective Identity, Social Conflict and Institutionalisation', in C. Mar-Molinero and A. Smith (eds), *Nationalism and the Nation in the Iberian Peninsula: Competing and Conflicting Identities*. Oxford and Washington D.C.: Berg, pp. 221–36.

Urla, Jaqueline. 2012. *Reclaiming Basque: Language, Nation, and Cultural Activism*. Reno: University of Nevada Press.

Valle, Teresa del. 1994. *Korrika: Basque Ritual for Ethnic Identity*. Reno: University of Nevada Press.

Part IV

SCHOLARS MAKING BORDERS

CHAPTER 10

The Controversial Concept of
European Identity

Mats Andrén

A wave of significant identity-making swept through Europe in the second half of the nineteenth century. The establishment of a system of national identities had been completed in the first half of the century. Europe would afterwards be presented as a continent of homogeneous nation-states, and the borders on the map seemed to be clearly demarcated. Now globalization, migration processes and minority movements have launched a second wave of identity-making. National identities have been complemented by other cultural identities following the fall of Communism, the emergence of the European Union, regionalization and a stronger emphasis on local government. Identity politics have been presented as one of the distinguishing characteristics of our time (Meyer 2002).

The cultural boundaries of the new Europe offer a changing landscape. Some of them are being enhanced while others are being created or re-created. Europe has more languages than are officially recognized, and they are spoken by many more people than after the Second World War. The same goes for religions. In addition to several denominations of Christianity, Islam, Buddhism and Hinduism are now fully established in Europe, New Age beliefs are widely practised, and even Syncretism has been brought to Europe by American and African migrants. This is a paradox: when the goal has been to dismantle political, legal and economic borders, visible cultural boundaries have become stronger and more numerous.

Notes for this section begin on page 168.

So there seem to be good reasons for seeking a European identity that could transcend the cultural borders and hold a multicultural EU together. Such a common identity would help to merge the cultures of Europe, just as politics, law and economies are tending to integrate and become more homogeneous. The concept of European identity would appear to be rather straightforward. Europeans think and act as inhabitants of a particular continent, just as Americans, Africans and Asians do. However, such generalizations are shaky, given that differences within a continent can be quite large. As long as the discussion is about Europe in general, the assumption of a common identity would appear to be valid. But as soon as the focus shifts to content, things become problematic. The ostensibly simple question of what characterizes Europe and Europeans turns out to be an Achilles heel for the European identity project.

'European identity' has been established as a catchphrase. The term is widely used in different contexts these days – often in political programmes, as when the European Parliament seeks to create a European identity, or when advocating solutions to European crises, but also in exploring analyses of contemporary Europe (euobserver 2012; Spiegel Online 2012; Venet and Baranes 2013).

Descriptive inquiries are often interwoven with normative proclamations in a way that makes it hard to distinguish them from each other. This dynamic is common in initiatives undertaken by the European Commission for research on European identity (European Commission 2012; Comenius Project 2012). In public debate, European identity is often presented as a necessary phenomenon that has actually arrived along with peace and freedom; a common identity is already in place and all it needs is to acquire greater substance to become fully installed in the collective consciousness. This is the standpoint of people like Umberto Eco, who says that the current European identity is still shallow but is growing deeper one step at a time. Eco is confident that 'we're now all culturally European'; and despite the European debt crisis, he is convinced that 'we will remain a federation' (*Guardian* 2012).

However, there is no consensus on what European identity is. Although there is a great deal of talk about it, a common definition is not any closer. The notion is very complex and has become highly politicized (Karolewski and Kaina 2006; Checkel and Katzenstein 2009). This chapter does not discuss what such an identity is or might be, or attempt to describe its characteristics (as e.g. Pedersen 2008). The chapter is not a history of the phenomenon we refer to as Europe. Three such valuable studies are Davies (1996), Delanty (1995) and Rietbergen (1998). It does not address the question of whether a European identity is in the making or whether it is expanding.[1] Instead it looks at the use of the concept of European identity.

More specifically, the novel approach of this chapter is to view the concept as controversial, and highlights its use as a performative action (Kuus 2007). The crucial question is: How does discussion about a European identity affect the image of Europe?

This chapter analyses the connotations of the contemporary concept of European identity. It starts off with the meanings assigned to the phrase 'European identity' by prominent scholars in the intellectual debate of the 1990s. This approach permits clarification of three ideal definitions and one dismissal. The analysis is followed by remarks on the broader use of the concept. Finally, the ideal definitions are discussed and critiqued.

Three Definitions and One Dismissal

The following exposition starts from three ideal-typical definitions of the basic tenets of European identity. They tend to differ from each other; together they offer a view of European identity as an essentially contested concept. The key question of separating the definitions from each other looks at European heritage and the emergence of contemporary European issues: How old is European heritage and how old are the prerequisites for the present structure of Europe? There have been three clearly distinguishable ideal types.

(1). The first definition invokes a long historical tradition, starting with Antiquity and the Middle Ages. One illustration can be taken from Jacques Le Goff, the French historian who specialized in the Middle Ages and its thinking. There are other examples in which the length of the tradition invoked may be different, but it always goes back a long way; however, Le Goff is typical. A book that he published in the early 1990s looks at contemporary Europe. From this historical vantage point, he argues that European identity has a kind of continuity from its earliest days, through modern times, and up to the present. Ancient Greece contributed the concepts of reason, science, freedom and the critical spirit. The heritage from the Roman Empire is Christianity and a dichotomy between the Latin West and the Greek East that characterized Christianity in the Early Middle Ages and drew a line across Europe.

Le Goff indicates the Catholic Church as the common denominator of Western Europe throughout the Middle Ages, as well as the divide between kingdoms, languages and ethnic groups. Political unity was created by the Frankish Empire, which reached its zenith at the beginning of the ninth century. Its division established the boundary between France and Germany. Starting in the Late Middle Ages, Le Goff identifies two movements of

European identity. The first is the quest for a way of defending Europe and excluding others. This often evolved into a passion for self-cleansing, illustrated by the treatment of heretics, Jews and homosexuals. The other movement was expansionistic, as in the Crusades, the commercial boom of Genoa and Venice, the reconquest of Spain and overseas expansion. Le Goff concludes that there is an obvious *longue durée* of European identity based on the striving for unity and preservation of diversity (Le Goff 1996: 53).

(2). The second definition also attempts to chronicle a long history of European identity. However, its basic tenet is the assertion of a culturalist definition. It assumes original identities that live on through the centuries without changing in any substantial way. European history is described in terms of a linear progression from Classical Greece to the Enlightenment. Former French president Valery Giscard d'Estaing defines Europe on the basis of its ancient heritage and the creativity of the Renaissance. The ingredients were there from the very beginning and only needed time and space to evolve, leading to a homogeneous, contemporary European culture shared by both citizens and countries. Thus, it is not possible for a country that has been defined as non-European, such as Turkey, to become European in the future (Giscard d'Estaing 2002).

Joseph Ratzinger – Pope Benedict XVI – emphasizes two cultures that characterize Europe. One is Christian and recognizes the moral power of humanity. The other is secular and nihilistic, believing in the powers bequeathed by technology and scientific rationality. The latter culture has provided major opportunities, but also threatens the extinction of the human race. Ratzinger's conclusion is that European identity should be grounded in the Christian culture that sustains eternal values and human dignity. He recognizes that the potential exists in other religions as well, but argues that Christianity has brought eternal values and human dignity to Europe (Ratzinger 2005).

(3). The third definition of European identity alludes to its modernity. The definition stands in sharp contrast to the other two. British historian Timothy Garton Ash proposes abandonment of the teleological mythology of national history when talking about European identity. A new narrative is needed that focuses on the goals of European societies – he mentions 'freedom, peace, law, prosperity, diversity and solidarity'. His brief remarks are typical of the postwar era (Garton Ash 2007).

Jürgen Habermas is the main advocate of the modernist definition. He rejects any suggestion of an identity that has been upheld through the centuries since Antiquity. His idea is that European identity is partly a result of developments in the eighteenth and nineteenth centuries. It was during this time that state and society became secularized and a bourgeois urban lifestyle emerged. This is also a period characterized by the breakthrough of ideas regarding justice, solidarity, individual rights and human rights. Habermas sees European identity as a partial product of contemporary history, including the Second World War, Fascism and the evolution of the welfare state. Europe differs from the United States, as its people enjoy a high standard of living and well-developed safety net. He sees European identity in the light of the European Union, which has urged its members to act for the common good and not as individual nation-states. Habermas is not very surprised; Enlightenment ideals combined with the experiences and achievements of the past fifty years have forged a European identity (Habermas 2001).

English sociologist Gerard Delanty has launched a concept of European identity that is very much in line with the previous one. Delanty argues that European identity is of a fundamentally different character from national identities because of its cosmopolitanism and reflexivity. It largely manifests in post-national consciousness and should be open to a self-critical dimension. In a sense, Delanty emphasizes the social aspects of European identity even more than Habermas does, presenting it as embedded in social achievements and justice (Delanty 2009).

Having described the three definitions, the postmodernist dismissal of European identity should also be noted. French philosopher Étienne Balibar approves of European identity as a modernist construct, very much akin to the policies of the European Union. However, he argues that such a fictional identity serves the purpose of excluding and limiting democracy in Europe, and states that leaders seem to be avoiding the political issues associated with the concept of European identity. He discusses mechanisms that exclude people from the rights of citizenship and others that include people in the economy and workforce, resulting in a kind of apartheid system. Thus, he concludes that extension and expansion of citizenship rights is inconsistent with the establishment of European identity. Balibar dismisses the very idea of European identity, emphasizing the lack of fixed borders around Europe. Neither Europe nor its neighbours have boundaries that are historically or culturally continuous. He argues that Europe is a borderline in itself, containing layer upon layer of different borders, thereby sharing histories and cultures with much of the rest of the world (Balibar 2009: 20, 184, 245).

The Various Discourses on European Identity

Le Goff, Habermas and Ratzinger presented their definitions after the fall of Communism in Central and Eastern Europe in the hope of fostering a deeper integration of the EU and in an effort to expand upon the original group of member states. The definitions can also be seen as part of the extension of several discourses on Europe and European identity that preceded the 1990s and that continue in some respects in the twenty-first century. The decade before the fall of the Berlin Wall saw a more intense discussion of Central Europe and its identity. Central European intellectuals Milan Kundera, Vaclav Havel, György Konrad, Adam Michnik and others recognized the idea of Central Europe as conducive to values such as freedom and truth, which are fundamental to Europe (Matejka et al. 1982–1990). The relationship between Russia and Europe was posited as a central tenet during the perestroika of the 1980s. Gorbachev argued strongly that Russia had a place in the 'house of Europe', while others both inside and outside of Russia stressed fundamental differences between the two areas (Neumann 1996: 160–79). The relationship between several European countries and Europe as a whole can pose a similar issue when it comes to member states, accession states and other bordering states. Several discourses on Europe emerged, and some with roots in the nineteenth and twentieth centuries continue to this day.

Habermas and Le Goff are both strongly in favour of European integration. Their arguments should primarily be related to the ideas of European identity that have been developed and emphasized within the EU discourse since the 1980s. An EU declaration from 1973 stated that economic integration should go hand in hand with an evolving European identity. But the making of such an identity was regarded as a consequence of economic integration. During the 1980s, the emphasis was on identity in relation to a shared European culture. Proposals by the European Commission talked about supporting 'European consciousness'. The lack of European identity was considered to be a problem. It was the only piece of the puzzle that was missing in the attempt to forge an integrated Europe. European identity was considered necessary for the sake of citizen loyalty to the EU, as well as for its badly needed legitimacy (Shore 2000: 15–65; Stråth 2002).

It is questionable whether the EU process actually contributes to a shared European identity. More likely it is increasing the significance of cultural borders. The EU has stressed the role of regions and in some cases strengthened the status of minority languages. This can also be seen in the definition of the European identity. An important theme of the identity policies that the EU has pursued is how to deal with differences. The expression 'unity in diversity' is often used as part of the EU discourse. Europe is presented as having a diverse culture, which is considered to be a positive thing, but also as a common heritage with shared values. The idea is that Europe enjoys cultural diversity within the framework of a common identity or civilization. This makes it possible for the EU to rhetorically affirm cultural borders (Hansen 2000: 51–71; Delanty 2003). It has been argued that the discourses of European identity are primarily related to establishing exclusionary characteristics. 'It is doubtful if this will do to ensure a smooth process of ongoing European integration and successfully address the challenges of the ongoing European societies', according to Dirk Jacobs and Robert Maier (1998).

An Open Question

The starting point for posing the question of European identity is the battle over its definition. There appear to be different answers. Whether the identity is assigned to the Middle Ages, Enlightenment or postwar period is important. A more radical understanding of the issue is to situate European identity in our time and argue that history is being used to affirm the various positions. It might be said that history has been reduced to building blocks or scenery for the construction of an ideology about European identity. But if European identity is interpreted as an ideology, the historical traditions must still be known in order to analyse it consciously on the basis of thorough knowledge.

A dual position is needed. Historical traditions exist. It is possible to give an account of events that have shaped Europe. It is also possible to explore processes of importance for European identity. It is significant that identity is being constructed in contemporary Europe and rewriting history. This is what the battle is all about. Given that the objective of this chapter is to think about the concept of European identity, it is necessary to start in the present and consider history as a battlefield of contemporary struggles. The goal must be to establish a distance from which to present contemporary ideologies.

History gives us different ways to talk about Europe that shed light on contemporary definitions of European identity. Both historical and modernistic definitions make use of the idea of progress. They see Europe as a place of progress and development. They are not one-sided, as they also emphasize negative aspects of contemporary Europe. Still, they essentially see the modern era as one of progress.

Another view of Europe is that it is in decline. Such a view is found in critiques of civilization from the Enlightenment onwards. Nietzsche spoke of European nihilism, which became a general theme in the early twentieth century (Wittrock and Andrén 2014). It seems obvious that contemporary Europe is part of a nihilistic global culture with a lifestyle that is accelerating climate change. Furthermore, France and the UK have nuclear weapons. Such a view of Europe is prominent in the culturalism represented by Ratzinger.

Both Ratzinger and Habermas make use of the traditional idea of Europe when talking about European identity. The idea of Europe has historically signified a special geographical area of the world, Christianity and a particular way of conducting politics. While Ratzinger emphasizes Christianity, Habermas posits a political description of Europe that accords special status to citizenship. An underlying similarity is that both of them make connections between European identity and moral or ethical standpoints. Habermas argues that politics has a moral foundation and advances an ethic of solidarity and social justice, while Ratzinger articulates a Christian morality (Habermas and Derrida 2003).

What is Hidden and What is being Promoted?

So what is the battle over European identity all about? Geographer Merje Kuus has stressed the performative aspect of identity-building in Europe. From this perspective, identity is not an attribute, a thing that defines a community and carries it forward. It is that which is performed in action, for instance by defining an identity.

> Performative approaches do not treat identity as an attribute or a property of the subject – something that subjects such as individuals or states express. It conceives subjectivity explicitly in processual terms, not as a source but as an effect of identity claims. Identity then is not something that states, groups or individuals have, but something that groups and individuals do. (Kuus 2007)

To make a fair assessment of the discourse on European identity, both that which is said and the act of its being said must be observed. The question is what purpose the discourse on European identity serves. A more specific question is what the EU discourse on European identity promotes: the idea is that it advances the quest for further integration, for constructing legitimacy and thereby for advocating democracy. The answers concern concrete political efforts, such as building infrastructure and securing the energy supply. Another question, harder to answer but still important, is what is hiding within the discourse on identity.

Having stated that the discourse is inherent to European history and has consequences, and having stressed that the discourse as such can serve a purpose, awareness is required of an important performative component of the definition of European identity, which is to hide some of Europe's cultural borders. Its historical heritage needs to be mentioned once again. What is hidden and what is promoted when European identity is assigned Christian roots? To hide Muslim aspects of European history and their presence in contemporary Europe, it is crucial to promote Europe as a homogenous Christian continent. It is a problematic approach, given the history of South East and South West Europe, the fact that Christianity and Islam share common roots, and the vital role played by Arabic intellectual culture in Medieval Europe. This approach hides the large population of contemporary Europe that comes from Islamic cultures. It hides the fact that both Islam and Christianity have strains of fundamentalism within their structures, but it also hides the tolerance and secularism that can be found in both Islam and Christianity.

Another question involves the Enlightenment. What is hidden and what is promoted by emphasizing this historical period? Secularism is promoted, as are freedom of the individual, rational thinking and science. Identifying that which is hidden is more complicated. Modern European history has dark episodes, such as colonization and brutality against both non-Europeans and Europeans. This is not necessarily hidden in modernistic definitions of European identity. Habermas emphasizes that Europe willingly contemplates the dark aspects of its modern incarnation. However, advocacy of a unified Europe seems to rely on a more one-sided view. An article published in 2003 by Habermas and Jacques Derrida on the necessity of a shared foreign policy underscores two aspects of Europe. On the one hand are the successful model of a welfare state and the striving for a Europe that transcends competing nation-states. On the other hand are cultural diversity and mutual acceptance of cultural differences (Habermas and Derrida 2003).

The stated objective of European identity is to take the focus off national sentiments and allegiances. However, it is important to consider the relationship between promotion of this identity and conflicts of class and ethnicity, inequality and segregation. To what extent does the former obscure the latter? The formula used in speeches and manifestos by the EU is 'unity in diversity', which is also employed by Le Goff when carving out a European duality that both creates unity and protects diversity. This principle conceals certain fundamental conflicts.

There are good reasons to be critical of the advocacy of European identity. The relationship between a European model for the welfare state and the cultural foundations of a shared identity must be considered. Habermas establishes an important interplay between European identity, the welfare state and cultural diversity. But that is where the idea of European identity needs to be scrutinized and questioned. Programmes for a European identity tend to obscure societal conflicts. It is highly uncertain what characteristics will be attributed to European identity in upcoming discussions about the future of Europe. It might very well be given culturalist attributes and play an important role in xenophobic and Islamophobic political programmes. The discourse on European identity might also contribute to discourses that question the welfare state or promote cultural homogenization.[2]

Mats Andrén is professor of history of ideas and science at the University of Gothenburg, and former director of the Centre of European Research at this same university (CERGU http://www.cergu.gu.se//); 2011–2016 he was the deputy dean. His latest book is *Nuclear Waste Management and Legitimacy: Nihilism and Responsibility* (Routledge, 2012), and he has published seven monographs and twelve anthologies. He is also guest editor for special issues – e.g. on European Nihilism in *European Review* 2 (2014), with Jon Wittrock.

Notes

1. As is studied by, for example, Michael Bruter (2005), and at research conferences such as 'Euroidentities. The Evolution of European Identity: Using Biographical Methods to Study the Development of European Identity'; http://www.euroidentities.org/ (accessed 3 September 2012).

2. The chapter is a revised and adapted version of 'Det som är gemensamt: talet om europeisk identitet' in Claes G. Alvstam, Birgitta Jännebring and Daniel Naurin (eds). 2011. *I Europamissionens tjänst: vänbok till Rutger Lindahl.* Gothenburg: Göteborgs universitet.

References

Balibar, E. 2009. *Vi, det europeiska folket? Reflektioner kring ett transnationellt medborgarskap* [We, the people of Europe? Reflections on transnational citizenship]. Stockholm: Tankekraftförlag.

Bruter, M. 2005. *Citizens of Europe? The Emergence of a Mass European Identity.* New York: Palgrave Macmillan.

Checkel, J.T., and P.J. Katzenstein (eds). 2009. *European Identity.* Cambridge: Cambridge University Press.

Comenius Project. 2012. 'Comenius – Towards a European Container, leaving the "National Container"'; http://www.tei-comenius.com/ (accessed 7 September 2012).

Davies, N. 1996. *Europe: A History.* Oxford: Oxford University Press.

Delanty, G. 1995. *Inventing Europe: Idea, Identity, Reality.* London: Macmillan.

———. 2003. 'Europe and the Idea of "Unity in Diversity"', in R. Lindahl (ed.), *Whither Europe? Borders, Boundaries, Frontiers in a Changing World.* Gothenburg: University of Gothenburg.

———. 2009. 'Models of European Identity: Reconciling Universalism and Particularism', *Perspectives on European Politics and Society* 3: 345–59.

Euobserver. 2012. 'We Need to Invest in a European Identity'; http://euobserver.com (accessed 7 September 2012).

Euroidentities. 2012. 'Euroidentities: The Evolution of European Identity: Using Biographical Methods to Study the Development of European Identity'; http://www.euroidentities. org/ (accessed 3 September 2012).

European Commision. 2012. 'The Development of European Identity: Policy and Research Issues'; http://ec.europa.eu/research/social-sciences/ (accessed 7 September 2012).

'European Identity and Cloud Conference 2013'; http://www.id-conf.com/ (accessed 3 September 2012).

Garton Ash, T. 2007. 'Europe's True Stories', *Prospect* 131 (February).

Giscard d'Estaing, V. 2002. 'Pour ou Contre l'Adhésion de la Turquie à l'Union Européenne', *Le Monde*, 8 November.

Guardian. 2012. 'Umberto Eco: "It's culture, not war, that cements European identity"', *Europa* 26 January 2012; http://www.guardian.co.uk/world/2012/jan/26/umberto-eco-culture-war-europa (accessed 3 September 2012).

Habermas, J. 2001. *Braucht Europa eine Verfassung?* in *Zeit der Übergänge: kleine politsche Schriften IX*. Frankfurt am Main: Suhrkamp.

Habermas, J., and J. Derrida. 2003. 'February 15, or What binds Europeans Together: A Plea for a Common Foreign Policy, Beginning in the Core of Europe', *Frankfurter Allgemeine Zeitung*, 31 May.

Hansen, P. 2000. *Europeans Only? Essays on Identity Politics and the European Union*. Umeå: Umeå University.

Jacobs, D., and R. Maier. 1998. 'European Identity: Construct, Fact and Fiction', in *A United Europe: A Quest for a Multifaceted Identity*, ed. M. Gastelaars and A. de Ruijter. Maastricht: Shaker.

Karolewski, I.P., and V. Kaina (eds). 2006. *European Identity: Theoretical Perspectives and Empirical Insights*. Berlin: LIT Verlag.

Kuus, M. 2007. 'Ubiquitous Identities and Elusive Subjects: Puzzles from Central Europe', *Transactions of the Institute of British Geographers* 32(1): 90–101.

Le Goff, J. 1996. *Das alte Europa und die Welt der Moderne*. Munich: Beck.

Matejka, L., et al. (eds). 1982–1990. *Cross Currents: A Yearbook of Central European Culture*. Ann Arbor, MI: University of Michigan.

Meyer, T. 2002. *Identitätspolitik: Vom Missbrauch kultureller Unterschiede*. Frankfurt am Main: Suhrkamp.

Neumann, I.B. 1996. *Russia and the Idea of Europe*. London: Routledge.

Pedersen, T. 2008. *When Culture Becomes Politics: European Identity in Perspective*. Aarhus: Aarhus University Press.

Ratzinger, J. 2005. 'Europa in der Krise der Kulturen', in Mercello Pera and Joseph Ratzinger, *Ohne Wurzeln: der Relativismus und die Krise der Europäischen Kultur*. Augsburg: Sankt Ulrich Verlag, pp. 62–84.

Rietbergen, P. 1998. *Europe: A Cultural History*. London: Routledge.

Shore, C. 2000. *Building Europe: The Cultural Politics of European Integration*. London: Routledge.

Spiegel Online International. 2012. 'How to Forge a Common European Identity'; http://www.spiegel.de/international/europe/ (accessed 7 September 2012).

Stråth, B. 2002. 'A European Identity: To the Historical Limits of a Concept', *European Journal of Social Theory* 5.

Venet, C., and B. Baranes (eds). 2013. *European Identity through Space: Space Activities and Programmes as a Tool to Invigorate the European Identity*. Vienna: Springer.

Wittrock, J., and M. Andrén. 2014. 'The Critique of European Nihilism: Interpretation, Responsibility, and Action', *European Review* 22(3): pp. 179–195.

CHAPTER 11

The EU as a 'Large Space'?

Carl Schmitt and the Contemporary Dilemmas of Political Rituals and Cultural Borders

JON WITTROCK

This chapter considers the relevance of Carl Schmitt's concept of *Großraum*, or 'large space', for the theme of cultural borders. This concept was formulated in a series of works from the 1930s onwards. Specifically, Schmitt's reflections on a type of political entity that is neither a modern state nor an empire bears on contemporary dilemmas pertaining to the relationship between territorial and cultural borders in Europe.

The EU as a whole has sought to define its outer borders and deal with the problems implied in patrolling and monitoring them, while internal territorial controls have diminished within the Schengen area. Nevertheless, member states retain formal sovereignty, even as EU law has come to be regarded, since the 1960s, as trumping national law when applicable. Furthermore, what seems very similar – but hardly identical – to a constitutional structure and the institutional arrangements of a democratic nation-state have been erected. Member states have agreed to give up a degree of their sovereign powers in exchange for the benefits of cooperation, but while the explicit aims of these manoeuvres have been peace and prosperity, they have simultaneously given rise to perceived political tensions between state sovereignty and EU influence, not least as played out on the symbolic plane, and concerning the reproduction of cultural borders by means of politicized historical narratives, as well as shared symbols and rituals.

During the last few decades Carl Schmitt has gone from being a controversial but relatively obscure thinker to a still controversial but increasingly

Notes for this section begin on page 181.

central source of inspiration within political theory, as well as in a number of other academic fields; his influence has grown to the point that one commentator speaks of a protracted 'rebirth of interest in Schmitt' (Strong in Schmitt 2007: xiii), observing that he attracts attention all over the theoretical and ideological field: from Chantal Mouffe's (2005: 20) suggestions for a revitalization of political pluralism and agonistic contests to the widespread influence of Schmitt in political-theoretical and legal debates in both the United States and Europe. One could of course also mention Agamben's (1998, 2005) works, as well as Ojakangas's (2006) succinct study, and Marder's (2010) philosophical engagement, to name a few in a constantly growing literature.

Furthermore, Schmitt has been continuously influential in constitutional debates in postwar France, Germany, and other European countries, as well as in the context of the foundation of the EEC (see Joerges 2003; a similar but brief appearance is made by Schmitt in Laughland 1998). An example of a systematic treatment from the perspective of jurisprudence is provided by Böckenförde in Dyzenhaus (1998). For treatments of Schmitt as a Catholic thinker and political theologian, see Eichhorn (1994), Wacker (1997) and Dahlheimer (1998).

Finally, Schmitt's works remain open to distinctly different interpretations, and remain a focal point for contestation within present-day political thought and debates over the future of Europe. The works of the thinker who proclaimed, (in)famously, that '[t]he specific political distinction to which political actions and motives can be reduced is that between friend and enemy' (Schmitt 2007: 26), and that 'all political concepts, images, and terms have a polemical meaning. They are focused on a specific conflict and are bound to a concrete situation' (ibid.: 30) have thus become, themselves, places of contestation, where his defenders and detractors meet, sometimes to wage their own wider wars of ideological confrontation and to promote their own respective political projects. To many on both the right and left, Schmitt's works have become a major source of alternative conceptions that challenge the perceived threats of a homogenous, liberal-democratic and capitalist universalism.

Schmitt was not exactly an unrelenting anti-democrat; he did legitimize the National Socialist regime, but before that, he tried to stop its takeover. Schmitt's 1923 *Die geistesgeschichtliche Lage des heutigen Parlamentarismus* (The Crisis of Parliamentary Democracy) contains a sharp polemic against liberal democratic parliamentarianism, arguing, instead, for the possibility of a democratic dictatorship based on the notion of democracy as consisting in the identity of the ruler and the ruled, rather than deliberation or parliamentary representation, neither of which contemporary parliaments, Schmitt claims, are able to provide in any convincing manner (see Schmitt

1988b). Throughout the Weimar years, however, Schmitt appeared some-what ambivalent. His 1928 *Verfassungslehre* (Constitutional Theory) formu-lates a stringent interpretation of the constitution of the Weimar Republic, although Schmitt consistently maintained that any political entity, whether incorporating components of parliamentarianism or not, ultimately rests on an instance of a political will transcending any formal system.

The normative and descriptive aspects of Schmitt's works are notori-ously difficult to separate from each other. Thus, Schmitt is often perceived to proceed from a more or less opaque political agenda, which frames his descriptive concepts and narratives as well (perhaps the best example, to provide an esoteric understanding, is in Meier 1995). On the other hand, his visions, even when they are polemically grounded, continue to appeal to several theorists with views far from his, and to observers with very different political agendas; Schmitt, it should be noted, not only openly supported Hitler after (but not before) the *Machtübernahme*, but he was also an unapolo-getic anti-Semite in some of his writings (see Gross 2000).

This would probably be a good place to immediately address some pressing issues. It should be noted that Schmitt's concepts, in the German original, are loaded with a contextual significance that is easily lost in English translation. This goes, of course, for Schmitt's usage of concepts like *Volk* and *Reich*, which were widely used by the National Socialist regime for propagandistic purposes. Thus, when we seek to determine Schmitt's con-temporary relevance, that also implies reading Schmitt with Schmitt as well as against him. Schmitt put forth his major theoretical outline of the *Großraum* in the spring of 1939, after the *Anschluss* of Austria but before the outbreak of the Second World War. In its origins, then, this Schmittian notion is hardly innocent, but the same could be said of any other political concepts – as Schmitt himself observed, they arise out of specific contexts, against the horizon of concrete struggles for power. But being aware of the original context also allows us to use concepts differently, and sometimes to seek to wrestle them out of the hands of their creator, and to find out whether we can put them to use ourselves.

So what is the relevance of Schmitt's model of large spaces for the making of cultural borders? Schmitt raises important questions concerning the relations between the cultural borders that are performed and embodied by political rituals and symbols, and territorial borders that are drawn and redrawn by both war and legislation. We may understand large spaces as being either normative or descriptive, and we shall explore both aspects – whether Schmitt's theory of large spaces seems an adequate description of some crucial features of the contemporary Europe and its cultural borders, and/or whether it depicts something desirable, towards which we would wish to strive, as a model to realize. Our answers, however, will not necessarily be in the form of consistent affirmations or rejections, but rather in degrees. This presupposes that we choose some main elements of Schmitt's understanding of large spaces to which we can then relate actual contemporary, European political developments.

Hence, in the following, I will initially attempt to reconstruct a more general understanding of large spaces. Thereafter, I will apply this general understanding to the specific context of the contemporary European Union and consider the tension between member states and the union in order to examine its *descriptive* utility, and finally, its eventual *normative* desirability. On the whole, I shall attempt to chart a course in between the extreme stances of either a general acceptance or rejection of Schmitt's concept, arguing for a somewhat more nuanced reception. While Mouffe (2007) defends the contemporary relevance of Schmitt's thought on global politics, along the lines of a global balancing of a potentially threatening, totalizing liberal Western project, Schmitt's large space implies considerably more than that, rendering its descriptive utility as well as its normative desirability, even as a source of inspiration, dubious.

A General Understanding of Large Spaces?

Schmitt's 1939 *Völkerrechtliche Großraumordnung mit Interventionsverbot für raumfremde Mächte* lays out the basic outline of a large space: it consists of a *Reich*, or core (literally: 'realm'), its major power, and a host of lesser powers, within a common *Großraum*, or 'large space'. Schmitt stresses that this arrangement does not simply comprise an extended state: there is a qualitative, not merely a quantitative, difference (see Schmitt 1995: 309). Concretely, however, what does this entail?

As a starting point, Schmitt refers to the US Monroe Doctrine of 1823, rejecting further colonization of the Americas by European powers. Whether or not and to what extent Schmitt's interpretation of this doctrine is correct is of lesser relevance to our concerns; what is of key interest is how Schmitt uses it to advance his own theoretical approach. Clearly, there is a political and polemical point in turning to this example for a legal theorist of the German Reich in 1939: praising American aspirations provides a cunning comparison, and Schmitt was hardly the only one making it. As Hooker (2009: 134) notes, 'Ribbentrop cited the Doctrine in March 1939 as a precedent for the partition of Poland, and Hitler himself deployed the analogy in a speech to the Reichstag in April 1939. Schmitt was apparently warned not to claim authorship of the idea so as to avoid offending the Führer's dignity'. Thus, Schmitt (1995: 281) claims: 'For us it is decisive, that the original Monroe Doctrine of 1823 is the first declaration in the history of modern public international law that speaks of a large space, and', he continues, crucially, 'establishes for it the basic principle of non-intervention of powers external to that space'.[1]

True, the Monroe Doctrine was about the non-intervention of external powers – which in itself is significant since a novel understanding of internal/external is established based on the declaration of the United States and its demarcation of a political understanding of the Western Hemisphere; but further developments resulted in corresponding instances of intervention by the US. This approach could then be applied on a global scale, as the sovereignty of other countries lapsed into ambiguity; as Schmitt (2003: 252) observes in his major later work, the 1950 *Der Nomos der Erde*, translated into English as *The* Nomos *of the Earth* (2003): 'The external territorial form with its linear boundaries was guaranteed, but not its substance'.

The immediate significance of Schmitt's musings on this development transcends the legal-historical context of US foreign policy: he is concerned with, above all, elaborating on large spaces as, in the first instance, comprising a type of political entity that is neither a state, nor an empire, in the sense of European, colonial empires. Thus, in *Völkerrechtliche Großraumordnung*, Schmitt (1995: 285–91) turns to the British Empire, having already examined the US, in a move that is still rhetorically and polemically grounded: the British strove to keep the sea lanes open, to control the oceans, but they also established a patchwork imperial system, binding together legally distinct units in a common whole. However, from the perspective of techniques of rule, there is one clear and decisive difference: while the American large space came to comprise a zone of intervention/non-intervention, rendering sovereignty ambiguous, the British maintained, for the most part, a Weberian (see Weber 1978: 314) monopoly on the use of force throughout their colonial territories. Schmitt, by the way, was a student of Weber's, but hardly a consistent follower (see Engelbrekt 2009). Thus, one analytical distinction that can be retrieved from Schmitt's analysis of empires and large spaces concerns 'techniques of rule': the consistent *occupation* of territories as opposed to policies of *intervention*.

Schmitt laments the development of the United States towards a universalistic, hegemonic power, rendering sovereignty ambiguous on a yet wider, global scale, while losing its ties to its specific, concrete foundations in the Western Hemisphere. The rising superpower had, with its proclamation of the 1939 Panama Declaration forbidding hostile powers to extend warfare to the Western Hemisphere, sown the seeds of a homogeneous, geometrically determined global surface, open to economic exploitation and military intervention. This new proclamation extended three hundred miles out to the sea, drastically transcending the customary European three-mile limit of coastal, territorial waters, as opposed to open oceans:

As long as one understood by 'Western Hemisphere' only a continental land-mass, it was linked with a mathematical-physical line of division, as well as with a geographical-physical and historical form. But its expansion and displacement to the sea made the concept of 'Western Hemisphere' even more abstract in the sense of an empty and overwhelming, mathematically and geographically determined spatial dimension. (Schmitt 2003: 283)

As Schmitt observes, in 1939, '[u]niversalistic, world-encompassing general concepts are, within public international law, the typical weapons of interventionism' (Schmitt 1995: 285).[2] Schmitt (ibid.: 306) himself put forth, as an alternative, 'The new concept of order of a new public international law', which is 'our concept of the Reich', supposedly supported by a specific people (*Volk*).[3] However, are there other traits of large spaces that can render them somewhat more meaningful? Here, we may turn to the notions of the 'political idea' (*politische Idee*) which 'radiates' (*ausstrahlt*) throughout a large space. Sadly, however, Schmitt remains frustratingly vague on both of these notions (ibid.: 296). Furthermore, Schmitt envisages four kinds of legal-political interrelations according to his 'large space' model: between different large spaces; between cores (*Reiche*); between the composite ethnic-cultural (*völkisch*) groups within a large space; and between such groups across the borders of large spaces (ibid.: 305). However, since the core determines the external orientation of a large space as a whole, other relations transcending the territorial borderlines of a large space would be subsumed under its over-arching considerations. Again, Schmitt is not exactly clear on how this is sup-posed to work. The Reich, he maintains, must be grasped in contrast to the ethnic diversity of the late Roman Empire, as well as to that of the empires of the Western democracies (ibid.: 297). It is a fiercely particularistic notion, resisting the universalizing ambitions of great powers opposed to German interests. It is also, however, an unclear one as to its actual implications.

To conclude, then, the theory of large spaces may, on the one hand, have been put forth in 1939 by Schmitt as an attempt either to justify German power-political ambitions, or to bolster his own popularity with the regime – something he was urgently in need of doing. Schmitt had fallen out of favour with the regime by the late 1930s, and not even his explicit attempts at posing as a committed anti-Semite seemed to help (this is not to say, of course, that Schmitt was *not* an anti-Semite, but merely that him being so did not earn him any lasting popularity with the regime (see Bendersky 1983: 248–49).

According to this reading, Schmitt's theorizing on the large space amounts, either way, to little more than an exercise in opportunism (see Hooker 2009: 138–39). On the other hand, Schmitt could be understood as sketching out a more general theory, both in 1939 and in the 1950 *Der Nomos der Erde*. However, such a more general understanding is difficult to render precisely; it remains a sketch. So to what extent is this theoretical understanding of large spaces applicable to concrete contemporary developments in Europe?

The European Union as a Large Space?

As Joerges (2003: 171) observes, 'even if one acknowledges a constructive dimension in Carl Schmitt's "European Monroe doctrine", it is nevertheless striking that he himself remained largely silent as to the *internal order* of the *Großraum*'. Furthermore, 'Schmitt was not capable of identifying, and his opponents did not even want to identify, the structures that would replace the autonomy which the sovereignty principle in international law had protected' (ibid.: 185).

In the case of the EU, there is no one, single core; rather, there are several cores, different ones for different policy areas, that do appear to render the sovereignty of peripheral entities ambiguous to a certain, albeit limited, extent. In economic policy and especially in the eurozone, Germany and/or the European Central Bank can be seen as a core, whereas in the common security and defence policy, all member states retain a core of sovereignty but, through the Solidarity Clause, agree to intervene in support of each other. Regarding EU legislation, the purely geographical 'cores' would be Brussels/Strasbourg and Luxembourg, whereas the actual political cores could be found in terms of both formal institutions and informal networks. Concerning those areas where EU law applies, its primacy in relation to the legal orders of the member states would seem to render the latter a periphery in regard to the EU. Also, in the early decades of the EU, a Franco-German core was conceivable, and is occasionally resurrected; however, with successive enlargements, the EU no longer retains a historical and cultural core based on, or legitimized by, recourse to the ancient empire of Charlemagne or a Western European core of the founding states. However, if we conceive of the EU as a whole, the EU itself would then be the core, whereas neighbouring countries would constitute a periphery, open to domination by means of 'soft' power, or what some have called 'soft imperialism' (see Hettne and Söderbaum 2005). Finally, as noted above, Schmitt's notion of Reich is contrasted by him to the ethnical diversity of competing imperial models. In other words, my usage above has indeed considerably stretched the Schmittian notion of a Reich into a more abstract discussion of cores.

The EU, then, cannot easily be equated with Schmitt's notion of a large space. Nevertheless, the key questions Schmitt raises in conjunction with his works on large spaces do hit upon something significant pertaining to debates on which kind of political entity could complement and perhaps replace the nation-state, which techniques of rule are used in global politics, and what the relationship would be between political idea and technique of rule or domination. However, in the absence of a fully worked out explanation by Schmitt in *Völkerrechtliche Großraumordnung*, we are left to elaborate on our own, in the light of his other works.

Schmitt was concerned, throughout his career, with the problem of the political representation of authority and the collective manifestations of faith as opposed to its private, fragmented, and often apolitical effects. Already in *Political Romanticism* (originally *Politische Romantik*, 1919) Schmitt attacks the tendencies towards a disconnected, fragmented and politically ineffectual aestheticism among early nineteenth-century German intellectuals (and by way of extension, among his own contemporaries), resulting in an 'immanent occasionalism' whereby experiences are disjointed from predictable (heuristic and pragmatic) implications. He argues that '[s]ince any concrete item can be the *occasio* of an incalculable effect – for Mozart, a look at an orange can be the occasion for composing the duet *Là ci darem la mano* – this relationship is completely incommensurable, devoid of all objectivity, and non-rational. It is the relation of the fanciful' (Schmitt 2011: 83). Conversely, the imposition of a shared interpretative and ritual framework that ties the individual to the political entity, or to a community of faith coexisting with the political entity, is generally lauded by Schmitt. And while it is tempting to declare such concerns obsolete, this is not the case at a descriptive level: on the contrary, whether labelled as 'nationalism' or in the guise of 'civil religion', liberal democracies do retain a form of publicly supported collective worship, with its attendant symbolism (see Bellah 1970; Rousseau 1994). As Brubaker (1996: 16) notes, '[w]e should not ask: what is a nation, but rather: how is nationhood as a political and cultural form institutionalized within and among states?' Apart from obvious institutional frameworks (the educational and legal systems, military forces, etc.) nationhood is also reproduced by ceremonies and symbols, in both grand and less spectacular settings (see e.g. Billig 1995 for examples of the latter).

Schmitt's (2007: 26) understanding of 'the political' is well known, not to say infamous: 'The specific political distinction to which political actions and motives can be reduced is that between friend and enemy'. A 'political idea', then, separates friend from enemy, establishes a community as well as its demarcations discursively, but also in collective practices such as shared rituals. This is the basis for Schmitt's polemic against Hobbes in his 1938 treatise on *Leviathan*:

> Hobbes declares the question of wonder and miracle to be a matter of 'public' in contrast to 'private' reason; but on the basis of universal freedom of thought ... he leaves to the individual's private reason whether to believe or not to believe, and to preserve his own *judicium* in his heart... (Schmitt 2008b: 56)

And as a consequence, '[t]he distinction between private and public, faith and confession, *fides* and *confessio*, is introduced in a way from which everything else was logically derived in the century that ensued until the rise of the liberal constitutional state'. The political idea would thus have a performative aspect, like the common worship of Hobbes's commonwealth – indeed, Schmitt characterized Hobbes as the thinker who 'consummated the Reformation' by bringing the collective worship back together with the unity of the political entity (see Hobbes 1998: 302; Schmitt 2008a: 125–26). The political idea, however, would not necessarily be tied to Christianity. Analytically, this is only what is to be expected since Schmitt's ambition is for his theory of large spaces to be developed in the direction of a more general utility (Schmitt 1995: 278).

Now, the question arises as to the interrelations between a shared collective worship, embodying a cultural community both in terms of a shared narrative horizon and in enacted rituals, and the constitution of legal-territorial borderlines. It may be easily observed that narratives of the nation have served to legitimize external borderlines, as well as criteria for membership, of European states. The typical understanding of nationalism entails that it refers to a political narrative that strives for the 'nation' to coincide with the 'state'. The two basic propositions of nationalism were summarized by classical scholars on the subject, like Kedourie (1993: 1), as, firstly, 'that humanity is naturally divided into nations', and secondly, 'that the only legitimate type of government is national self-government'; and according to Gellner (1993: 1), nationalism 'is primarily a political principle, which holds that the political and the national unit should be congruent'. But this is not simply a question of narratives, but also of ritual enactment around core symbols, such as the national flag and anthem. Here one should resist two temptations; the first is to conclude, with Guibernau (1996: 95), for example, that 'Fascism implied a new style in politics. One of the most prominent and distinctive features of Fascism was the use of symbols, ceremonies and rituals. A world of sacred objects was created and their worship effectively organized'. Such symbols and rituals are and have been utilized by liberal democracies as well; but, as Lane (1981), for example, has shown, they were also used by the regime in the USSR. Secondly, one should beware of concluding, for example with Breuilly (1982: 64), that 'nationalists celebrate themselves rather than some transcendent reality, whether this be located in another world or in a future society'. Nationalist narratives do incorporate a transcendence of sorts, transcending the present community by extending backwards into history while simultaneously anticipating the future. It is hardly surprising, then, that nationalist movements, with their collective rituals, core symbols, and historical narratives providing sources of meaning and community, have repeatedly been perceived as analogous to organized religion; Hayes (1960:

15) claims that nationalism was needed since industrialization created 'a kind of religious void ... for large numbers of people in modern Europe and the contemporary world ... [A]ny such void is unnatural, and an urge arises to fill the void with some new faith'. Parker (1984: 231) states that 'Europeans ... seemed increasingly to need in politics, as they once had needed in religion, an intercessor between the individual and the universal, an object of tangible love on a grand scale'. More recently, both Anderson (1991: 5) and Smith (2001: 35), for example, have stressed the similarities between nationalist and religious movements. Such features were to be officially sanctioned by the Constitutional Treaty, but as Piris (2010: 23) observes, '[t]he use of words such as "laws", "minister", "flag" or "anthem", and ... "constitution" indeed had a powerful political effect. Using these words provoked a psychological shock, which proved to be much larger than the legal nature and substantive content of the Constitutional Treaty'.

We are then faced with two questions: first, ought a political community built upon liberal democracy, including basic rights, open deliberation, and contested elections, to include also a kind of collective worship – one that is publicly endorsed, even if it is not enforced? If so, ought it to be restricted to the member states of the EU, or ought it to exist also at the EU-level?

There is no easy answer in addressing this tension. We should simply be aware that it exists, and that it mirrors similar tensions regarding the status of the legal structure of the EU (is it 'quasi-constitutional', and if so ought the EU to have a constitution – itself an important symbol, some have argued), its economic policies (as a regulatory state as opposed to increased redistributive flows), and its lack of an actual shared public sphere (see e.g. Weiler 2002; Follesdal and Hix 2006).

Conclusion: Sovereign Borders and Collective Symbolism

While the notion of a large space fails to fully capture the EU, and while a closer reading reveals troubling aspects rendering it an undesirable notion normatively, there is much to be said for the continuing importance of the questions that Schmitt raises: the distinction he implies between forms of domination – territorial occupation as opposed to rendering sovereignty ambiguous within a sphere of influence – remains relevant. Furthermore, however, and even more directly, the status of the collective worship of the political community in relation to the areas affected by it remains a highly pertinent and still unresolved issue within the context of the development of the EU. If the 'political idea' of a unified Europe, with its own quasi-supranational symbols – a flag, an anthem – indeed 'radiates' all across the 'periphery' (the constituent member states) it does so weakly. Ought these elements to be abolished? Or should we finally accept, rather, that the EU does constitute a united entity, and thus strengthen its ceremonial practices?

Either way, as long as these symbols remain, and as long as rhetoric reinforces the image of European cooperation as something more than simply economic integration, there is a political idea, and it does radiate, thereby colliding or fusing with the respective political ideas and symbolic imageries of the member states. To what extent the EU can indeed 'radiate' its political idea without acute collision with the ceremonies and symbolism of the member states, and to what extent, conversely, integration could proceed without the aid of symbolic imagery, remains an open question, but certainly not an irrelevant one.

Descriptively, then, Schmitt's large space cannot be applied exactly to the EU – there is too much discrepancy between the two. Nevertheless, Schmitt does raise important questions, especially concerning the connections between the external, territorial borderlines of the sovereign constructs and the cultural boundaries of their internal collective worship. In the context of the contemporary EU, the question concerning this relationship remains supremely relevant, and some of the core issues facing the union are tied to this very issue. There seems to have been a certain hesitation, after the failure of the Constitutional Treaty, to stress 'state-like' features; nevertheless, these remain in place. This development highlights the tension between allowing the EU to maintain and deepen the way in which its own 'political idea' radiates, as opposed to limiting it, while retaining the primary linkage between territorial nation-states and the collective worships of *their* respective political ideas. Ultimately, the question touched upon appears to be the following: to what extent can the EU intrude upon the sovereignty of its constituent member states, and to what extent can these latter continue to deepen their cooperation, *without* strengthening the capacity of the EU's political idea and its attendant symbolism to radiate throughout the union?

While Mouffe draws upon Schmitt in advocating a global balancing of a potentially threatening, totalizing liberal Western project, Schmitt's large space entails more than that. Above all, it is difficult to avoid the conclusion that it implies a form of domination of lesser powers that renders their sovereignty ambivalent. Such an influence, if unwanted by those affected, amounts to an insidious form of threat, and is hardly desirable. Furthermore, Schmitt remains unclear on the way in which the 'political idea of a large space radiates', but he does imply that it is the political idea of the core (or Reich) that radiates to the periphery. That would seem to entail a disjuncture between public legitimacy and collective symbolism for the periphery being influenced by the core.

Ultimately, neither processes of secularization nor the development of the EU, nor even the spread of liberal democracy in Europe and worldwide,

have rendered the questions of the cultural borders, performed and embodied by rituals and symbols, obsolete. On the contrary, as recent decades have
shown, national symbols and their attendant rituals remain a crucial obstacle to be overcome for those who desire to transcend the nation-state and
perhaps to 'consummate secularization' by doing away with publicly supported symbols and rituals altogether, just as Hobbes, according to Schmitt,
consummated the Reformation.

Jon Wittrock is senior lecturer at Södertörn University, School of Social
Sciences. His interests concern the intersection between the ambiguous
categories of religion and politics from a political-philosophical angle. He
has published several articles and book chapters on the thought of Hannah
Arendt, Carl Schmitt and Martin Heidegger, and has been co-editor for
special issues of *European Review* and *Telos*.

Notes

1. 'Für uns ist entscheidend, daß die ursprüngliche Monrolehre von 1823 die erste
Erklärung in der Geschichte des modernen Völkerrechts ist, die von einem Großraum spricht
und für ihn den Grundsatz der Nichtintervention raumfremder Mächte aufstellt.'
2. 'Universalistische, weltumfassende Allgemeinbegriffe sind im Völkerrecht die typis-
chen Waffen des Interventionismus.'
3. 'Der neue Ordnungsbegriff eines neun Völkerrechts ist unser Begriff des Reiches.'

References

Agamben, G. 1998. *Homo Sacer: Sovereign Power and Bare Life*. Stanford, CA: Stanford
University Press.
———. 2005. *State of Exception*. Chicago and London: The University of Chicago Press.
Anderson, B. 1991. *Imagined Communities: Reflections on the Origin and Spread of Nationalism*.
London and New York: Verso.
Bellah, R.N. 1970. *Beyond Belief: Essays on Religion in a Post-Traditional World*. New York:
Harper & Row.
Bendersky, J. 1983. *Carl Schmitt: Theorist for the Reich*. Princeton, NJ: Princeton University
Press.
Billig, M. 1995. *Banal Nationalism*. London: Sage.
Breuilly, J. 1982. *Nationalism and the State*. Manchester: Manchester University Press.
Brubaker, R. 1996. *Nationalism Reframed: Nationhood and the National Question in the New
Europe*. Cambridge: Cambridge University Press.
Dahlheimer, M. 1998. *Carl Schmitt und die deutsche Katholizismus 1888–1936*. Paderborn:
Ferdinand Schöningh.
Dyzenhaus, D. (ed.). 1998. *Law as Politics: Carl Schmitt's Critique of Liberalism*. Durham, NC
and London: Duke University Press.

Eichhorn, M. 1994. *Es wird regiert! Der Staat im Denken Karl Barths und Carl Schmitts in den Jahren 1919 bis 1938*. Berlin: Duncker & Humblot.

Engelbrekt, K. 2009. 'What Carl Schmitt Picked Up in Weber's Seminar: A Historical Controversy Revisited', *The European Legacy* 14(6): 667–84.

Follesdal, A., and S. Hix. 2006. 'Why There is a Democratic Deficit in the EU: A Response to Majone and Moravcsik', *Journal of Common Market Studies* 44(3): 533–62.

Gellner, E. 1993. *Nations and Nationalism*. Oxford: Blackwell.

Gross, R. 2000. *Carl Schmitt und die Juden: Eine Deutsche Rechtslehre*. Frankfurt am Main: Suhrkamp.

Guibernau, M. 1996. *The Nation-State and Nationalism in the Twentieth Century*. Cambridge: Polity Press.

Hayes, C. 1960. *Nationalism: A Religion*. New York: Macmillan.

Hettne, B., and F. Söderbaum. 2005. 'Civilian Power or Soft Imperialism? The EU as a Global Actor and the Role of Interregionalism', *European Foreign Affairs Review* 10(4): 535–52.

Hobbes, T. 1998. *Man and Citizen* (De Homine *and* De Cive). Indianapolis, IN: Hackett.

Hooker, W. 2009. *Carl Schmitt's International Thought: Order and Orientation*. Cambridge: Cambridge University Press.

Joerges, C. 2003. 'Europe a Großraum? Shifting Legal Conceptualisations of the Integration Project', in *Darker Legacies of Law in Europe: The Shadow of National Socialism and Fascism over Europe and its Legal Traditions*, ed. C. Joerges and N.S. Ghaleigh. Oxford: Hart Publishing, pp. 167–192.

Kedourie, E. 1993. *Nationalism*. Oxford: Blackwell.

Lane, C. 1981. *The Rites of Rulers: Ritual in Industrial Society – The Soviet Case*. Cambridge: Cambridge University Press.

Laughland, J. 1998. *The Tainted Source: The Undemocratic Origins of the European Idea*. London: Warner Books.

Marder, M. 2010. *Groundless Existence: The Political Ontology of Carl Schmitt*. London and New York: Continuum.

Meier, H. 1995. *Carl Schmitt and Leo Strauss: The Hidden Dialogue*. Chicago and London: The University of Chicago Press.

Mouffe, C. 2005. *On the Political*. Milton Park: Routledge.

———. 2007. 'Carl Schmitt's Warning on the Dangers of a Unipolar World', in *The International Political Thought of Carl Schmitt: Terror, Liberal War and the Crisis of Global Order*, ed. L. Odysseos and F. Petito. New York: Routledge.

Ojakangas, M. 2006. *A Philosophy of Concrete Life: Carl Schmitt and the Political Thought of Late Modernity*. Bern: Peter Lang.

Parker, W. 1984. *Europe, America and the Wider World: Essays on the Economic History of Western Capitalism, Volume 1: Europe and the World Economy*. Cambridge: Cambridge University Press.

Piris, J.-C. 2010. *The Lisbon Treaty: A Legal and Political Analysis*. Cambridge: Cambridge University Press.

Rousseau, J.-J. 1994. *The Collected Writings of Rousseau: Vol. 4*. Hanover: University Press of New England.

Schmitt, C. 1988a. *Der Nomos der Erde im Völkerrecht des Jus Publicum Europaeum*. Berlin: Duncker & Humblot.

———. 1988b. *The Crisis of Parliamentary Democracy*. Cambridge, MA: MIT Press.

———. 1995. *Staat, Großraum, Nomos: Arbeiten aus den Jahren 1916–1969*. Berlin: Duncker & Humblot.

———. 2003. *The Nomos of the Earth in the International Law of the Jus Publicum Europaeum*. New York: Telos Press.

———. 2007. *The Concept of the Political: Expanded Edition.* Chicago and London: The University of Chicago Press.

———. 2008a. *Political Theology II: The Myth of the Closure of any Political Theology.* Cambridge: Polity Press.

———. 2008b. *The Leviathan in the State Theory of Thomas Hobbes: Meaning and Failure of a Political Symbol.* Chicago and London: The University of Chicago Press.

———. 2011. *Political Romanticism.* New Brunswick and London: Transaction Publishers.

Smith, A. 2001. *Nationalism: Theory, Ideology, History.* Cambridge: Polity Press.

Wacker, B. (ed.). 1997. *Die eigentlich katholische Verschärfung: Konfession, Theologie und Politik im Werk Carl Schmitts.* Munich: Wilhelm Fink.

Weber, M. 1978. *Economy and Society: Outline of an Interpretative Sociology.* Berkeley: University of California Press.

Weiler, J. 2002. 'A Constitution for Europe? Some Hard Choices', *Journal of Common Market Studies* 40(4): 563–80 .

CHAPTER 12

How Prehistory Becomes Crucial for Border Making

PER CORNELL

Questions of nation, state and border are intricate and complex. There are issues of terminology, as well as problems in understanding the variations in the workings of states and nations and their implications for larger social, economic and political processes. There are various dimensions to these problems. When discussing borders, we speak both of the physical geographical limits and complex social, cultural and political borders in a wider sense. The understanding of a cultural 'unit' depends largely on how we describe its characteristics. Further, in traditional border thinking, not least in certain strands of German discourse, there has been the idea of a core area for a particular given culture. In such a discussion, the location and character of the core area is a crucial point in defining 'authenticity' and borders. In this case, we will address such a discussion related to archaeological discourse, which has wider implications beyond archaeology and prehistory as such. The extent to which archaeology merely reflects a general trend or may help to define it is beyond our scope. However, it will become evident that archaeological scholarship has had implications for the general trends. The examples are from German-speaking contexts during the first half of the twentieth century and relate to two key archaeologists: Gustaf Kossinna (1858–1931) and Oswald Menghin (1888–1973). Kossinna was born in a small town in Prussia, close to the present-day Lithuanian border, an area that was part of the Russian Empire in 1858. The north European location of his birthplace may be of certain relevance to the archaeology he later developed, assigning a special role to the Nordic–Baltic area. Menghin was born in the southern Tyrol region of the Austro-Hungarian Empire. His archaeology may also have been influenced by his birthplace, assigning a major role to areas of Central Europe.

Both Kossinna and Menghin seem to belong to the past, despite limited attempts to reconsider their work. However, identifying elements of past debates may help us to avoid certain pitfalls. It is important to look more closely at arguments about identity and borders, avoiding certain gross generalizations that would stand in the way of understanding the complex issues involved. Let us look at the archaeologies they developed.

Gustaf Kossinna, Prussian Archaeologist

Kossinna was interested in languages and history before he ventured into archaeology. He had a great impact on German archaeology long before 1908, when he launched his journal *Mannus*, which came to be highly influential. *Siedlungsarchäologie* was largely his creation. In a sense, Kossinna was responsible for the breakthrough of a spatial method; he was instrumental in lending a 'spatial turn' to archaeology. The use of the word *Siedlung* had to do with geographical location, the place inhabited by a particular culture, people or tribe. *Siedlung* should be read in this case as resembling *Heimat*, another frequent term in Kossinna's oeuvre, and equally complex. The question of *Heimat* was strongly linked during this period to *Blut* and *Boden*, blood and soil. The issue of soil is paramount and should be interpreted literally in Kossinna's writing. People of true authenticity and value to Kossina must be linked to terrain, earth and soil.

Kossina plotted particular archaeological findings, such as flint axes or certain types of ceramics, on maps. The maps were generally scaled to include large parts of Northern Europe and relatively few artefacts. Given his knowledge of chronology (often taken from Swedish archaeologist Montelius), the maps were used to identify the origin and distribution of a particular culture or people. An artefact was, often with little or no argument, taken to represent particular peoples or ethnic groups, such as 'Germans' during the Stone Age.

Kossina explicitly states that archaeology is only concerned with Europe, particularly Germany. He excludes other parts of the world a priori as topics for archaeology (Kossinna 1911, 1928). This attribution of special importance to a particular area, even to the point of excluding others, is a very important element in his way of thinking about archaeology (and the world, it might be added). Kossinna's mindset was not unusual among German scholars. Martin Heidegger, in his 1927 *Being and Time*, wrote about the importance of earth and soil, and the danger of losing such a connection (*Bodenlosigkeit*, Heidegger 1977: 21–22, cf. 177–78, 418–19).[1]

Kossinna did not construct his method out of thin air. His approach had borrowed many related ideas, particularly about mapping, from geographers and others working in the Humboldtian tradition, not to meniton *Kulturkreislehre*, an approach developed mainly by ethnographers and archaeologists. The concept of 'people' was used by many scholars, including archaeologists, in the nineteenth century, but rather diffusely. In analysing stratigraphy, each major stratum was often taken to indicate the presence of a new people that had taken over a specific area from another group. Kossinna also used racist theory and 'science' from Britain, France and Germany. The development of racist arguments in biology played an important role. Kossinna and Eugen Fischer, a leading German biologist working on 'race', shared many interests (cf. Gessler 2000). Fischer even ventured into archaeology at times, while Kossinna tried his hand at human skulls and their alleged racial characteristics.

Kossinna, however, created a particular blend, which became *Siedlungsarchäologie*. He did not like general ideas of human evolution, but instead stressed the particularities of *Heimat*, and the connection to earth, soil and blood.

To illustrate Kossinna's way of arguing, we will briefly summarize his views concerning the origins of the Germans based on a book from 1928 (*Ursprung und Verbreitung der Germanen in vor- und frühgeschichtlischer Zeit*). The argument recapitulates several previous studies by Kossinna from 1909–10 and 1912 (1914). Kossinna dedicated a large part of his 1928 study to arguments about racial characteristics, comparing contemporary populations to Stone Age skulls, allegedly identifying various groups in Germany, Friesland and the Nordic countries. He continues with a discussion of archaeological material from the more recent Stone Age, focusing mainly on ceramics, stone axes and various types of burial ceremonies. He then proceeds to various 'cultures' he believes to have identified in this archaeological material, as well as discussions of their chronology. It is often difficult to see how he connects empirics to his pre-historical reconstructions. His scenario is more or less as illustrated below.

A primitive hunter-gatherer population is replaced by an Indogermanic population centre in Jutland (today's Denmark) and Schleswig-Holstein, eventually expanding to parts of southern and western Sweden and Germany. This population appears at the end of what we call the Mesolithic period (the 'Ertebölle' phase) and eventually builds megalithic monuments. In Kossinna's archaeology, migration is a main element and the Indogermans undertook several migratory movements as far as today's Southern Germany.

An 'Arctic Dobbertinner pre-Finn' culture (survivors of the old hunter-gather population) arrives from the north. This arctic population are particularly well adapted to cold climates and are good warriors. They settle down in Jutland and southern Scandinavia, eventually mingling with the Indogermans. The Finno-Indogermans emerge from this mix (Kossinna 1928: 216) and come to dominate southern Scandinavia and Denmark, while 'pure' (previously migrated) Indogermans survive in Halle and other regions of Germany. The Finno-Indogermans use boat axes and corded ware ceramics, burying their dead in individual tombs of relatively simple construction (as compared to the megaliths). They eventually migrate to Germany and mix with pure Indogermans. The Germans emerge from this mix, a culturally unified people, in 2000 BCE, shortly before the beginning of the Bronze Age (ibid.: 297).

Thus, the Germans were to have emerged from two distinct Nordic populations. Two observations should be made. One is that Kossinna believed that certain particular cultural and racial mixes were positive. However, in the case of the Germans, there is a higher percentage of Indogermans, and a smaller element of the 'pre-Finns'. The other observation is that Kossinna had many hyperborean beliefs: he proceeded from Nordic thinking. That which is good comes from the north. The 'pre-Finns' lived, according to Kossinna's maps, in parts of present-day Norway, Sweden and Finland. It is interesting that he uses the complex term 'Finns'. Kossinna knew Finland, as well as Finnmark in Norway. He makes a point of separating pre-Finns from Finno-Ugrians, who appeared later – less positive in Kossinna's opinion. The use of the term Finns was certainly intentional.

Keeping Kossinna's archaeological perspective in mind, we will look briefly at his involvement in politics.

Kossinna's Politics

Kossinna engaged in the political debates of his time. He wrote political pamphlets, notably at the end of the First World War, in which he used his archaeology for political purposes. As an example of political intervention, we can mention an article on the region around the River Vistula ('Weischsel' in German, running through Krakow, in present-day Poland), which was an old *Heimatboden* for Germans, visible in Neolithic ceramics. The text was entitled 'Weichselland'. An ancient German *Heimat*-land of 1919, intended as a critique of the Versailles Treaty, has been reprinted with political motifs, on various occasions, notably in 1940 (Kossinna 1940). Hans Reinerth, a German archaeologist and one of Kossinna's students, was responsible for the new edition. In his introduction he states that '*Weichselland*

is free. Through the deeds of the Führer, old German Folkland … has been
to be been brought back to the Reich' (p. III). Note the year of publication;
the introduction was signed in December 1939. This quotation shows how
directly archaeology is linked to politics in official rhetoric, particularly the
use of the word free, thereby contributing to a political narrative on borders
bordering narrative.

The 1928 book by Kossinna helped to stabilize his career. But it also
had obvious political intentions, largely coinciding with his career ambitions.
The book opens with a photograph from 1915 in which Kossinna was giving
a lecture to General Field Marshal Hindenburg. In 1928, Hindenburg was
Reichspresident of Germany. The closing words of the book also relate to
Germany of the 1920s. Hindenburg is mentioned, and Kossinna speaks of
the Germans of the Neolithic period, characterized by stunning weaponry
(axes and daggers), as a 'weapon-happy' and 'weapon-proud' people – '[e]
ven today, only weapon-proud can our poor People get their lost freedom
back' (Kossinna 1928: 302). For Kossinna, archaeology is not only a reflection of, or support for, the German national project, but a vital and constructive element in its making. The case of Kossinna illustrates how one can
pursue an academic career, and it shows how particular academic developments may exert a general, though limited, political influence.

We may also add that by 1928 Kossinna was a member of the *Kampfbund
für Deutsches Kultur* (cf. Grünert 2002; Wijworra 2006), which was under
the protection of Alfred Rosenberg, later minister of culture in the NSDAP
government and the protector of the *Reichsbund für Deutsche Vorgeschichte*. A
general observation about Kossinna is that he is very keen on stressing the
role of the Nordic, even at the expense of the southern parts of Germany,
such as Bavaria.[2] Kossinna would never have been wholeheartedly accepted
in the wider circles of Catholic Bavaria. There is actually something of a
Prussian in Kossinna. The whole scenario of Nordic development, in his
view, unfolded in a limited area of the north (the Nordic countries, northern
Germany, Friesland and the Baltic countries). There was no major 'external'
element. The Deutsch was Nordic Deutsch. Kossinna was a major defender
of Nordic Thought, a movement that insisted on the importance of the
Nordic elements of German culture. The movement was heterogenous,
including authors from varied backgrounds and argumentative ability (cf.
Günther 1922; Wirth 1931; Strzygowski 1940; for a general discussion, cf.
Lutzhöft 1971; Arvidsson 2000, 2001; Dahl 2006). Kossinna's ideas came
to play a major role in the 1930s. With the rise of the Nazi government,
Kossinna's archaeology became official party line (as seen in an official pre-
history published by the NSDAP, cf. Reinerth 1940).

After these brief comments about Kossinna, let us turn to the Austrian
scholar Menghin.

Oswald Menghin, Austrian Archaeologist

Menghin, as mentioned, was born in Meran in the southern Tyrol, which was part of the Austro-Hungarian Empire; it is a German-speaking area located in present-day Italy. He was appointed academic lecturer in 1913. He became a university professor at the Prehistoric Department of the University of Vienna in 1917, remaining there until 1945. From 1930 to 1933, he was a professor at the University of Cairo. In 1935–36 he had an appointment as rector at the University of Vienna. After the Second World War, Menghin escaped from an indictment in Nürnberg, and succeeded in establishing a second career in Argentina (cf. Arenas 1990).

Among Menghin's publications was a study of the prehistory of Böhmen and Mähren, published as part of the *Sudetendeutsche Heimatforschung* series (1926); his magnum opus *Weltgeschichte der Steinzeit* (1931); and publications about field archaeology in Egypt, including *The Excavations of the Egyptian University in the Neolithic Site at Maadi* (1932, with Amer Mustafa). Compared to some of the more speculative German writings of the period (e.g. Hermann Wirth), Menghin was relatively consistent and logical, defending a rather systematic scientific approach. He stressed the importance of stratigraphy and fieldwork. Menghin's major contribution to the bordering discourse was his theoretical framework, the *Kulturkreislehre*, developed by ethnologists such as Fritz Graebner in Germany and the Jesuit Wilhelm Schmidt in Austria and Switzerland (cf. Roberts and Vander Linden 2011). Menghin's study of what he calls the world history of the Stone Age is broad in scope, and the size of the bibliography is truly impressive. It formally includes all of the populated continents, including Africa, the Americas, Australia and New Guinea, not to mention 'the Old World'. There are also references to archaeologists in India and the Arab world, which was not common at the time. Several different languages appear in the bibliography, including German, French, Italian, Spanish, English and Scandinavian. Clearly, a lot of work was put into publishing such an ambitious work. Several of his arguments are logically consistent, though difficult to follow at times.

Menghin, to some extent reflecting a general cultural trend of the period, is sceptical of the notion of progress. People always have a wish to return to their roots, their faraway and primitive past (Menghin 1931: 616). He is not explicit in his position on this question: there is no general condemnation of such an urge, as in Frazer (1920). In a certain sense, Menghin is close to Heidegger's desire to take a leap backwards in order to find the future. Turning to Kossinna, the primitive is there, tangible and direct in the Germany of the twentieth century, and it is a positive asset of the German character to harbour this primitive instinct.

There are several similarities between Kossinna and Menghin: both stress the cultural border; both plot cultural variables on large-scale maps; both have a strong belief in the existence of easily defined cultures; and both place German characteristics at the centre of world history. To Menghin, Nordic traits are the cultural expression of Indogermanic nature, another similarity with Kossinna. Like Kossinna, Menghin largely excludes the Mediterranean region and West Asia in his discussion of German origins. However, he is much more diffuse when placing the Indogermans and Nordic culture in Europe. In a discussion of the origins of the Indogermans, he relies on particular ideas of culture and essence. He argues that the 'Band-ceramic complex' (often referred to as Linear Band Keramik in today's archaeology) cannot correspond to the Indogermans since they lack the necessary expansive and dominating force (Menghin 1931: 554). Similarly, Menghin argues in *Geist und Blut* (1934) that a black person is always black. This particular example has been discussed by Geerh (1986: 21); this type of thinking of absolute essence seems to be a cornerstone of Menghin's ideology.

In a map designed to show the alleged distribution of Nordic culture in 2000 BCE, there is a much greater focus on southern Germany than in the corresponding map by Kossinna. The Nordic culture is the German one, not Scandinavian or Nordic in a geographic sense. By 2000 BCE, the Nordic German people were already in the Balkans, Upper Tyrol, the French frontier and Belgium, as well as the Volga and Dnieper to the east. Menghin worked little on Nordic questions. He even states that the Indogermans, through their expansion, 'even made Scandinavia Nordic' (Menghin 1931: 475). Thus, Scandinavia has no role in the making of Nordic culture, in sharp contrast to Kossinna. In general terms, geography matters a great deal to Menghin, but not in the sense of giving an absolute privilege to one specific area to the extent Kossinna did.

Menghin also speaks about the importance of several 'undercurrents' that play a role in the definition of a particular expression of Nordic culture. Even 'Arctic' appears – an argument apparently borrowed from Kossinna. There are also other cultural movements with a certain impact on Scandinavia, though of less significance. Menghin dwells on the 'Bell Beaker Complex', a late Stone Age ceramic material found on the Atlantic coast of Europe, from Spain northwards. According to Menghin, this is an expression of a North African–Nilotic culture. Menghin notes that the material is also found in southern Scandinavia, regarding it as an enigmatic, widely dispersed phenomenon with no lasting effects (Menghin 1931: 474).[3]

Menghin's Politics

Menghin is a complex figure. Some of his archaeological work is systematic, logical and consistent. His work in Egypt includes direct, open collaboration with Egyptian archaeologists, which was not very common during this period. He also established close links with Argentinian archaeologists.

In his famous 1935 speech delivered in Vienna, Edmund Husserl addresses the question of European identity. Somewhat bewilderingly, he refers positively to Menghin. Husserl says that when addressing European prehistory it is necessary to turn to Menghin and his significant work, which is so 'rich in thought', and presents a world history of the Stone Age (Husserl 1954: 319). Whatever Husserl's reasons may have been for using this text, the reference indicates great admiration for Menghin.[4] It may also be mentioned that Heidegger's *Being and Time* criticizes the notion of a general world history (cf. Heidegger 1977: 381, discussing the 'vulgar' notion of world history). This may suggest another point of coincidence between Heidegger and Kossinna, as opposed to Husserl. But the philosophical arguments are complex, and this issue must be scrutinized in greater detail.

In his previously mentioned 1934 publication entitled *Geist und Blut*, Menghin downplays the role of biological race in human society. However, he insists on the relevance of culture essence. In Menghin's thinking, cultures are essential units. There are only two possibilities: a culture either exists or has become extinct. He argues at length concerning the question of Jews in Austria, insisting that there is no place for Jewish culture there.

Menghin participated in various political and cultural movements. From 1919 to 1926, he was a member of Deutsche Gemeinschaft (German Fellowship), which brought together German nationalists and Catholics who were working for 'Germanhood' (Stadler 2001: 563; cf. on Austrian parties during this period, Simon 1984 and Kriechbaumer 1996), and later on became a member of other similar organizations. It was in such circles that he first got to know Arthur Seyß-Inquart, an important Nazi politician and administrator during the war. In the 1930s, Menghin continued to participate in organizations that advocated for closer links between Germany and Austria. He formed part of the 'Catholic Nationalist' movement, which was sympathetic to National Socialism (cf. Haag 1980). Throughout his Austrian career, Menghin argued for a larger Germany in which Austria would be but a province.

As an academic, Menghin actively participated in organized campaigns against intellectuals such as Sigmund Freud,[5] as well as against the Vienna Circle of Logical Empiricism. Menghin's name figures in several studies on the latter, including Stadler's well-known stud about the school being a major enemy of Austria (Stadler 2001).

At the time of the *Anschluss*, Menghin temporarily served as minister of education in the cabinet formed by Seyß-Inquart, and was responsible for introducing laws that limited the access of certain ethnic groups to posts in higher education (Rosenkrantz 1990; cf. Lichtenberger-Fenz 1988; Urban 1996: 9). Menghin signed the laws personally. The result was the discharge of many scholars from universities and other institutions of higher education. Throughout his Austrian career, Menghin actively participated in draining Austrian universities of highly competent, internationally acclaimed scholars.

Menghin edited the *Prehistoric Journal of Vienna*, publishing a note in the 1938 issue that spoke of the new possibilities of the larger Germany, and stressing the tasks that were emerging from the joining of Österreich to the Deutsches Reich and the Führer Adolf Hitler (Menghin 1938: 3).

With respect to the reception of Menghin in Nazi circles, his lack of enthusiasm for the Kossinnian version of *Nordische Gedanke* seems to have been a problem. His previous involvement in a Catholic-oriented political party, and his contacts with Catholic circles in Austria, also seem to have been a major problem (Kriechbaumer 2001: 54–75; cf. Geerh 1986; Kohl and Perez-Gollan 2002). The Italian annexation of southern Tyrol after the Hitler-Mussolini pact, making his own *Heimat*-land Italian, may also have a major blow to Menghin.

Menghin was regarded as an important asset in Nazi circles, but there was controversy. At times he was not trusted to have any important position in the party (Kriechbaumer 2001: 743). However, as of 1940, Menghin was a party member (Fontán 2005: 50). An internal investigation scrutiny by high-ranking officials of the Nazi government found him to be highly reliable (ibid.: 82). However, although Menghin had contact with the SS-Ahnenerbe during the later Nazi period, he never became an important figure in the Nazi archaeological propaganda. He was indicted at Nuremberg as one of the instigators of the Second World War (Fontán 2005), and incarcerated in a prison camp. He finally escaped the indictment and went to Argentina in 1948, where he started a second career.

Kossinna and Menghin: A Comparison

In summary, we can compare Kossinna and Menghin. Both worked on German prehistory and both were highly political in their visions of the past, and supported German military expansionism through their archaeology. They also shared a geographical approach by which culture always corresponded to a given core area, from which the culture had been secondarily distributed. The idea of culture as particularity and essence is common to them. Both adopted the idea of primitiveness in the present (also discussed by British scholars of the period, including Lubbock 1872 and Frazer 1920), a notion that is particularly salient in Kossinna.

There are important differences between Kossinna and Menghin that have certain relevance in relation to questions of cultural borders and Europe. While Kossinna is obsessed with the idea of Nordic Thought, and places all important historical events related to the creation of German culture in the Nordic sphere, excluding the rest of the world, Menghin places the origin of the Germans in Central Europe. He tries to create a prehistoric world placing Germans there.

In addressing the reasons for the differences, the distinction between the national project in Germany and the Austro-Hungarian Empire is certainly relevant. Birthplace is also important, as well as the issue of Protestantism for Kossinna and Catholicism for Menghin. The reason that Kossinna was so acclaimed by Nazi officials should be further explored in future studies. In some ways, Menghin might have been an equally good choice for the Nazis, assigning larger geographical areas of the German-speaking world a place in the making of German culture.

Per Cornell is professor of archaeology at the University of Gothenburg, and has led several large projects funded by the Swedish Research Council. His latest books are *Encounters, Materialities, Confrontations: Archaeologies of Social Space and Interaction* (Cambridge Scholars Press 2007, ed. with Fredrik Fahlander), and *Eric Boman: La figura del explorador y científico en el noroeste argentino* (Barco Edita 2016, with Patricia Arenas).

Notes

1. The use of a particular kind of spatial thinking in German colonies (somewhat similar to the archaeology of Kossinna and Menghin) cannot be addressed in this context. Cf. Noyes (1992), discussion of German South West Africa.

2. The importance of *Nordische Gedanke* in Nazi-German propaganda is, at first sight, rather strange. Why did Bavarian or Austrian Nazis accept this argument, which made their earthly 'homelands' secondary in the official historical perspective? Bavaria was a stronghold of Nazism, so this point should be studied in greater detail. *Nordische Gedanke* evidently contained some very important message, even in Bavaria and Austria. On the notion of *Nordische Gedanke*, cf. below.

3. In passing, it may be noted that the Bell Beaker is widely discussed in contemporary archaeology, but few researchers talk about it as African. However, there are Bell Beaker ceramics in North African deposits, which Menghin seems to have noted. The Bell Beaker materials from North Africa have not been studied much. There is a certain tendency to engage in more advanced work in the region. Still, in several introductory books on archaeology, distribution maps on the Bell Beaker do not include the North African material. Concerning the effects of the 'Bell Beaker tradition', many archaeologists stress its importance

as a predecessor to the introduction of the Bronze Age along the Atlantic coast of Europe, including Scandinavia.

4. This speech of Husserl is often quoted in the context of the European Union, cf. www.ellopos.net/politics/eu_links, 'The European Prospect', with European Union Select Internet resources, for links to this speech (consulted 18 October 2011). Although highly interesting, it is far beyond the scope of this chapter to analyse Husserl's use of Menghin in greater detail.

5. The relationship between the thinking of Freud and that of Menghin is intricate. It is well known that Freud often referred to prehistory, and there are certain similarities to their approaches. Still, there are major differences that merit further scrutiny.

References

Arenas, Patricia. 1990. *Antropología en la Argentina: El aporte de los científicos de habla alemana.* Buenos Aires: Institución Cultural Argentino-Germana/Museo Etnográfico 'J.B. Ambrosetti', Facultad de Filosofia y Letras de la U.B.A.

Arvidsson, Stefan. 2000. *Ariska idoler.* Stockholm and Stehag: Symposion.

———. 2001. 'I skuggan av kors och hakkors', in *Myter om det nordiska,* ed. C. Raudvere, A. Andrén and K. Jennbert. Lund: Nordic Academic Press, pp. 91–110.

Chakrabarty, Dipesh. 1992. 'Postcoloniality and the Artifice of History: Who Speaks for "Indian" pasts?', *Representations* 37: 1–26.

Cornell, Per. 2007. 'Unhomely Space: Confronting Badiou and Bhabha', in *Encounters/Materialities/Confrontations: Archaeologies of Social Space and Interaction,* ed. P. Cornell and F. Fahlander. Newcastle: CSP, pp. 100–22.

Dahl, Göran, 2006, *Radikalare än Hitler.* Stockholm: Atlantis.

Fontán, Marcelino. 2005. *Oswald Menghin: ciencia y nazismo.* Buenos Aires: Fundación Memoria del Holocausto.

Frazer, James. 1920. 'The Scope of Social Anthropology', in *Psyche's Task and the Scope of Social Anthropology.* London: Macmillan, pp. 157–76.

Geerh, Richard S. 1986. 'Oswald Menghin, ein Vertreter der Katolischen Nationalen', in *Geistiges Leben im Österreich der ersten Republik,* ed. I. Ackerl and R. Neck. Munich: Oldenbourg, pp. 9–24.

Gessler, Bernhard. 2000. *Eugen Fischer (1884–1967).* Freiburg: P.hD. Dissertation, University of Freiburg (Breisgau).

Grünert, Heinz. 2002. *Gustaf Kossinna (1858–1931): vom Germanisten zum Prähistoriker. Ein Wissenschaftler im Kaiserreich und in der Weimarer Republik.* Rahden/Westfalen: Leidorf.

Günther, Hans Friedrich Karl. 1922. *Rassenkunde des deutschen Volkes.* Munich: Lehmann.

Haag, John. 1980. 'Marginal Men and the Dream of the Reich: Eight Austrian National-Catholic Intellectuals, 1918–1938', in *Who were the Fascists: Social Roots of European Fascim,* ed. S.U. Larsen, B. Hagtvet and J.P. Myklebust. Bergen: Universitetsforlaget, pp. 239–48.

Heidegger, Martin. (1927) 1977. *Gesamtausgabe: Veröffentlichte Schriften 1914–1970. Abt. 1, Veröffentlichte Schriften 1914–1970. Bd 2, Sein und Zeit.* Frankfurt am Main: Klostermann.

Husserl, Edmund. (1935) 1954. 'Die Krisis des europäischen Menschentums und die Philosophie', *Husserliana, gesammelte Werke, vol. 6,* ed. W. Biemel. Dordrecht: Nijhoff, pp. 314–48.

Kohl, Philip L., and José Perez-Gollan. 2002. 'Religion, Politics and Prehistory: Reassessing the Lingering Legacy of Oswald Menghin', *Current Anthropology* 43: 561–86.

Kossinna, Gustaf. 1909/1910. 'Der Ursprung der Urfinnen und der Urindogermanen und ihre Ausbreitung nach dem Osten', *Mannus* 1 (1909): 17–52, 225–45 and *Mannus* 2 (1910): 59–108.

———. 1911. 'Anmerkungen zum heutigen Stand der Vorgeschichtsforschung', *Mannus* 3: 127–30.

———. 1928. *Ursprung und Verbreitung der Germanen in vor- und frühgeschichtlicher Zeit.* Leipzig: Germanenverlag.

———. 1940. *Das Weichselland, ein uralter Heimatboden der Germanen.* Leipzig: Kabitzsch.

Kriechbaumer, Robert. 2001. *Die Grossen Erzählungen der Politik.* Vienna: Böhlau.

Lichtenberger-Fenz, Brigitte. 1988. 'Österreichs Hochschulen und Universitäten und das NS-regime', in *NS-Herrschaft in Österreich 1938–1945*, ed. E. Tàlos, E. Hanisch and W. Neugebauer. Vienna: Verlag für Gesellschaftskritik, pp. 269–82.

Lubbock, John. 1872. *Prehistoric Times, as Illustrated by Ancient Remains, and the Manners and Customs of Modern Savages.* London: Williams & Norgate.

Lutzhöft, Hans-Jürgen. 1971. *Der Nordische Gedanke in Deutschland 1920–1940.* Stuttgart: Klett.

Menghin, Oswald. 1926. 'Einführung in die Urgeschichte Böhmens und Mährens', *Anstalt für Sudetendeutsche Heimatforschung, Vorgeschichtliche Abteilung* 1. Reichenberg: Anstalt für Sudetendeutsche Heimatforschung.

———. 1931. *Weltgeschichte der Steinzeit.* Vienna: Anton Schroll & Co.

———. 1934. *Geist und Blut: Grundsätzliches um Rasse, Sprache, Kultur und Volkstum.* Vienna: Anton Schroll & Co.

———. 1938. '25 Jahre Wiener Prähistorische Gesellschaft', *Wiener Prähistorische Zeitschrift* 25: 1–3.

Menghin, Oswald, and Amer Mustafa. 1932. *The Excavations of the Egyptian University in the Neolithic Site at Maadi.* Cairo: Government Publishers.

Noyes, John. 1992. *Colonial Space: Spatiality in the Discourse of German South West Africa 1884–1895.* Chur: Harwood.

Reinerth, Hans. 1940. 'Die Urgermanen', *Vorgeschichte der Deutschen Stämme* 1, ed. H. Reinerth. Reichsbund für Deutsche Vorgeschichte & Reichsamt für Vorgeschichte der NSDAP. Leipzig and Berlin: NSDAP Verlag, pp. 1–64.

Roberts, Benjamin, and Marc Vander Linden (eds). 2011. *Investigating Archaeological Cultures: Material Culture, Variability, and Transmission.* New York: Springer.

Rosenkrantz, Herbert. 1990. 'Entrechtung, Verfolgung und Selbsthilfe der Juden in Österreich, März bis Oktober 1938', in *Österreich, Deutschland und ihre Mächte: Internationale und Österreichische Aspekte des 'Anschluss' vom März 1938*, ed. G. Stourzh and B. Zaar. Vienna: Verlag der Österreichischen Akademie der Wissenschaften, pp. 367–417.

Simon, Walter B. 1984. *Österreich 1918–1938: Ideologien und Politik.* Vienna: Böhlau.

Stadler, Friedrich. 1996. *Studien zur Wienerkreis: Usprung, Entwicklung und Wirkung des Logischen Empirismus im Kontext.* Frankfurt am Main: Suhrkamp.

Strzygowski, Josef. 1940. *Die Deutsche Nordsee: Das Bekenntnis eines Kunstforschers.* Vienna and Leipzig: Luser.

Urban, Otto Helmut. 1996. 'Er war der Mann zwischen den Fronten: Oswald Menghin und das Urgeschichtliche Institut der Universität Wien während der Nazizeit', *Archaeologia Austriaca* 80: 8–14.

Wijworra, Ingo. 2006. *Der Germanenmythos: Kontruktion einer Weltanschauung in der Alterturmsforschung der 19 Jahrhunderts.* Darmstadt: Wissenschaftliche Buchgesellschaft.

Wirth, Hermann. 1931. *Der Aufgang der Menschheit: Untersuchungen zur Geschichte der Religion, Symbolik und Schrift der atlantisch-nordischen Rasse.* Jena: Eugen Diederichs Verlag.

Conclusion

Thomas Lindkvist and Katharina Vajta

In this volume the linguistic, cultural and political diversity in Europe has been discussed from different perspectives in twelve studies. Borders and their role in defining and reproducing identities have been examined by scholars from many different disciplines, thus representing diverging viewpoints, theoretical traditions and empirical ranges. Europe and its cultural borders are found at the crossroads of these hypotheses. The first hypothesis is that borders are to be seen as constructed narratives, concepts and practices. According to the second, the search for the starting point of nations is crucial to the making and definition of European borders. Finally, borders are Janus-faced: they may divide and unify at the same time. The chapters of this anthology confirm this. The first hypothesis indicates that cultural borders differ fundamentally from geopolitical frontiers. It has been shown that cultural perceptions such as imaginary, literary, linguistic and religious representations are historically constructed as narratives, concepts and practices. The second hypothesis deals with the myth of the origin and the search for this myth. That search may be in the fields of archaeology, history, ideology or just a plain longing for uniqueness, which reoccurs throughout this book. The third hypothesis brings up the two sides of the coin that constitute European culture – unity and diversity. These characteristics and the tension between them are fundamental to contemporary Europe. Which borders divide and which unite? This question has been brought up in many of the case studies.

The different perspectives in this volume, whether the author's own discipline is history, linguistics, sociology, or something else, can all be considered as pointing more or less in the same direction. The construction of borders is marked by multifaceted and complex dimensions, and today we must manage cultural borders that are constantly moving and changing, thus needing to be redefined – if possible, in order to consider how they impact both individuals and society. Borders carry differences, and they bring the narratives of differences. As Andrén (Chapter 10) points out, visible cultural borders have become stronger and more numerous, and this might in turn also imply that the differences have become more important. The question then becomes how shall we deal with them – are there ways of elaborating upon non-hegemonic narratives? Hence the importance of narratives promoting inclusive aspects of cultural borders (Larsson and Spielhaus, Chapter 2), and of rituals and border practices in the construction of identity (Järlehed, Chapter 9).

However, the possibility of a European identity is not only a rather recent phenomenon; it can also be seen as a narrative in itself. Several authors go back to the end of the Western Roman Empire and the Middle Ages. Here, Larsson and Spielhaus (Chapter 2) make a crucial point when observing that the Muslim presence in Europe is often considered to be a recent phenomenon, even if that presence is much older, and even if medievalists have shown that Muslims have been a part of European history for a long time. Grinell (Chapter 3) shows us that Christian traditions are not the only ones that have been built upon a European inheritance, but that in fact both European thinking and Islam have a common heritage in Athens and Jerusalem. The cultural border between Islam and Christianity, which today is increasingly stressed within Europe and the Western world, is thus a modern historical construction of an evolving narrative implying new risks of furthering a bipolar world when emphasizing the Christian roots of Europe (Andrén, Chapter 10).

The making of identities and thus the creation of borders is a matter of defining what things have in common and what must be excluded. The national identities that emerged as politically determined imagined communities were constituted by common elements, such as language, confession or a common narrative of the past. The making of identities is always a question of defining a 'we' and 'the others'. Therefore identities are changing. These changes depend on shifting political and social conjectures. Politically created identities need to be legitimized, and stating an origin, a point of beginning, has often been considered necessary. Pinning down the origin of a nation has always been seen as a necessity. This was the case during the formation of the modern nation-states during the nineteenth century, but also in the new – or renewed – states formed in the dissolved USSR and Yugoslavia.

The creation of the origins of nations had the purpose to stress cultural coherence. This also implies that valuations and exclusions have been made. From the chapters in this volume it is evident how elusive and arbitrary the quest for an origin can be. To place, as has been done, the origins of Europe in the High Middle Ages is convenient, since the geographical space of that culture, defined through the Roman Church, corresponds roughly to the European Union. The elusive origins only mean something to those who invent them.

The chapters in this book discuss identities with diverging content. Thus, the borders are imagined differently. The matrix is the nation-state, but the emergence of larger political entities, like the European Union, raises a problem of whether they 'could complement and perhaps replace the nation-state' (Wittrock, Chapter 11). Could the symbols, ritual and ceremonies produced to legitimize the nation-states be transferred to a larger space like the EU? Is the EU something more or something less than the sum of the member states? This important problem is raised in Wittrock's chapter, based upon a study of Carl Schmitt's theory from the interwar period – and thus in another political context – of the *Großraum* (Larger Space).

Languages could potentially be seen as crossing and transgressing national borders, unifying beyond them. Loester (Chapter 5) asks the classic question of what is a dialect, what is a language – where are their borders? She observes that today the linguistic variety of Bavarian is spoken in Germany, Austria and Northern Italy, and even in the United States, thus showing that linguistic cultural borders are broader than national borders. The mere spelling of the same word can establish and reflect differences: Bayern-Baiern. Dichotomies between 'us' and 'them' can be found in many different contexts and at different levels. Multiculturality is not easily handled by nations that stress national unity to a mosaic of different cultures, religions and languages. Few countries allow their citizens the opportunity to hold dual citizenship, as Luxembourg does. Fehlen (Chapter 7) analyses how this European nation exploits its borders as a unifying component of its identity, and how borderlands can function as unifiers, but also how the language becomes an excluding factor; fading national borders risk giving way to new borders, symbolized by national language. We can see that the border has been moved from territory to language, and a new narrative is constructed regarding Luxembourgish as a national language. Hereby a common and unique language as a vital part of a national identity and culture has been supplemented in Luxembourg. However, Järlehed (Chapter 9) observes quite the contrary, when writing that the Basque language 'seems to lose importance as an identity marker'. Is this perhaps an example of an evolving, moving cultural border? This sort of narrative about cultural practices can thus be constructed and reinforced at different levels: for instance in language text books, failing to further the intended intercultural approach, replacing it with a discourse on stereotypes, and confirming and reproducing the narrative of national borders (Vajta, Chapter 4).

Throughout, the authors come back to the notion of cultural belonging and citizenship, however less often to nationality. Leppänen (Chapter 8) is the first to mention this concept, and brings up the issue of loyalty in relation to borders, thus stressing the problems that arise when one belongs to more than one side of a border. Indeed, borders can be embodied and can dwell within the individual, as was clearly the case for Aino Kallas.

It becomes necessary to see borders not only as dividers, but also – and maybe mostly – as unifiers; in other words, to see that they are Janus-faced. A growing number of differences make it more and more difficult to keep them apart, since people live their lives in cultural borderlands 'where the analytical categories of politics and religion are not distinguishable from each other', as Grinell (Chapter 3) points out. Berg (Chapter 1) shows that it is possible with different identifications, at different levels, and Söhrman (Chapter 6) gives examples of different possibilities to have simultaneous identities. The different sides of the border(s) make up a whole, and Grinell underlines the common heritage in Europe built on Christian, Jewish and Muslim traditions – narratives of inclusion and exclusion become interdependent (Larsson and Spielhaus, Chapter 2).

This puts forward the performative aspect of identity. Theoretically, there is the possibility of choice: we are free to try to go beyond borders, thus creating a meeting point between cultural borders where a 'Mischkultur' embodies how something new may arise. This implies leaving the 'geographical approach' of Kossina and Menghin, 'in which culture always corresponds to a given geography' (Cornell, Chapter 12). It opens up the possibility of seeing 'the borderland as a place to have a full identity', as Grinell says when quoting Anzaldúa (Chapter 3), following Söhrman's 'holistic idea' (Chapter 6). Identities are thus forged within and outside the frames of cultural borders, and the example of Kallas, whose family and own self carry the tension between different cultures, nationalism and internationalism (and whose gender can also be seen as a cultural border since she has to give up her Finnish nationality). This shows the ultimate way of reconciling different belongings when taking on a literary alias (Leppänen, Chapter 8).

This leads to the final concern – intersectionality. Who are the agents that make identities and borders? The development of Europe after the Second World War has in many respects changed the conditions of identity building, and made cultural borders more complex. Political borders are less appropriate to stressing cultural coherence. There are tendencies to prioritize regional borders before nation-states like the EU (Wittrock, Chapter 11), or to construct cultural entities that transgress nation-states (Cornell, Chapter

12). But identities and borders are never one-dimensional. Groups and individuals, like Kallas, must create and apprehend their identities and thus their own borders, within or without the borders set by cultural, political and economic processes.

Thomas Lindkvist was Professor of Medieval History at the University of Gothenburg from 1999-2016. His latest publication is *Trade and Civilization: Economic Networks and Cultural Ties, from Prehistory to the Early Modern Era*, coedited with Kristian Kristiansen and Janken Myrdal (Cambridge University Press, 2018). He gained his PhD at Uppsala University.

Katharina Vajta is senior lecturer in French at the Department of Languages and Literatures at the University of Gothenburg, where she is also Head of Department. Her main research interests are within the fields of sociolinguistics, language and identity, the French-speaking world and intercultural education. She is a member of the steering group for the Centre for European Research at Gothenburg University.

Index

MAKING SENSE OF HISTORY
Studies in Historical Cultures
General Editor: Stefan Berger
Founding Editor: Jörn Rüsen

Bridging the gap between historical theory and the study of historical memory, this series crosses the boundaries between both academic disciplines and cultural, social, political and historical contexts. In an age of rapid globalization, which tends to manifest itself on an economic and political level, locating the cultural practices involved in generating its underlying historical sense is an increasingly urgent task.